MW00626347

Introduction to Cybercrime

Introduction to Cybercrime

Computer Crimes, Laws, and Policing in the 21st Century

Joshua B. Hill and Nancy E. Marion

Praeger Security International Textbook

 PRAEGER™

An Imprint of ABC-CLIO, LLC
Santa Barbara, California • Denver, Colorado

Copyright © 2016 by Joshua B. Hill and Nancy E. Marion

All rights reserved. No part of this publication may be reproduced, stored in a retrieval system, or transmitted, in any form or by any means, electronic, mechanical, photocopying, recording, or otherwise, except for the inclusion of brief quotations in a review, without prior permission in writing from the publisher.

Library of Congress Cataloging-in-Publication Data

Names: Hill, Joshua. | Marion, Nancy E.
Title: Introduction to cybercrime : computer crimes, laws, and policing in the 21st century / Joshua B. Hill, Nancy E. Marion.
Description: Santa Barbara, CA : Praeger, 2016. | Series: Praeger security international textbook | Includes bibliographical references.
Identifiers: LCCN 2015036592| ISBN 9781440832734 (hardback) | ISBN 9781440835339 (paperback) | ISBN 9781440832741 (ebook)
Subjects: LCSH: Computer crimes. | Computer crimes—Prevention. | Internet—Security measures. | BISAC: COMPUTERS / Internet / Security. | LAW / Communications.
Classification: LCC HV6773 .H554 2016 | DDC 364.16/8--dc23 LC record available at http://lccn.loc.gov/2015036592

ISBN: 978-1-4408-3273-4
Paperback ISBN: 978-1-4408-3533-9
EISBN: 978-1-4408-3274-1

20 19 18 17 16   1 2 3 4 5

This book is also available on the World Wide Web as an eBook.
Visit www.abc-clio.com for details.

Praeger
An Imprint of ABC-CLIO, LLC

ABC-CLIO, LLC
130 Cremona Drive, P.O. Box 1911
Santa Barbara, California 93116-1911

This book is printed on acid-free paper ∞
Manufactured in the United States of America

To Madeline Noca Francis-Hill!

Contents

CHAPTER ONE

Introduction

Introduction: Target Breach

IN DECEMBER 2013, AT THE PEAK OF THE holiday shopping season, U.S. retailer Target announced that the company had suffered a major security breach and that, as a result, about 40 million customers had their payment card details stolen (including their card numbers, expiration dates, CVV security codes, and PINs), and another 70 million customers were at risk of losing personal records such as email addresses. Those responsible for the theft could, in turn, sell the stolen information on the black market where it could be used to cause further damage to the original victims. Target officials attempted to diminish the impact of the damage by reporting that the stolen PIN data was encrypted at the terminal as the customer entered their information, and that the encryption key was not stored on Target's systems but instead by the payment processor. Since the key was not stolen in the breach, the possible danger to victims was limited, according to Target.[1]

It was later discovered that the information was stolen using Kaptoxa malware (a derivative of BlackPOS, a point of sale malware) that had been installed on Target's point-of-sale terminals. BlackPOS was originally created by a 17-year-old hacker from Russia who sold the software to cyber-criminals. These criminals then used the software to carry out cyberattacks on merchants. The attackers used credentials that they had stolen from a heating, ventilation, and air conditioning supplier, Fazio Mechanical Services, that had access for business reasons (i.e., electronic billing, contract submission and project management). Once the malware was installed on Target's machines, it went undetected for about 19 days, during which time the criminals continued to collect customers' data.

The attack on Target occurred in two stages. In the first, the hackers installed the malware on only a limited number of Target's point-of-sale systems as a way to test the software and see if it worked. After that, the criminals applied it to the majority of Target's systems. The stolen credit card and personal information was sent to a number of drop servers located within the United States and one located in Brazil. Here, the information could be readily accessed by cybercriminals located in Russia and Eastern Europe.[2]

The effects of the crime were far reaching. For Target itself, the breach led to a 46 percent drop in net profits during a critical holiday shopping season.[3] Estimates of the financial costs vary. According to the U.S. Consumer Bankers Association, the breach cost the company $200 million as they replaced customers' payment cards that may have been compromised.[4] Another estimate put Target's losses at $420 million, including reimbursement, the cost of reissuing millions of new cards, legal fees, and credit monitoring for those customers who demanded it.[5] Target officials estimated the financial costs to be $61 million, but $44 million was covered by insurance.[6]

Other ramifications were seen in the company. In March 2014, the chief information officer of Target, Beth Jacob, announced her resignation. Company officials replaced her with a new chief information security officer. Target has also made changes to its security and technology divisions and improved its cash registers. MasterCard and other card companies have increased security on credit cards by adding microchips to credit and debit cards that are almost impossible to copy. Moreover, when a user makes a purchase with a card, the chips in the card allows for a code that is used only one time. So the data, if stolen, is useless to anyone else.[7]

But the effects of the Target breach were much wider. Not long after the attacks, two banks (Green Bank from Houston, Texas, and Trustmaker National Bank from New York) announced that they had plans to sue Target as well as Trustwave, a security firm that was supposed to ensure security at Target. Officials from the banks explained that Trustwave failed to protect Target's customer data and that they were forced to spend $172 million to replace customer payment cards that had been compromised during the breach.

A settlement in April 2015 addressed these concerns. Target agreed to set aside up to $19 million for banks and credit unions that had issued the MasterCards involved in the breach and had to reissue the cards. The money would help the banks pay for the operating costs and losses on the cards that were affected. Not all banks were happy with the settlement, however. Smaller banks, which are typically forced to pay more for reissuing fees, wanted to see a higher settlement.[8]

Unfortunately, data shows that an increasing number of computer systems have been infected with the Kaptoxa malware that was used in the

Target attack. Damballa, a company of cybersecurity experts, reports that it found a 57 percent rise in Backoff detections (a "POS" or "point of sale" malware) during certain times of the year. Estimates provided by the U.S. Secret Service indicated that this has resulted in 1,000 firms being hit with a cyberattack.[9] In fact, after the Target breach, one cybercrime firm reported that it had uncovered at least six other attacks on different merchants in the United States whose credit card systems were also infected with the same malware.[10] Clearly this means that any company could become a victim of a cyberattack at any time, and such an attack would affect thousands of individuals alongside the targeted company.

Breaches like the one Target faced are not unusual in today's world. Cyberattacks appear in many forms and range from relatively harmless (such as changing the content on a website) to perilous (such as data being stolen and used to steal identities or trade secrets). Any organization, public or private, may be victimized by cybercriminals. Government agencies at all levels (federal, state, or local) have been victimized. Large and small companies in the United States and globally have had data stolen. Private individuals have also been victimized by cybercriminals. In essence, anyone who relies on a computer for daily activities can become a victim.

These attacks can cause great harm to business and individuals alike, including financial ruin and other long-term problems. In many of these attacks, victims have lost sensitive and confidential information, such as personal data and company secrets, leading to identity theft and monetary losses. Businesses have suffered not only from financial losses but also from damages related to lost business secrets and strategies. Government sites and politicians' accounts have been hacked, and the hackers have released political secrets to the public that resulted in tense relationships on the international front. Once victimized, individuals, businesses, and governments must pay thousands of dollars in response to these attacks as they attempt to recover.

Unfortunately, the techniques for committing cybercrime, such as the one against Target, are becoming increasingly sophisticated and specialized. Cybercriminals now have a wide variety of tools and techniques available to help them commit these crimes. Most cyberattacks happen quickly and can affect thousands of victims around the world, often without their knowledge.

Cybercrime

Cybercrimes are relatively new criminal offenses that are the result of recent advances in computer technology and the Internet. Today, the Internet is an essential part of everyday life for most people. Most businesses, governments, and individuals rely on this new technology as part of their daily routine. Computers are used in homes, businesses, medical offices, libraries, and schools. They have changed the way people work, communicate, and socialize in their daily lives. Many people use the Internet each day to conduct business, perform research, gather information, shop, entertain, pay for goods and services, carry out banking and financial tasks, send files and data to others, and communicate with friends and family around the world. In fact, it is estimated that about 31 percent of the Earth's population uses the Internet regularly.[11]

Many of the changes resulting from technology have clearly benefited society. We have seen advances in medicine, in the sciences, and in engineering. We have also improved communication between businesses and personnel. Documents are available more readily and are more secure. Many companies have "gone green" as a way to protect the environment. We have even seen changes in the workplace so that employees are no longer forced to work in an office setting for eight straight hours. Instead, they can work from home or another location any time of the day or night.

While advances in technology have benefited society, they have also created new opportunities for cybercriminals who use these innovations to cause harm to others. As technology has developed, so have new crimes that rely on that technology. Many of these crimes, such as computer hacking or the introduction of spyware, would not exist if it were not for computer technology. And as the computer technology becomes more advanced, so do the illegal activities. New criminal offenses are constantly being developed in the realm of cyberspace.

Not only have new crimes emerged but some more traditional crimes have also been transformed for the new medium. Traditional crimes such as fraud, theft, stalking, and bullying, which have been part of our society for years, now occur in new ways. Illegal drugs and child pornography, both of which existed before the development of network technology, are now sold via the Internet. Financial transactions (e.g., misuse of credit cards) and money-laundering offenses have evolved into new forms of crime. In some cases, the Internet has made commission of these crimes much simpler.

These new crimes are occurring because they are comparatively easy to commit. Cybercriminals can easily hack into computer systems anywhere in the world with little cost and little risk of being caught. They can alter records and information, steal money, or steal the identities of innocent victims. They can offer goods and products for sale that cannot be purchased elsewhere. Messages can be posted with the intent of harming a person's reputation. The software needed to carry out all of these malicious attacks can be purchased online for a small fee.

Because of the ease with which these offenses can be committed, they are on the rise. But they can also be very dangerous. In 2012, the World Economic Forum claimed that cybercrime is one of the biggest risks to global financial and political stability.[12] If successful, cybercriminals have the potential to cripple the global economy.

Definition of Terms

Many new terms have emerged in this new realm of cyberspace. Unfortunately, there is sometimes disagreement over the precise meanings of some of these terms, and they are used inconsistently. The meaning of the terms varies based on the region of the world or the time period in which a term was used. Many of the terms had distinct meanings at one point but are now largely used interchangeably. Because of this confusion, it is important to define the terms used throughout this book.

Cybercrime

"Cybercrime" is very a broad term that is often used to refer to different concepts. Consequently, there is some debate as to the exact meaning of the term.[13] For the purposes of this book, cybercrime can be thought of as crime that involves computers and computer networks.[14] Generally, it refers to acts that involve criminal uses of the Internet or other networked systems to cause harm to others or some form of a disturbance. It can include any criminal activity—not only on computers, networks, or the Internet but also on mobile phones or other personal devices—that is intended to cause harm to others.[15] These are illegal activities that are conducted through global electronic networks.[16] In short, the term "cybercrime" refers to methods by which computers or other electronic devices are used to carry out criminal activity and cause harm to others.

A cybercrime could be the misuse of computer systems or networks to carry out criminal offenses by unauthorized access to a computer system, illegal interception or alteration of data, or misuse of electronic devices. Other examples are the theft of intellectual property, that is, theft of a patent, trade secret, or anything protected by copyright laws. It can also include attacks against computers to deliberately disrupt processing or acts of espionage to make unauthorized copies of classified data. It includes downloading illegal music, stealing money from bank accounts, creating viruses, posting confidential business information on the Internet, committing identity theft or fraud, trafficking in child porn, money laundering and counterfeiting, and committing denial-of-service attacks. Other examples of cybercrimes include computer viruses; malware; fake emails or websites; identity theft; cyberbullying, stalking, or harassment; hacking; online scams (e.g., Nigerian scams); credit card theft; or phishing. These are all explained in more detail in chapter 2.

The term "cybercrime" often encompasses other, more specific categories of illegal behavior such as computer-assisted crimes and computer-focused crimes.[17] Other terms that refer to the same acts are computer crimes, digital crimes, techno-crimes, and high-tech crimes. These terms all refer to criminal activities that are committed by the use of emerging digital, network, or computer technologies, such as the Internet.

In the European Union, the Council of Europe provides a more complete definition of cybercrime. It describes cybercrime as "applied to three categories of criminal activities. The first covers traditional forms of crime such as fraud or forgery, though in a cybercrime context relates specifically to crimes committed over electronic communication networks and information systems. . . . The second concerns the publication of illegal content over electronic media (i.e., child sexual abuse material or incitement to racial hatred). The third includes crimes unique to electronic networks, that is, attacks against information systems, denial of service and hacking."[18] These types of attacks can also be directed against crucial critical infrastructures and affect existing rapid alert systems in many areas, with potentially disastrous consequences for the whole society. Common to each category of crime is that they may be committed on a mass scale and with a great geographical distance between the criminal act and its effects. Consequently the technical aspects of applied investigative methods are often the same across attack types.[19]

Cybercriminal

Cybercriminals are those who use mobile phones, laptop computers, or network servers to commit a cybercrime. For these offenders, the computers provide the means for committing crime. For example, a cybercriminal may hack into a computer network to disseminate a computer virus. Or an offender may use a computer to send child pornography to another user or steal another person's identity. An offender commits a computer crime when he or she uses a computer as the tool to commit a crime.[20] Although a criminal does not need special computer skills to commit a computer crime, he or she usually needs to have more than a basic level of computer knowledge to commit a computer crime.[21]

Because of the nature of technology, it is sometimes difficult to identify the person who is responsible for a virus, attack, or other cybercrime. Many cybercriminals are not caught. However, those that are investigated and arrested sometimes face severe penalties of both time in prison and large fines.

Drop Account

A drop account is an account that is opened by a criminal as a way to receive profits from his or her criminal activity. Most times, the accounts are opened with a false identity so they are difficult for law enforcement to track.

Advanced Persistent Threats

Advanced persistent threats (APTs) are attacks on computer systems that involve multiple techniques or approaches. In some instances, cybercriminals will use multiple techniques or methods in their attacks rather than a single method to ensure a particular result. This way, if one method is detected and blocked by security software, another means of attack will cause the intended harm.

Computer Forensics

The term "computer forensics" refers to the examination of computer components and their contents, including hard drives, external drives, compact disks, and printers, to investigate allegations of possible crimes and collect evidence of those crimes. The term is sometimes used to describe the forensic examination of all forms of digital evidence, including data traveling over networks, which is sometimes referred to as "network forensics" or "digital investigations."

Recently, the term "computer forensics" has been expanded by some professionals in the information security community to describe activities related to protecting computer systems rather than simply gathering evidence of possible crimes.

Subdisciplines of computer forensics include malware forensics and mobile device forensics. These subdisciplines are focused on collecting evidence of wrongdoing by use of malware and mobile devices (i.e., cell phones), respectively.

Malware

The term "malware," which is short for "malicious software," is a general term for software programs that affect how a computer functions.

Many early forms of malware were written as experiments and were intended to be annoying or funny rather than cause serious damage to files or a computer system. However, most malware programs today are written for malevolent purposes and intend to cause harm to computers and/or provide a profit for the criminal. In the legal field, malware may also be referred to as "computer contaminant."

Most malware is spread through an email attachment. When the receiver opens the attachment, the malware installs itself onto the victim's computer. Once on the computer, the malware can have many effects. It can be programmed to damage the computer itself or to delete files. It can also steal information by acting as a "keylogger" to capture information typed into a computer (i.e., passwords or account information), or it can copy files. Another common attack is to hijack a system, allowing the attacker to remotely control the system.[22] All of these actions clearly interfere with the daily operation of that computer.[23] If serious enough, the malware can prevent an organization or website from operating or shut down computer networks for a short time.

One danger with malware is that the receivers are often unaware that malware has been attached to their computer. Experts estimate that 54 days pass between the time the malware is placed on a computer and when it is detected. Further, about 15 percent of malware goes undetected for 180 days.[24] This gives criminals access to user information such as passwords and bank account numbers over a long period of time.

Malware typically includes computer viruses, worms, adware, spyware, keyloggers, logic bombs, rootkits, and Trojan horse programs that seek to alter functions within computer programs and files. Many attacks that use malware are blended attacks in which multiple types of malware are used at the same time.

Reports indicate that the volume of malware that is detected each year is increasing. Some point to this and argue that malware will be the largest security threat to computer users in the future.[25] In the past 10 years the amount of malware intended to attack mobile devices has grown. Recent attacks have proliferated on the Android system. A virus geared toward Android devices was recently spread through a free app that was downloaded by users all around the world more than 250,000 times in the span of just a few days.[26]

Crimeware

Crimeware refers to the software that is used to commit acts of cybercrime. The term encompasses a multitude of different malicious, or potentially malicious, software products. Examples of crimeware are bots and Trojan horses.

Botnet

One form of malware is a botnet, or bot network. These are comprised of many computers that have been infected with malware that allows them to be controlled remotely through commands sent through the Internet, possibly from thousands of miles away. In some cases, thousands of infected computers can be controlled by one person as a way to disrupt or block Internet traffic. It can also be used to steal information or distribute other malware. The infected computers are sometimes referred to as "zombie computers."

Packet Sniffers

Packet sniffers are small pieces of malware that are attached to computer systems and have the capability of "sniffing out" or inspecting data that is being sent along a computer network. If an important piece of data is detected, such as a password, that information is recorded and sent to the criminal.

Personally Identifiable Information

Personally identifiable information (PII), refers to any information that can be used to identify an individual. If stolen, a criminal can use this information to steal that person's identity or cause other harm to them. Examples of PIIs are a person's full name, Social Security number (or other federal identification number, such as a passport number or driver's license number), birth date and place of birth, credit card account numbers, and bank account information. Even simple things such as sex, race, place of employment, education, or criminal record can be considered PII because when it is used in conjunction with other pieces of information it can permit a criminal to identify an individual.

Cyberterrorism

Cyberterrorism is the use of the Internet by terrorist groups who are attempting to affect a nation's policies. As defined by the Federal Emergency Management Agency, cyberterrorism is the "unlawful attacks and threats of attack against computers, networks and the information stored therein when done to intimidate or coerce a government or its people in furtherance of political or social objectives." Cyberterrorism is covered in more detail in chapter 7.

Zero-Day Exploit

A zero-day exploit occurs when a computer hacker is able to uncover a weakness in a software program that is unknown to the owner or business and has not been exploited by a cybercriminal. Criminals may be able to initiate a malicious attack that takes advantage of the weakness before the program can be corrected or a security patch can be issued by the software vendor. In 2013, Symantec found 23 zero-day vulnerabilities in websites owned by businesses, an increase of 61 percent over the previous year.[27]

Exploit Kits

Exploit kits are malicious programs that allow criminals to identify vulnerabilities in computer systems and then spread malware to those computers. Exploit kits can be sold or rented, either individually or in bundles, on the cyber black market. Many of the exploit kits available today originate for relatively low prices in such countries as Russia and China, where the black markets for malware are more popular. Exploit kits are encrypted so that they are not detected by security systems. According to the Internet Crime Complaint Center, the most popularly purchased exploit kit is Blackhole, which was created in Russia. With this exploit kit, a computer may be infected with the malware for a long period without the user knowing.[28]

Cyber Black Markets/Darknets

Cyber black markets are online stores that provide criminals with the materials or tools they need to carry out cybercrimes. According to many reports, the cyber black market economy is thriving. The sites have storefronts with instant messaging chat rooms, like a typical retail website. For the most part, they cater to unskilled or beginning hackers who many not have a good understanding of computer systems, but with the use of the tools and products on the black market, they are able to launch more advanced attacks. The tools are generally not expensive. On one site, botnets were sold for as low as $50. The sites also provide education and training to the purchaser.[29] Consulting services for setting up a botnet can range from $350 to $400; for advice on spreading a virus, the fees are around $100 per 1,000 installs. To arrange to have email spam sent, it will cost around $40 per 20,000 emails.[30] If someone wishes a more complex or elaborate attack, the prices will be higher.[31]

Script Kiddies

Hackers who do not possess the technical skills to carry out complicated attacks are sometimes called "script kiddies." Their attacks are often aimed at systems with weak security. They tend to make more mistakes and are not as capable at hiding their attacks, which makes it easier for law enforcement officials to track them down. But they also tend to carry out most of the computer crimes and use the crimeware tools that are available on black market sites. Because they are not serious attacks, script kiddies usually cause only minor vandalism.[32]

Motives of Cybercriminals

Why do people commit cybercrime? That is a tough question to answer. Every cybercriminal is different and has a different reason for his or her illicit behavior. Cybercriminals carry out their attacks or commit crimes on the Internet to achieve many goals, some of which are described in the sections that follow.

Financial Reasons

One goal of many cybercriminals is to make a profit. Many cybercriminals successfully do this through online fraud or by stealing assets or funds from a company or an individual. In order to carry out these crimes, they must break into a computer system and alter data or steal personal information from others like passwords or other confidential credentials. With this information, criminals are able to steal money from bank accounts. To make it easier, cybercriminals will often seek out vulnerable victims, such as the elderly, whom they can easily exploit.

Disrupt Business

Some cybercriminals seek to disrupt the daily business operations of a company or in some other way cause harm to a business or an individual. They may seek to affect as many people as they can in a short amount of time. To do this, they may write a virus in a way that will remain undetected for many months or that will spread easily from one computer to another. This way, the largest number of users possible will be affected by the malware.

Terrorism

Terrorists around the world use advanced technology to recruit new members. They also use the Internet to communicate with other terrorist groups about future activities, including possible attacks. They use the Internet to raise money by soliciting donations, and they publish training materials and other propaganda that favors their group. They can encourage others to carry out acts of violence by providing tips on the Internet or by adding instructions on how to build a bomb to their literature.

Theft (Nonfinancial)

Some cybercriminals carry out crimes as a way to steal valuable intellectual property or trade secrets. They can steal from other businesses, other individuals, or other governments. They can profit from selling or using the information.

Political Reasons

Some cyberattacks are politically motivated. The attackers may hack into a computer system as a way to get attention for their cause, show their support for a particular cause, raise donations, or persuade people to join their group. In some cases, governments will hack into the systems of other governments as a way to commit espionage or steal secrets (especially technology secrets). Every country engages in espionage against other nations to some extent, but China and Russia are more well known for this. Many countries, such as China and Sweden, permit warrantless wiretapping with other nations. Russia has the SORM monitoring programs; the United Kingdom has the Government Communications Headquarters, which provides signals intelligence and taps fiber-optic cables for secret access to communications; Germany and the Netherlands use wiretaps.[33] In 2012, the United States filed charges of cyberactivity against the Chinese government for hacking, a charge the Chinese deny. Box 1.1 includes some cases of state-sponsored cyberespionage.

Box 1.1 Cyberespionage Cases

- March 20, 2014: A group called DarkSeoul attacked South Korean assets. Although reports about events are inconsistent. it appears that the group attacked two banks and a television broadcast station. The malware was coded to begin at a specific time to wipe the master boot record and other records. The multistaged attacks caused a great deal of damage.[a]
- Prism: The United States has developed a Prism program implemented by the National Security Agency in an attempt to trace foreign communications. The most intelligence being gathered by the United States is from Iran, followed by Pakistan, Jordan, Egypt, and India.[b]
- China: The cyberespionage group APT1 was accused of being Unit Number 61398 of the Chinese People's Liberation Army. It was also accused of being responsible for stealing hundreds of terabytes of data from over 140 organizations across the English-speaking world. APT1 is staffed by hundreds of people who are trained in computer security and speak English proficiently. The group controls thousands of computer systems and is able to steal technology secrets and other proprietary manufacturing information.[c]
- April 2007: Estonia was attacked by the Russian government in what may have been the first cyberwar. The primary targets were the Estonian president and parliament, two of the country's largest banks, and the three largest news outlets. It was done after the Estonian officials removed a 1947 statue that commemorated an unknown Russian soldier. The attackers used hundreds of botnets and distributed denial-of-service attacks that overloaded networks with phony requests for information. The attacks involved about a million computers and lasted about three weeks.[d]

[a]Department of Homeland Security, US-CERT, "South Korean Malware Attack," available at https://www.us-cert.gov/sites/default/files/publications/South%20Korean%20Malware%20Attack_1.pdf.

[b]Bernard Everett, "Optically Transparent: The Rise of Industrial Espionage and State-Sponsored Hacking," *Computer Fraud and Security*, October 2013, 13–16, www.computerfraudandsecurity.com.

[c]Tim Ring, "A Breach Too Far?" *Computer Fraud and Security*, June 2013, 5–9, www.computerfraudandsecurity.com.

[d]Nancy Marion, Kelley Cronin, and Willard M. Oliver, *Homeland Security* (Durham, NC: Carolina Academic Press, 2015).

Amusement/Curiosity/Challenge

One motive for many cybercriminals is simply curiosity or amusement. They see hacking into a secure system as a challenge and do so simply to see if they are able to break into a system. Many cybercriminals in this category do not intend to cause harm, and many are not technologically skilled. Nonetheless, their actions can cause a significant amount of damage.

Organized Crime

Members of organized crime carry out cybercrimes as a way to increase their power and wealth. They see cybercrime as an easy way to make a profit, partly because it is easier to carry out crimes on the Internet than to physically break into a building or facility.[34] They have used the Internet to traffic in drugs, even making alliances with drug traffickers in the Middle East and other locations to increase their supply and market. Some groups have used cybercrime as a way to launder money or traffic in child pornography, illegal weapons, and even humans.[35] Organized cybercrime will be covered in more detail in chapter 6.

Locating Victims

Some offenders use the Internet and other social media outlets to locate potential victims for their crimes. The offenders enter chat rooms and, by using pseudonyms and fake profiles that make them more attractive, meet potential victims, build a level of trust with them, and then arrange to meet them in person where they can carry out brutal acts of violence, sometimes even murder.

Cybercriminals often use social websites to meet victims. These sites frequently include personal information about an offender that criminals can use to reach out to the victim. And many are successful in doing so. Locating potential victims via that Internet is becoming easier. Many people now use the Internet to communicate and socialize with others through social media sites such as Facebook and Twitter. According to the Norton Report,[36] 21 percent of adults who use online social media sites have become victims of cybercrime. Moreover, 15 percent of social network users reported that their profiles had been hacked and found that strangers were pretending to be them. About one-tenth of those who use social network sites reported that they had fallen for a scam or fake link. Although most users (75 percent) realize that cybercriminals use social networks for victims, only about 44 percent use security software and only 49 percent use privacy settings as a means to limit what information they share.[37]

People also give out information through professional websites, such as LinkedIn. These sites provide a person's place of employment and job title, educational background, previous employers and where the person went to school and lives. While these sites help people keep in touch with family and friends and make professional contacts, they can also be used for harm. Many users post personal information, including phone numbers, birthdays, or employment information that can then be used by criminals to gather information to identify potential victims. These sites give criminals enough information to enable them to commit crimes, such as identity theft and phishing schemes. An example of someone who used the Internet to find victims is in Box 1.2.

Box 1.2   Criminals Who Used the Internet to Find Victims

Peter Chapman was a serial rapist who used Facebook to meet young women. Chapman, a 33-year-old, nearly toothless, homeless man, met 17-year-old Ashleigh Hall online and arranged to meet her in person. When he did, he sexually assaulted and killed her.[a]

John E. Robinson, who was also known as "Slavemaster," used the Internet to meet women who enjoyed a submissive role during sex. He concealed his true identity, pretending to be a wealthy businessman, and convinced Sheila Faith to move in with him. Robinson cashed her pension checks for seven years. He then met 21-year-old Izabella Lewicka and offered her a job. Later he met Suzette Trouten. All three women disappeared. Robinson was arrested in 2000. The bodies of the three women were later found in chemical drums. All three had been killed by blows to the head by a hammer. Robinson was later convicted and sentenced to death.[b]

In Ohio, 53-year-old Richard Beasley and 16-year-old Brogan Rafferty used Craig'slist to lure men to their home under the pretense of a job. Three men were killed and one survived. Beasley was sentenced to death.[c]

[a]Helen Carter, "Facebook Murderer Who Posed as Teenager to Lure Victim Jailed for Life," *The Guardian*, May 19, 2014, http://www.theguardian.com /uk/2010/mar/08/peter-chapman-facebook-ashleigh-hall.

[b]Sue Wiltz, *Slave Master* (New York: Pinnacle Books, 2004).

[c]Kim Palmer, "Ohio Judge Sentences 'Craig'slist' Killer to Death," Reuters, April 4, 2013, http://www.reuters.com/article/2013/04/04/us-usa-crime-craigslist -idUSBRE9330LS20130404.

Effects of Cybercrime

The victims of cybercrime, whether they are businesses or individuals, face many repercussions, both in the short term and the long term.

Individuals

Some victims of cybercrime suffer great harm if they fall prey to cybercrime. They will often spend months, if not years, to clear their credit records. In some cases, the damages go beyond a damaged credit history. Computer crimes can result in significant monetary loss for the victims. The people whose information is stolen must sometimes pay thousands of dollars to have their records cleared up. More severe crimes can lead to death as some victims of cyber offenses have committed suicide as a result of their victimization. One of those victims was Phoebe Prince, who moved to Massachusetts from Ireland. After being the target of constant cyberbullying by her peers, she took her own life.

Part of the problem is that many personal or home computers do not have even simple security systems that help block malware from installing in their systems. Many adults are not aware of the dangers that lurk online and do not feel the need to install firewalls or other systems to block malware. The Norton Report showed that many adults who use the Internet reported that they do not know how to recognize different types of malware and the effects they can have on their computers. About half, or 40 percent of adults, claimed that they did not realize it was possible for malware to be installed on a computer unknowingly.[38]

The yearly Norton Report estimated that the cost of cybercrimes committed against individuals cost is about $100 billion a year. This was based on events reported by people in 24 different countries. This estimate may actually be low, as a significant number of cybercrime victims do not report the offenses, and many others do not realize they have been victimized. Moreover, the report estimated that there are about 1.5 million cybercrime victims each day, and the average loss to a victim of cybercrime is $197. In the United States, that average is $290.[39]

Businesses

If a business is attacked by cybercriminals, it could be disastrous. While some cyberattacks result in little or no damage, others cause damages so extensive that a company may never recover. Not only could they lose profits from an attack but it can also impact a company's image, reputation, and brand image, resulting in a loss of confidence by investors and customers. The company may be forced to shut down temporarily because of malware installed in their computer systems. Even a small attack can compromise a large business.

The financial losses of a cyberattack could be massive. It is difficult, if not impossible, to put an exact cost estimate on an attack, as the earlier Target example shows. The extent of the losses will depend partly on the size and type of attack as well as the extent and duration. The primary cost resulting from a data breach is informing customers that their data may have been stolen and compromised in some fashion. Other costs include the actual damage caused to computers, the loss of sales, and the potential fines a company might face for losses and damages. Then there is a threat of regulatory penalties and legal action, fines, and an interruption of daily business. There may also be a loss of trade secrets or other business information.

Sometimes a company may be forced to shut down so malware can be removed from its computers. Cybercriminals can use stolen credit card information to run up huge bills, causing the credit card company significant losses. There are also the expenses related to security software purchased and personnel hired in an effort to protect against possible attacks.[40] In 2013, cyberattacks cost the world an estimated $113 billion.[41]

Box 1.3   The Ashley Madison Hack

While most cybercriminals engage in their crimes for personal gain, some engage in cybercrime for other reasons. The recent hacking of the website AshleyMadison.com, which caters to married people who want to find someone to cheat on their partner with, illustrates this point.

In July 2015, hackers gained access to the personal information of Ashley Madison's users. Other websites were also breached in the hack, all owned by the same company as Ashley Madison, Avid Life Media, Inc. The other sites whose users' names and other identifying information were also stolen included Cougar Life, which is geared toward older women seeking younger men, and Established Men, which is designed to couple older men with younger women.

While breaches of websites to gain access to personal information are not unusual, what was unique about the Ashley Madison breach was the fact that the group who hacked the site, calling themselves the Impact Team, was not interested in selling the information they got. Rather, they demanded that Ashley Madison be taken down permanently.

The Impact Team left a lengthy manifesto that, along with calling the men using the site "cheating dirtbags," also cited the fact that the company did not delete user data appropriately when a user left the site. In response to these perceived problems, the group publically released some of the user data they had gathered and threated to release more each day until the site was taken down.

While certainly a cybercrime, the unique elements of the Ashley Madison hack represent the fine line between ideas like "hacktivism" and general cybercrime. Here the motivation for the criminal activity was not personal gain, at least in terms of money, but rather damaging a company with its users and the public. While the full rationale of the Impact Team may never be discovered, the publicity of the hack, and the type of data it targeted, may indicate an area of increasing concern for practitioners and users alike.

Source: W. P. Nobles III, "Online Cheaters Exposed after Hackers Access Ashley Madison Hookup Site," *Washington Post*, July 20, 2015, http://www.washington post.com/news/morning-mix/wp/2015/07/20/online-cheaters-exposed -after-hackers-access-ashleymadison-hookup-site/?tid=sm_fb.

Cybercrimes can be particularly harmful to those in the banking and financial industries, where computers are used every day to send and receive funds. It is estimated that the number of cybercrimes in financial firms is more than double the number of cybercrimes in other industries. Specifically, it has been estimated that 39 percent of companies that provide financial services suffered from cybercrime compared with 17 percent in other industries.[42] It is estimated that banking institutions lose billions of dollars each year through fraudulent transactions.

The financial cost of a computer attack for a business is difficult to quantify, and it is difficult to determine the total cost of a cyberattack. Some costs can be easily calculated, whereas others must be estimated. Direct financial costs include things like technical personnel, who must spend time investigating a potential breach or legal costs. These costs are directly attached to the occurrence of the breach. However, there are also indirect costs that are not directly related to the breach. This may include a loss of productivity, which is more difficult to measure.

It is estimated that the APT attack against the Oak Ridge National Laboratory cost the U.S. Department of Energy more than $2 million. The attack against the Sony PlayStation Network, which resulted in the theft of personal information from about 77 million accounts, was estimated to cost that company approximately $171 million.[43]

One group attempted to put a cost on a cyberattack. The 2013 *Annual Cost of Failed Trust Report: Threats and Attacks* gathered responses from Global 2000 organizations based in Australia, France, Germany, the United Kingdom, and the United States. The researchers reported the total possible cost of security threats over a 24-month period to be $398 million per organization.[44]

A study by the Ponemon Institute attempted to put a value on the damage to a company's reputation caused by cyberattacks. The results of this study showed that the cost of an attack to the brand value can be anywhere from $184 million to $339 million. Depending on the attack, companies may lose anywhere between 12 to 25 percent of their brand value after a breach. This can mean a loss of millions of dollars.[45]

Another study estimated that attacks cost companies approximately $214,000. The expenses cover things like the forensic investigation, investments in technology that must be made as a result of the breach, and brand recovery costs.[46]

Current Book

Because of the potential harm that can occur as a result of cybercrime, it is crucial that people increase their knowledge and understanding of it. This book will introduce readers to the basic concepts and trends in cybercrime. The authors assume that the reader has no prior knowledge of cybercrime but rather just an interest in learning more.

A short history of cybercrime is presented in chapter 2, which will provide background on the current state of cybercrime. The different types of cybercrime are described in chapter 3, along with a description of their frequency. Of course, there are many legal concerns regarding Internet crimes, some of which are emerging alongside the technology. Chapter 4 covers the amount of cybercrime occurring—insofar as that is possible. Law enforcement's response and the difficulty of tracking offenders are the subjects of chapter 5.

Chapter 6 provides readers with a view of the role of organized crime groups participating in cybercrime and examines some organizational types. Terrorists also rely on the Internet to recruit members and carry out crimes, which is the focus of chapter 7. In chapter 8, information about cyberwars is presented, and the question of how nation-states can use the Internet and other networks for warfare is examined. Legislatures have responded to the emerging crimes in the United States and internationally. The domestic response is the focus of chapter 9, and the international response is the focus of chapter 10. A conclusion to the material in the book and some predictions for the future are presented in chapter 11.

A Note on the Social Elements of Cybercrime

Any book on cybercrime would be remiss to not acknowledge that, at least to some degree, the fear the public feels about cybercrime is conditioned on the way society sees it. While there appears to be good reason to be afraid of some cybercrimes, particularly crimes like fraud and identity theft, there remain a large number of cybercrimes that, while potentially threatening, have yet to occur on any large scale.

Box 1.4   Cybercrime in the Movies

Cybercrime, and particularly hackers, have been part of popular culture for at least four decades. In fact, the original idea of a hacker can be traced back to the genre of cyberpunk, which came of age in the 1970s. David S. Wall argues that there were three phases to the development of pop culture's version of cybercrime. The first, the original cyberpunk literature, developed in the 1970s and early 1980s and featured dystopic societies with highly advanced technology. Also prominent in these stories, which included novels like the Neuromancer trilogy, was crime. In some ways, the cyberpunk genre defined how we see cybercrime today.

By the late 1980s the development of pop culture surrounding cybercrime had changed. Rather than the dystopic versions of reality prominent in cyberpunk, facilitation of crimes using computer technology became prominent. In movies like the original *The Italian Job*, hackers were used as tools to further normal criminal activity. However, by the 1990s a second strain of "haxploitation" movies had taken hold, which developed more out of the cyberpunk genre, and these focused on the hacker as a lone individual fighting against a corrupt system through his or her technological prowess. Movies like *Real Genius* are examples of this type of film.

A third strain of haxploitation movies developed more recently. Films like *The Matrix* showed a world that was entirely generated by computer technology, and therefore, both the hacker and the hack took place in this simulated environment.

In all of these genres, the issue of crime committed via networks, or cybercrime, is featured prominently. In fact, Wall argues that these depictions, and others related to them, continue to shape our view of cybercrime and the space in which it happens. This powerful influence is difficult to shift away from, as new movies continue to emphasize the power hackers, and others engaged in technocrime, have to influence the world around us.

Source: David S. Wall, "Cybercrime and the Culture of Fear: Social Science Fiction(s) and the Production of Knowledge about Cybercrime," *Information, Communication & Society* 11 (2011): 861–884.

In his 2011 work, *Cybercrime and the Culture of Fear*, David S. Wall suggests that the fear we feel as a society is predicated on elements of pop culture that surround us. Specifically, Wall references the types of movies that feature hackers or other technologically mysterious (to most of us) characters and notes that the world they operate in, the world that most people are exposed to in terms of cybercrime, is one that is naturally criminogenic and dangerous.

This can easily be seen in popular movies like *Hackers* and *Swordfish*. In those films, and others like it, hackers have the ability to penetrate any system and cause any number of insidious things to happen to innocent, or not so innocent, people. This omnipotent super-hacker ideal is, by and large, both outmoded in terms of pop culture and inaccurate to begin with. Nevertheless, it still drives a significant amount of the public discourse regarding cybercrime.[47] A more complete explanation of the culture of fear surrounding cybercrime is examined in Box 1.4.

While this general fear, by itself, is not worrisome, its effects on society could be momentous. Politicians often use fear as a driver to allow for broadened security agendas,[48] and some businesses profit from products meant to ameliorate this fear. Indeed, some hackers have now become businesspeople, relying on the fear possible data theft engenders to become wealthy.

One of the reasons a book like this is helpful is because it helps dispel some of these myths about cybercrime without denying the reality of the problem. The more students and others are informed about the topic of cybercrime, the less likely the fear is to be the primary driver of behavior. Additionally, we hope the information in the book helps prevent victimization.

Review Questions

1. What are the definitions of some of the key terms related to cybercrime?
2. What is malware and why is it important?
3. If someone called you a script kiddie, what would that mean?
4. Describe the motives of cybercriminals.
5. What are the long-term and short-term effects of cybercrimes on individuals? On businesses?

Key Terms

Advanced persistent threat (APT)
Botnet
Computer crime
Computer forensics
Crimeware
Cyber black market
Cybercrime
Cybercriminal
Cyberterrorism
Darknet
Digital crime
Digital investigation
Drop account
Exploit kit
High-tech crime
Malware
Packet sniffer
Personally identifiable information (PII)
Script kiddie
Zero-day exploit

Notes

1. "Target and Snapchat Suffer Major Data Breaches," *Computer Fraud and Security*, January 2014, 1–3.
2. "Retailers Hit by Malware-Based Hacking Attacks," *Computer Fraud and Security*, February 2014, 1–3.

3. Susan Berfield, "From Cyber Crime to Canada, Target Had a Very Bad Year," *Bloomberg Business*, February 26, 2014, http://www.bloomberg.com/bw/articles /2014-02-26/from-cyber-crime-to-canada-target-had-a-very-bad-year.

4. Tracey Caldwell, "The True Cost of Being Hacked," *Computer Fraud and Security*, June 2014, 8–13.

5. "Target Hackers Broke in Via HVAC Company," Krebs on Security, February 14, 2014, http://krebsonsecurity.com/2014/02/target-hackers-broke-in-via-hvac -company/.

6. Caldwell, "True Cost of Being Hacked," 10.

7. Boston Globe, "Target Settles Data Breach Lawsuit with MasterCard for $19M," *New York Times*, April 16, 2015, https://www.bostonglobe.com /business/2015/04/15/target-settles-data-breach-lawsuit-with-mastercard-for /63fwFAprKcW8imQ88bpbXI/story.html.

8. Robin Sidel, "After Target and Home Depot Breaches, Small Lenders Object to Settlements," *Wall Street Journal*, April 27, 2015, http://www.wsj.com/articles /after-target-and-home-depot-breaches-small-lenders-object-to-settlements -1430175638.

9. "Retailers under Sustained Attack," *Computer Fraud and Security*, November 2014, 3.

10. Reuters, "Firm Uncovers More Hacks on US Retailers," *Chicago Tribune*, January 17, 2014, http//articles.chicagotribune.com/2014-01-17/business/chi -hacking-retailers-20140117_1_u-s-retailers-law-enforcement-attacks; Jim Finkle, "Exclusive: Cybercrime Firm Says Uncovers Six Active Attacks on U.S. Merchants," *Chicago Tribune*, January 17, 2014, http://articles.chicagotribune .com/2014-01-17/business/sns-rt-us-target-databreach-20140117_1_payment -card-data-law-enforcement-retailers.

11. Maria Eriksen-Jensen, "Holding Back the Tidal Wave of Cybercrime," *Computer Fraud and Security*, March 2013, 10–15.

12. Ibid.

13. D. S. Wall, "Cybercrimes: New Wine, No Bottles?," in *Invisible Crimes: Their Victims and Their Regulation*, ed. P. Davies, P. Francis, and V. Jupp (London: Macmillan, 1999), 105–139; M. Williams, *Virtually Criminal* (New York: Routledge, 2006).

14. E. Casey, *Digital Evidence and Computer Crime* (London: Academic Press, 2000), 8.

15. Grainne Kirwan and Andrew Power, *The Psychology of Cyber Crime: Concepts and Principles* (Hershey, PA: Information Science Reference, 2012), 1–2.

16. D. Thomas and B. D. Loader, "Introduction—Cybercrime: Law Enforcement, Security and Surveillance in the Information Age," in *Cybercrime: Law Enforcement, Security and Surveillance in the Information Age*, ed. D. Thomas and B. D. Loader (London: England: Routledge, 2000), 3.

17. S. Furnell, *Cyber Crime: Vandalizing the Information Society* (London: Addison Wesley, 2002), 22.

18. Council of Europe, The commission communication "towards a general policy on the fight against cyber crime," 2007, retrieved from http://europa.eu /rapid/press-release_MEMO-07-199_en.pdf.

19. Council of Europe, Convention on Cybercrime, 2001, http://www .conventions.coe.int/Treaty/en/Treaties/Html/185.htm.

20. Casey, *Digital Evidence*, X.

21. L. D. Carter and J. A. Katz, *Computer Crime: An Emerging Challenge for Law Enforcement* (East Lansing: Michigan State University, 1997).

22. S. Furnell, "Hackers, Viruses and Malicious Software," in *Handbook of Internet Crime*, ed. Yvonne Jewkes and Majid Yar (Cullompton, England: Willan, 2010), 173–193.

23. Kirwan and Power, *Psychology of Cyber Crime*, 74.

24. Zahra Salehi, Ashkan Sami, and Mahboobe Ghiasi, "Using Feature Generation from API Calls for Malware Detection," *Computer Fraud and Security*, September 2014, 9–18.

25. Ibid.

26. Eddy Willems, "Android under Attack," *Computer Fraud and Security*, November 2013, 13–14.

27. Symantec, Internet Security Threat Report, 2014, http://www.symantec .com/connect/app#!/blogs/symantec-2014-internet-security-threat-report.

28. Florian Malecki, "Defending Your Business from Exploit Kits," *Computer Fraud and Security*, June 2013, 19–20.

29. "Cyber 'Black Markets' Have Become Mature Economies, Say Researchers," *Computer Fraud and Security*, April 2014, 3; Derek Manky, "Cybercrime as a Service: A Very Modern Business," *Computer Fraud and Security*, June 2013, 9–13.

30. Manky, "Cybercrime as a Service," 9–13.

31. Ibid.

32. Reid Skibell, "Cybercrimes and Misdemeanors: A Reevaluation of the Computer Fraud and Abuse Act," *Berkeley Technology Law Journal* 18 (2003): 909–944.

33. Bernard Everett, "Optically Transparent: The Rise of Industrial Espionage and State-Sponsored Hacking," *Computer Fraud and Security*, October 2013, 13–16.

34. Will Gragido, Daniel Molina, John Pirc, and Nick Selby, *Blackhatonomics* (New York: Syngress, 2012).

35. Rob McCusker, "Transnational Organized Cybercrime: Distinguishing Threat from Reality," *Crime, Law and Social Change* 46 (2006): 257–273; D. L. Speer, "Redefining Borders: The Challenges of Cybercrime Crime," *Law and Social Change* 34 (2000): 259–273; Kim-Kwang Choo, "Organized Crime Groups in Cyberspace: A Typology," *Trends in Organized Crime* 11, no. 3 (2008): 270–295.

36. Norton, 2013, 2013 Norton Report, http://www.yle.fi/tvuutiset/uutiset /upics/liitetiedostot/norton_raportti.pdf.

37. "Cybercrime Costs $110bn a Year—Maybe More," *Computer Fraud and Security*, September 2012, 3, 20.

38. Ibid.

39. Ibid.

40. Nigel Pearson, "A Larger Problem: Financial and Reputational Risks," *Computer Fraud and Security*, April 2014, 11–13.

41. Christine Hall, "The Hidden Cost of Cyber Crime," *Forbes*, March 20, 2014, http://www.forbes.com/sites/sungardas/2014/03/20/the-hidden-cost-of-cyber -crime.

42. Reuters, "Cybercrime Hits Financial Firms Hardest: Survey," March 3, 2014, http://www.reuters.com/article/us-banks-cybercrime-idUSBREA2300520140304.

43. Rafal Leszczyna, "Cost Assessment of Computer Security Activities," *Computer Fraud and Security*, July 2013, 11–16.

44. "Organisations Losing Money Because of Trust Failures," *Computer Fraud and Security*, March 2013, 3.

45. "Breaches Hit Firms' Brand Value Hard," *Computer Fraud and Security*, November 2011, 3.

46. Rafal Leszczyna, "Cost Assessment of Computer Security Activities," *Computer Fraud and Security*, July 2013, 11–16.

47. David S. Wall, "Cybercrime and the Culture of Fear: Social Science Fiction(s) and the Production of Knowledge about Cybercrime," *Information, Communication & Society* 11 (2011): 861–884.

48. David Altheide, *Terrorism and the Politics of Fear* (Oxford: AltaMira, 2006).

CHAPTER TWO

History of Cybercrime

Introduction

WHILE CYBERCRIME IS A RELATIVELY NEW PHENOMENON, some key people and events have been critical in defining this emerging field. By understanding these events, it is possible to gain a better perspective on current events and trends in cybercrime. In this chapter, the history of computer crime is described to show how computer crimes have evolved over the past few decades. This chapter will describe critical events and influential people that have helped to shape current policy and thus will provide a foundation to understand the current status of computer crimes.

Pre-1970

The Internet can be traced back to events in the 1950s when the United States was preoccupied with the Cold War and the Soviet Union. In 1957, the Soviets launched the satellite Sputnik into space, thereby winning the space race. As a way to advance American technology and prevent the Soviets from getting any further ahead, in 1958 the U.S. government created a new agency, the Advanced Research Projects Agency (ARPA), with the responsibility of developing new technologies to be used for military purposes. In 1962, a new division of ARPA was formed, the Information Processing Techniques Office, and a scientist from MIT, J. C. R. Licklider, was appointed to lead the new agency. He proposed a network of interconnected computers that scientists could use to share research and work jointly on projects. The idea lay dormant for a time, as few people had the expertise to carry out the plans. The next director of the agency picked up the idea again and formed the Advanced Research Projects Agency Network (ARPANet), an early precursor of the Internet. Ray Tomlinson, an engineer, was the first person to send an email over the ARPANet. He was also the first person to use the @ symbol in one of those communications. In 1990, ARPANet became the Internet.

In the 1960s and 1970s, there was little computer crime as the technology was neither widely available nor used by the general population. At that time, computer use was largely restricted to the military and to researchers at universities and other scientific labs. Most unauthorized hacking events were simply pranks carried out on computer systems at universities by inquisitive students who did not intend to cause any harm. The viruses they left behind were easily identified and removed. These hackers sought to discover kinks in the system and then use that information to make improvements. The events generally caused minimal damage to computers or data, if any at all. The entire purpose of hacking in those days was simply for fun—to prove that a person had the technological savvy and skills to break into a supposedly secure system. At the time, there were few laws that criminalized these activities, so they were not considered to be crimes, and few people were prosecuted for these acts. In fact, offenders often signed their names to a virus.

Some may argue that the first person to recognize and study computer crime and security issues was Donn B. Parker. During the early 1970s, as the Internet was evolving, Parker researched computer crime and security issues. He became a senior computer security consultant at the Stanford Research Institute and, in that position, wrote the first federal manual on computer crime, *Computer Crime—Criminal Justice Resource Manual*, in 1970. This was a manual for law enforcement officials, who were beginning to see more complaints of computer crimes. An example of early hacking is described in Box 2.1.

Box 2.1   An Early Example of Cyber Hacking

Magician and inventor Nevil Maskelyne, who was born in 1863, was fascinated by the expanding technology of the wireless telegraph. Maskelyne knew that British physicist John Ambrose Fleming had scheduled an appearance at the lecture theater of London's Royal Institution in June 1903, to demonstrate a modern communications system that would allow a person to send and receive Morse code wirelessly over long distances. Fleming had positioned his friend Guglielmo Marconi on top of a cliff in Poldhu, Cornwall, England. Marconi was to send a message to Maskelyne using Morse code, which Maskelyne would receive in the theater.

But even before Marconi sent his message to Maskelyne, the machine began to receive a message. At first, the message was only one word that was repeated over and over: *rats*. Then the message changed to a limerick: "There was a young fellow of Italy, who diddled the public quite prettily."

Clearly, Fleming was embarrassed at the failure of his technology. Neither he nor Marconi could account for the strange messages received, but it was quickly apparent that Marconi's assertion regarding the privacy and security of this new technology was not accurate. In today's terms, Fleming and Marconi had been hacked. Some time later Maskelyne announced that he had sent the messages through the projector in the auditorium. In other words, Maskelyne was the hacker.

The 1970s

During the 1970s, technology was rapidly advancing. Cybercriminals were likewise learning more about computer systems and their vulnerabilities, all the while honing their hacking skills. Throughout the decade, hackers' intentions and purposes were quickly changing. No longer were hackers finding ways into systems for fun; now they intended to cause harm. One of the first computer viruses designed to damage systems appeared in 1971. Called Creeper, the virus was released in the ARPANet. A computer infected with the virus displayed a message on the screen indicating that the system was infected and the identity of those responsible for creating the virus.

The first computer crimes also appeared during the 1970s. The first types of computer crimes to be recognized were computer intrusions and fraud.[1] Likewise, one of the first identified cybercrimes occurred in 1973, when a chief teller at Union Dime Savings Bank embezzled money from the company by manipulating account data in the bank's computer system.

In the 1970s the use of computer hacking expanded, and computerized phone systems became a prime target of "phreakers." These technologically savvy people could break into a system, discover the correct codes and tones, and get free long-distance service. One of those phreakers, John Draper (also known as Cap'n Crunch), discovered that a toy whistle he found in a box of Cap'n Crunch cereal was the same frequency as the

AT&T phone network. Using the free whistle, he was able to configure the system so that thousands of people got free phone calls from AT&T.

While computer crimes like Draper's were slowly emerging, the majority of the population remained largely unaware of crimes committed via computers and the Internet. Consequently, the impact of these events went mostly unnoticed by the general public.[2] However, to those who were more aware of computers and their increased vulnerabilities, it was clear that there was a potential for similar crimes to be committed at any organization that relied on computers.

In response, state legislators began to respond to the newly emerging crimes. They proposed and debated new legislation that sought to define specific computer operations as illegal. The first computer crime law that focused on cybercrime was the Florida Computer Crimes Act of 1978. The law was passed after it was discovered that employees at the Flagler Dog Track had used a computer to print fraudulent winning tickets. The new law defined all unauthorized access of a computer as a crime, even if the person committing the crime had no malicious intent.[3] New laws also meant that offenders could be, and were, arrested and prosecuted for computer crimes, but because of the novelty of these crimes (and partly because criminal justice personnel were unfamiliar with the technology), there were few actual prosecutions for computer crimes.

Few cybercrime laws were passed at the federal level. However, some in the federal government were beginning to recognize the potential dangers of the Internet. In 1977, the General Accounting Office (now known as the General Accountability Office) recommended that the U.S. government should limit the number of federal employees who used a computer. This would reduce the likelihood of a computer attack or security breach.

The 1980s

By the 1980s, computers and technology had become more mainstream. The Internet was rapidly expanding, and computers were being used in more businesses, government offices, and homes. Companies were beginning to use the Internet so they could reach out to users not only in the United States but also internationally to expand their markets. Because computers were becoming more widely used, computer crimes were becoming more frequent.

Moreover, offenders were also changing. Their intent was no longer to break into a computer system just for the fun of it. Many viruses and hacking attacks were now meant to cause critical harm to computer systems or result in theft of data. The crimes quickly became serious threats to businesses, financial institutions, and government offices. As crimes grew in intensity, courts began to recognize the dangers of computer crime and punished offenders with harsher sentences in terms of lengthier prison terms and higher fines. As a result, the Federal Bureau of Investigation (FBI) was assigned the task of overseeing credit card and computer fraud.

During this period, some significant trends became apparent, such as the growth of new viruses, more convictions for those guilty of computer crimes, the emergence of hacking groups, the use of cybercrime as entertainment, the publication of hacking magazines, and an international perspective.

Viruses/New Offenses

The first widely known viruses circulated in 1981. The Apple I, II, and III viruses, for example, targeted the Apple II operating system. They first appeared at the computer system of Texas A&M University and spread to other users when they downloaded pirated computer games. This action involved two crimes: the release of the computer virus and the pirating (or theft) of the software.

Malicious Hacking and Increased Punishments

The first person convicted of a felony for a computer crime was Ian Murphy, also known as Captain Zap. In 1981, Murphy and three of his friends broke into the AT&T computer system and changed the internal clocks. At that time, phone rates varied depending on the time of day. Phone calls made in the evening were cheaper than those made during the day. By changing the clocks at the company, users were charged incorrect rates for phone usage. Some callers using the phone during peak day times were charged late-night, discounted rates. Some who made phone calls in the evenings to take advantage of lower rates were charged higher rates. Clearly, this cost the company money and frustrated users. Murphy was eventually convicted of computer crimes and sentenced to 1,000 hours of community service and 30 months on probation.

One of the first arrests for computer hacking also occurred around this time. In 1983, a group of teenagers who called themselves the 414s (after their area code in Milwaukee, Wisconsin) hacked into the computer systems of Memorial Sloan Kettering Cancer Center in Manhattan, New York, and the Los Alamos National Laboratory in New Mexico. They were quickly arrested by FBI agents and charged with multiple counts of breaking into computer systems. One teen was granted immunity from prosecution in exchange for cooperating with authorities. The others were each given five years of probation.

This was a landmark case because it is one of the earliest incidents of an arrest resulting from hacking. At the time, there were few laws regarding cybercrime, and most law enforcement agents did not have the knowledge to investigate allegations of computer crimes. Moreover, until this case, most businesses did not give much credence to the need for security measures. Since cybercrime was not fully understood by the business community, and many in the information technology community did not recognize the potential for harm from hacking.

Throughout the 1980s, computer crime continued to advance, as did the punishments for it. In 1986, Herbert Zinn (aka Shadow Hawk) was a teenager who lived in New Jersey. He hacked into the computer systems of AT&T to steal computer data. Zinn was eventually convicted and sentenced to nine months in jail, largely based on new legislation passed in Congress: the Computer Fraud and Abuse Act of 1986. Before this law was passed, a defendant found guilty of computer hacking would probably have been sentenced to a term of community service and probation. With the new law, however, courts were beginning to view computer crimes as real crimes whose offenders deserved real punishment.

Box 2.2   Profile of Herbert Zinn

In 1989, Herbert Zinn, who went by the hacker name Shadow Hawk, became the first person convicted under the Computer Fraud and Abuse Act. Though a break-in to the computer systems of AT&T and defense systems, including NATO, were the ultimate cause of the charges, Zinn had been arrested several times before for breaking into systems at the Keller Graduate School of Management.

Ultimately, Zinn was charged with the theft of software, valued at over $1 million, from AT&T. He was discovered because he had bragged on a hacker bulletin board that he had breached AT&T's security, had access to the company's files, and wished to create a Trojan horse to place on their network. On a separate board, he posted the information required to gain access to the network so that others could use the information.

One of the boards Zinn posted information on was known as Phreak Class-2600. The stated purpose of the board was to "to educate computer enthusiasts . . . to penetrate industrial and government sector computer systems."

Zinn plead guilty to the charges and received a nine-month sentence. In part, the leniency of the sentence was because he was a minor when he committed the offenses. However, the arrest and prosecution were clearly meant to send a message to other hackers. One of the U.S. attorneys in charge of the prosecution stated that "The only way to convince these people that this is not a game, not Pac-Man, is to prosecute them."

While Zinn's arrest and prosecution were important because they were the first of its kind, the case has proved to be paradigmatic for prosecutions of hackers all over the country and is therefore not unique. Though the laws have evolved, and certainly the technology has changed dramatically, hackers like Shadow Hawk are still willing to violate the law.

Source: John Gorman, "Teenager Charged in Computer Hacking," *Chicago Tribune*, August 9, 1988, http://articles.chicagotribune.com/1988-08-09/news /8801210455_1_computer-break-ins-computer-hacking-herbert-zinn.

Another serious punishment for computer crime was handed out in 1988 to Robert Morris, the son of a high-ranking scientist at the U.S. National Computer Security Center and a graduate student at Cornell University. He launched a worm that infected over 6,000 computers by exploiting security flaws and holes in the Unix operating system. By the time the virus was stopped, it had caused an estimated $100 million in damages. At the time of Morris's offense, the law specified a sentence of up to five years in prison and a $250,000 fine. However, Morris was sentenced to three years of probation, 400 hours of community service, and a $10,000 fine.

In 1989, hacker Kevin Mitnick was accused of stealing software from Digital Equipment Corporation and long-distance phone codes from MCI. His case made headlines because he was the first person to be charged and convicted under a new law passed by Congress that made interstate computer hacking a federal offense. Because of that, Mitnick was sentenced to one year in prison but was told that he could not use a computer or associate with other hackers until 2001, though he fought that stipulation in court. More information on Mitnick is provided in Box 2.3.

Box 2.3   Profile of Kevin Mitnick

Early in his hacking career, Kevin Mitnick was involved in phone phreaking and other simple but malicious activities. He broke into computers at Digital Equipment Corporation and Pacific Bell. He and his friend Lewis De Payne were able to do this through a technique called "social engineering," whereby victims are tricked into giving up personal information that helps facilitate hacking. In 1987, Mitnick broke into the computers of the Santa Cruz Operation, producers of SCO Unix. He was arrested, convicted, and sentenced to three years of probation. The following year, Mitnick and another friend, Lenny DiCicco, hacked the computers at the University of Southern California and stole hundreds of megabytes of disk space (a lot at the time) to store VAX VMS source code. After being charged and arrested, Mitnick claimed that he suffered from a disorder that caused him to have no impulse control. Despite this, the judge sentenced Mitnick to a year in prison and six months of rehabilitation.

Upon his release, Mitnick attempted to become a private investigator and security specialist, but those in the information security community did not trust him and did not treat him well. In 1992, the FBI issued a warrant for his arrest for allegedly stealing computer time from a phone company. Mitnick went underground again but was found two years later after he left a series of insulting messages on a voice-mail of Tsutomu Shimomura, a physicist and Internet security expert.

Shimomura helped law enforcement officials track Mitnick to North Carolina, where he was arrested in 1995 and held in prison while awaiting his trial on federal charges. In August 1999, Mitnick was convicted of four counts of wire fraud, two counts of computer fraud, and one count of illegally intercepting a wire communication in the Central District Court of California and sentenced to almost four years in prison. He was sentenced to an additional 22 months in prison for having cloned cellular phones in his possession when he was arrested and for violating terms of his parole. Mitnick was released from prison in September 2000 and placed on parole for three years. During this time, his access to computers was to be restricted. He gave talks about his criminal past and wrote several books on computer crime, but profits he received from his speaking or writing were to be given to his victims. Mitnick eventually created his own computer security consulting firm.

Sources: Thomas C. Greene, "Chapter One: Kevin Mitnick's Story," *The Register*, January 13, 2003, http://www.theregister.co.uk/2003/01/13/chapter_one_kevin _mitnicks_story/; Jonathan Littman, *The Fugitive Game: Online with Kevin Mitnick—The Inside Story of the Great Cyberchase* (Boston: Little, Brown and Co., 1996); A. N. Mayorkas and T. Mrozek, "Kevin Mitnick Sentenced to Nearly Four Years in Prison; Computer Hacker Ordered to Pay Restitution to Victim Companies Whose Systems Were Compromised," press release, U.S. Department of Justice, U.S. Attorney's Office, August 9, 1999, http://www.usdoj.gov /criminal/cybercrime/mitnick.htm.

Hacking Groups

During the 1980s, people who enjoyed hacking into computer systems, either for fun or for other reasons, began to join groups as a way to advance their knowledge of the art of hacking. In 1981, a group of German computer enthusiasts who had a strong radical political orientation formed the Chaos Computer Club in Hamburg, Germany. They were able to hack into the German post office and, through the exploitation of security flaws, transfer a sizable amount of money into their own bank accounts. They soon returned the money to the bank but used the opportunity to make a political statement regarding ineffective government action regarding cybersecurity. The group held meetings called the Chaos Communication Congress.

Two groups of hackers formed in the United States were the Legion of Doom (LOD) and the Masters of Deception.[4] The LOD hacking group, founded by Vincent Louis Gelormine under the alias "Lex Luthor," got its name from popular DC comics; members were a group of phone phreakers who later became hackers.[5] The members of LOD enjoyed the process of hacking, supported others who wanted to get involved, and were eager to share their knowledge of hacking. They even published the *Legion of Doom Technical Journal*, which contained guiding principles, code, and programming examples as well as other information of interest to hackers around the world.[6] In the late 1980s, LOD actually helped law enforcement by restraining malicious hackers.

Gelormine had a reputation for attracting the best hackers to his group. The members of LOD were flagrant and enjoyed the publicity they sometimes received for their actions. However, a spat between two members,

Mark Abene (aka Phiber Optik) and Chris Goggans (aka Erik Bloodaxe), an editor of *Phrak* magazine, led to significant change. Abene left LOD and, along with some friends, formed a new group they called the Masters of Deception (MOD). Also helping to form the group was Eli Ladopoulos (aka Acid Phreak) and Paul Stira (aka Scorpion).

MOD often disagreed with the members of LOD, resulting in a two-year dispute known as the "hacker war."[7] Throughout the dispute, hackers from both groups attacked each other using the Internet and telephone networks. They jammed each other's phone lines and monitored each other's computer calls. Allegedly, members of LOD went so far as to establish an Internet security consultancy group that was available to assist corporations who had been victims of MOD. Members of the groups sometimes switched their allegiance.[8]

Later, a third group appeared on the hacking scene. The Cult of Dead Cow (cDc) was originally founded in Lubbock, Texas, in 1984 by Swamp Ratte ("Grandmaster Ratte"), Franken Gibe, and Sid Vicious.[9] The members of cDc encouraged others to hack. Over time, the group's members established a secret elite group, the Ninja Strike Force. While the other groups fought with each other, cDc continued to grow its membership and increase interest in hacking.[10]

The cDc was known for its use of humor, and members would sometimes wear clothing with amusing (although, to some, offensive) cartoons such as that of a crucified cow. In its later years, the cDc became an important proponent of hacktivism, or using hacking techniques for political purposes. The group also released numerous hacking tools, of which Back Orifice (BO) and especially Back Orifice 2000 (BO2K) were notorious examples. BO2K was a Trojan horse that allowed remote control of infected machines.

In the early 1990s, members of LOD and MOD were indicted for their illegal hacking activities. Abene was sent to prison for one year after pleading guilty in federal court to conspiracy and unauthorized access to federal-interest computers. Many members of the hacking community protested Abene's punishment,[11] and upon his release, he was named one of New York City's 100 smartest people. Most cDc members remained free from punishment.[12]

Entertainment

As computers and computer crimes became more easily identified by the public, it became a theme for popular entertainment outlets, making the topic even more established. In 1983, the movie *WarGames* told the story of a high school student who accidentally hacked into the computer systems of North American Defense Command in Colorado Springs, Colorado. The film became a top movie and showed viewers the potential harm that could result from a cybercriminal. After the movie opened, there was an increase in hacker activity.

In 1984, William Gibson wrote a science fiction novel about a computer hacker: *Neuromancer*. He was the first to coin the word "cyberspace."

In 1984, the hacking magazine *2600: The Hacker Quarterly* was first published by Eric Corley (aka Emmanuel Goldstein after a character in George Orwell's *1984*). When this happened, those in the hacking community became public figures and their hacking activities more well-known. The editors published many articles that explained the process of exploiting certain vulnerabilities in a variety of operating systems and application environments. The magazine also gave tips about how to carry out hacking attacks and phone phreak attacks. The magazine provided enough information that even novices could learn the basic skills needed to carry out a hacking crime. The magazine is still published today and contains a great deal of useful information for those interested in hacking.

Another magazine, *Phrack*, appeared in 1985. In the beginning, a new issue came out every month or two. One of the most widely read issues included what came to be known as the Hacker Manifesto. Published in 1986, it was written by Loyd Blankenship (aka the Mentor). It was written shortly after he was arrested and describes the conscience of a hacker (see Box 2.4).

Box 2.4   The Hacker's Manifesto by the Mentor

The following was written shortly after my arrest. . .

\/\The Conscience of a Hacker/\/
By
+++The Mentor+++
Written on January 8, 1986

Another one got caught today, it's all over the papers. "Teenager Arrested in Computer Crime Scandal," "Hacker Arrested after Bank Tampering". . . . Damn kids. They're all alike.

But did you, in your three-piece psychology and 1950's techno-brain, ever take a look behind the eyes of the hacker? Did you ever wonder what made him tick, what forces shaped him, what may have molded him?

I am a hacker, enter my world. . . .

Mine is a world that begins with school. . . . I'm smarter than most of the other kids, this crap they teach us bores me. . . .

Damn underachiever. They're all alike.

I'm in junior high or high school. I've listened to teachers explain for the fifteenth time how to reduce a fraction. I understand it. "No, Ms. Smith, I didn't show my work. I did it in my head. . . ."

Damn kid. Probably copied it. They're all alike.

I made a discovery today. I found a computer. Wait a second, this is cool. It does what I want it to. If it makes a mistake, it's because I screwed it up. Not because it doesn't like me . . .

Or feels threatened by me . . .
Or thinks I'm a smart ass . . .
Or doesn't like teaching and shouldn't be here . . .

Damn kid. All he does is play games. They're all alike.

And then it happened . . . a door opened to a world . . . rushing through the phone line like heroin through an addict's veins, an electronic pulse is sent out, a refuge from the day-to-day incompetencies is sought . . . a board is found.

"This is it . . . this is where I belong. . . ."

I know everyone here . . . even if I've never met them, never talked to them, may never hear from them again. . . . I know you all. . . .

Damn kid. Tying up the phone line again. They're all alike. . . .

You bet your ass we're all alike . . . we've been spoon-fed baby food at school when we hungered for steak . . . the bits of meat that you did let slip through were pre-chewed and tasteless. We've been dominated by sadists, or ignored by the apathetic. The few that had something to teach found us willing pupils, but those few are like drops of water in the desert.

This is our world now . . . the world of the electron and the switch, the beauty of the baud. We make use of a service already existing without paying for what could be dirt-cheap if it wasn't run by profiteering gluttons, and you call us criminals. We explore . . . and you call us criminals. We seek after knowledge . . . and you call us criminals. We exist without skin color, without nationality, without religious bias . . . and you call us criminals. You build atomic bombs, you wage wars, you murder, cheat, and lie to us and try to make us believe it's for our own good, yet we're the criminals.

Yes, I am a criminal. My crime is that of curiosity. My crime is that of judging people by what they say and think, not what they look like. My crime is that of outsmarting you, something that you will never forgive me for.

I am a hacker, and this is my manifesto. You may stop this individual, but you can't stop us all . . . after all, we're all alike.

+++The Mentor+++

Source: Loyd Blankenship, "Hacker's Manifesto." Originally published in *Phrack Magazine*, Volume One, Issue 7, Phile 3 of 10, September 25, 1986. Copyright © 1986 by Loyd Blankenship. Used with permission.

Box 2.5   The Mentor's Form Letter

The Mentor's Manifesto text has been used on multiple occasions in print and the movies. The Mentor's email address is included in the end credits of the movie Hackers, *in which a portion of it was used as dialogue. Also, a poster of the work also appears in Mark Zuckerberg's dorm room in the movie* The Social Network. *As a result, the Mentor receives numerous emails each month, the great majority of which are variants of "teach me to break into my school computer." This form letter is his response to such queries.*

A kind of disturbing trend in the whole popularization of the net is the mass influx of people who claim they want to be "hackers." This desire usually stems from bad Hollywood portrayals of computer hackers and too many X-Files episodes. Since the movie *Hackers* came out with my email address in it, I get 10–20 pieces of mail a week from people clamoring for me to "teach them to hack." With that in mind, I've been working on a small FAQ for people who think they want to be hackers.

No one can teach you how to be a hacker. Hacking is not just "breaking into my school's computer." Hacking is borne out of a real passion for computers that at times is all-consuming. I don't mean all-consuming in the sense of playing *Civilization* for 72 straight hours—while fun (and I've done it), this isn't really going to further your knowledge of computers.

You don't have to break the law to be a hacker. The first piece of advice I try to offer someone is "find a cheap system and install Linux, and get it working. Learn how to program. Teach yourself something."

The net is rife with text files on hacking; some are good, some are not. Begin by doing a search for "Phrack." That should provide you enough links to keep you busy for months.

Do some basic reading on telecom & networking. Hacking (in the sense that most people emailing me mean it) involves iterations of the following steps:

Step 1: Find a computer you want to get into.
Step 2: Get in.
Step 3: Don't get caught.

While this all seems basic, a surprising number of people don't have a good grasp of these steps.

The tricky steps are, of course, steps 2 and 3. Step 2 is very difficult to generalize, as there are tons of different systems that you will want to play with. But hacking can still be fun, even if you don't get into many systems.

Step 3, unfortunately, is the one you will have the most trouble with. Without going out on a limb too much, I think that 99% of the people moved to try these steps will get caught early and easily. It will be expensive for them and their parents, and they'll come away from the whole experience worse for the wear.

Why is this? With near-universal digital switching, tracing a number is so incredibly easy it is mind-numbing. Don't believe the Hollywood bullshit about needing to keep someone on the line for a certain length of time. Add to this the increased public profile of the net, and the fact that people are taking enforcement much more seriously, and you have a dangerous hacking environment. This is why I suggest starting out legal with one of the free *nix implementations—just to see if you really enjoy this kind of thing.

There will be those who insist on trying this anyway. To them, I offer the following advice: Never hack your own country. Preferably, make it appear like you're never hacking *from* your own country. If you do both, your career may last a bit longer.

Mentor

p.s. The above is for informational purposes only. I personally recommend you take up something soothing like tropical fish.

Source: Copyright © 1986 by Loyd Blankenship. Used with permission.

In 1990, the magazine published a confidential document from Bell South that the magazine found by hacking into the company's computer systems. By the 1990s, the magazine was released every six months. The final regularly released issue was published in August 2005, but special issues were later published in May 2007 and April 2008.

Government Response

Because new cybercrimes were emerging in the 1980s and the general public was gaining a better understanding of the potential dangers of computer crimes, legislatures in the United States and around the world began to pass new laws to deter potential offenders and punish those convicted of these new crimes. The Canadian government was the first country to enact a national law to address computer crime when they amended their Criminal Code in 1983.[13] The Australian Crimes Act was amended in 1989 to include Offenses Relating to Computers (Section 76), and the Australian states enacted similar laws at around the same time. In Britain, the Computer Abuse Act was passed in 1990 to criminalize computer intrusions.[14] In the United States, the Federal Computer Fraud and Abuse Act was passed by Congress in 1984 and then amended in 1986, 1988, 1989, and 1990.

In the United States, Congressman Dan Glickman (D-KS) called for hearings to examine computer hackers after the 414s broke into the computer systems of national agencies,[15] but no action was taken. However, the government did later take action by creating the Computer Emergency Response Team Coordination Center (CERT/CC) in 1988. This agency is a central reporting center for Internet security problems.

Cyberespionage

The year 1989 was pivotal in the evolution of computer crime as it contained the first incident of cyberespionage. Five people from West Germany were arrested and accused of hacking into government and university computer systems and stealing data. Three of the offenders then sold the stolen information to the Soviet government. Even though there may have been other incidents preceding it, this was the first that became widely known.

The 1990s

The 1990s was a period of transition when it came to cybercrime. The use of the Internet continued to grow, and it was now commonly used in schools and homes. More businesses continued to put their information online because they now had the ability to conduct business in the global economy, 24 hours a day, seven days a week. Geographic boundaries were no longer prohibitive for businesses, and they took advantage of their extended reach.

Consequently, the online economy expanded. According to the Digital Research Initiative, e-commerce first began on August 11, 1994, when Net-Market made the first online transaction. The first item purchased through a website protected by commercially available data encryption technology was the CD *Ten Summoner's Tales* by Sting. The buyer used a credit card and paid $12.48, plus shipping costs.

Since the Internet was more accessible to a wider band of people during the 1990s, there were more attempts to commit crimes. The term "cybercrime" became more commonly used as people became more aware of hacking, viruses, and other forms of computer crime. Cybercriminals took advantage of vulnerabilities in computer systems around the globe. As cybercrime and malware became more widely recognized and feared by users, antivirus programs were developed that were more capable of detecting harmful malware. In turn, this meant hackers and criminals needed to increase their technical skills in order to carry out their attacks. They started to make malware that was more complex, so that it went undetected by antivirus programs. One method criminals developed to subvert anti-malware programs was polymorphism. In this type of a virus, each new iteration of the malware evolves so that a new characteristic will appear that does not affect the original code.

In 1997, tools that would allow unskilled people to carry out computer crimes were made readily available online. That year a utility called AOLHell was released. The free application allowed virtually anyone to launch attacks on America Online (AOL). For days, AOL chat rooms were clogged with spam, and the email boxes of AOL users were overwhelmed with spam. Since that year, many more such tools have been released on the Internet.

Despite the increased security measures, the number of cybercrimes exploded during the 1990s, and the crimes that took place were far more devastating than previous crimes. The number of financial crimes committed through computer systems increased as many computer hackers shifted their online activities to stealing credit card numbers, passwords, PIN numbers, and other personal data that could then be used to commit crimes like identity theft. Illegitimate applications of email grew rapidly, generating lots of unsolicited commercial and fraudulent email, or spam. Identity theft was rising by the late 1990s, causing great concern for consumers and law enforcement alike.

It quickly became apparent that many hackers no longer broke into computer systems for the challenge or a sense of thrill, and they did not seek attention for their crimes as hackers did in the 1980s. The new group of hackers was much more dangerous. They sought to make a profit and cause harm to others.

Some key events occurred in the 1990s that pointed to the dangers of cybercrime. These included new viruses, more cases of hacking, cybercrime as entertainment, government action, hacking groups, and international events.

Viruses

One virus that was transmitted during the 1990s was the Michelangelo virus, which would install itself on a computer but then remain dormant in an infected computer for many weeks before attacking. The virus was written to trigger on Michelangelo's birthday and attacked the boot sector of the hard drive or floppy drive. For the most part, the virus left data largely untouched, so it did not cause much damage.

In 1999, the Melissa virus was released. Created by David Smith, it caused an estimated $500 million in damages. Smith was eventually convicted of writing the virus and given a five-year prison sentence. This case was the first to have caused so much damage, but it is also key because of the sentence the offender received. This showed that courts were beginning to take computer crime more seriously and to sentence perpetrators accordingly.

Hacking

The practice of hacking into computer systems continued in the 1990s. In 1994, a 16-year-old boy from the United Kingdom known as Data Stream hacked into many government sites, including Griffiss Air Force Base, NASA, and the Korean Atomic Energy Research Institute. Even though his victims were located in North America and Asia (and he was located in Europe), he was identified by Scotland Yard officials. This case was critical because it clearly identified the need for international cooperation between law enforcement agencies when it came to investigating cybercrime. Clearly, cybercrime was indeed global and no longer bound by geographic borders.

Another case that showed the growing importance of international cooperation in cybercrime occurred in 1995. Vladimir Levin, a graduate of St. Petersburg Tekhnologichesky University, was arrested and charged with being the head of a group of Russian hackers. The group allegedly stole almost $10 million from Citibank. Levin was arrested by Interpol at Heathrow Airport and extradited to the United States where he was convicted of the charges against him. He was sentenced to spend three years in prison and pay Citibank $240,015, the amount he profited from his crime.

Hacking in the United States was not only done for profit but also for other reasons during the 1990s. One of those reasons was political. In 1996, a computer hacker associated with a white-supremacist group disabled a Massachusetts Internet service provider (ISP) and damaged data on its system. The ISP attempted to stop the hacker from sending out worldwide racist messages under the ISP's name. The hacker signed off with the threat, "You have yet to see true electronic terrorism. This is a promise." While this attack caused very little damage, it was an example of how some hacking events were ideologically driven and were done to send a message in support of the hacktivist.

Hackers also broke into systems as a way to damage a business. In 1997, the Network Solutions Internet domain registry was hacked by a business rival, causing the company a great deal of damage and havoc. Eugene Kashpureff, the owner of a competing business called Alter-NiC, eventually pleaded guilty to carrying out the offense. This case is of interest because it was a clear example of how hacking could be used in a dispute between rival businesses. One company used hacking to subvert the business practices and success of a competing business. This was clearly a case of corporate warfare that was carried out through the Internet.

Entertainment

Hacking continued to be the focus of popular movies. In 1992, the movie *Sneakers* was released. In this movie, security experts are black-mailed and forced to steal a universal decoder for encryption systems. Another movie, *Hackers* (1995), was about a young boy who writes a new computer virus and is arrested by Secret Service agents. When he is older, he tries to prevent a dangerous virus from being unleashed. In 1995, *The Net* was released. This was about a software analyst who unwittingly becomes involved in a conspiracy. Her identity is stolen and she fights to get it returned. All three movies glorified the hacking community and highlighted potential dangers that the increasing reliance on the Internet created.

Government

The federal government continued to recognize the dangers posed by the exploitation of the Internet as multiple government agencies became the victims of cyberattacks. In 1996, hackers broke into the computer systems of the Department of Justice, the CIA, and the Air Force. They did little damage but changed the content of the websites. Then in 1998, a series of attacks on the Department of Defense, called Solar Sunrise, focused on more than 500 federal computers and resulted in the loss of sensitive government data. The hack was eventually traced to three California teenagers.

In May 1990, the General Accountability Office (GAO) reported that the Computer Security Act of 1987 was insufficient to protect government data from hackers. The GAO recognized that the lack of a sufficient budget helped contribute to this vulnerability and called for new laws and more money to address the potential dangers associated with the Internet.[16] The White House had similar concerns. In February 1991, Michelle Van Cleave, the White House assistant director for national security at the time stated that the theft of data from the U.S. government was a "serious strategic threat to national security."[17]

Members of Congress were also growing more concerned about cybercrime. In July 1996, the chairman of the House of Representatives Government Reform subcommittee, Stephen Horn (R-CA), issued a report entitled *Year 2000 Readiness Report Card*, which reviewed the potential ability of agencies to protect their data. The report gave many agencies failing grades, clearly indicating that their computer systems were not secure and were open to attack. In response, President Clinton created the President's

Commission on Critical Infrastructure Protection. This agency was given the task of coordinating and protecting the nation's infrastructure (i.e., the power grid, water services, and transportation) from possible cyberattack.[18]

Some members of Congress learned more about cybercrime in 1998 when seven members of the hacker think-tank known as L0pht testified in front of the congressional Government Affairs Committee. They informed the members about weak computer security in the government.

The FBI reacted to increasing instances of cybercrime, including the increase in the availability of online child pornography, by creating its Innocent Images National Initiative in 1995. Through this, agents could investigate and prosecute groups of online pedophiles. At that time, most people were not aware of the serious dangers the Internet could pose for children. In 1998, Attorney General Janet Reno announced the creation of the National Infrastructure Protection Center (NIPC) within the FBI. The NIPC has grown into the primary organization responsible for protecting the country's infrastructure networks and systems from attack (including viruses and hacking attacks).

At the same time, law enforcement officials began to take computer crime more seriously. In 1990, the Secret Service launched Operation Sundevil, which had a goal of catching computer hackers. The operation involved local law enforcement agents working in conjunction with federal Secret Service agents who performed raids in 15 states and seized computer equipment. Because they only arrested three people, some think the operation was a failure, or at least expended more resources than it was worth. That is a valid criticism. However, it was the first major federal operation directed at computer crime. It would take time for traditional law-enforcement officers to learn to properly investigate and combat computer-based crime.

Legislators also continued to pass new laws to punish those who committed cybercrimes and to deter future cybercriminals. One of the first laws designed to attack child pornography available on the Internet was passed in 1992 and was called Operation Long Arm. The legislation was proposed after it was discovered that people in the United States were obtaining child pornography from a Danish bulletin board system.[19]

Hacking Groups

In 1991, the aforementioned Mark Abene (aka Phiber Optik), a member of MOD, was arrested and accused of computer tampering and computer trespass. Law enforcement officials placed wiretaps on telephones to collect evidence against him that recorded conversations between different members of MOD. This case was significant because it was the first time law enforcement relied on wiretaps to record conversations of cybercrime-related offenders. In the end, Abene was prosecuted and sentenced to one year in jail.

In 1992, Kevin Poulsen was arrested for the first time after it was discovered that he had hacked into the computer systems of a radio station and rigged it so that he would win two Porsches, $20,000 in cash, and a trip to Hawaii. At the time of his offenses, Poulsen was hiding from law enforcement because of other computer hacking charges. He had also hacked into computer systems of law enforcement agencies and the military. After breaking into the military sites, Poulsen was charged with federal espionage charges because he obtained classified information. Poulsen was in prison for three years while he awaited his trial for hacking into the radio station. In the end, the federal espionage charges were dropped and Poulsen pled guilty to computer fraud counts related to the original contest fraud. Poulsen received a sentence of 51 months, and spent more time in prison than any other cybercriminal. He was released in June 1996 on probation, after agreeing not to use any computer for three years. More information on Poulsen is presented in Box 2.6.

Box 2.6 Profile of Kevin Poulsen

Seventeen-year-old Kevin Poulsen first became well-known publicly in 1982, after he gained unauthorized access to computers on the ARPANet system. Poulsen was not criminally charged but instead was hired as a programmer and computer security supervisor for SRI International, a company located in Menlo Park, California. He later went to work as a network administrator at Sun Microsystems. A few years later, in 1987, security agents at the Pacific Bell Company discovered that Poulsen and his friends had been hacking into their computers. After a brief investigation, the FBI began to watch Poulsen for espionage. When Poulsen found out, he ran from the law. While on the run from the FBI, he was able to learn about the FBI's electronic surveillance methods. At one point, he supported himself by breaking into computer systems at Pacific Bell, which allowed him to cheat at radio-station phone-in contests.

Poulsen was arrested in April 1992 as he shopped for groceries in Van Nuys. His case had been on television's *Unsolved Mysteries* twice by then. He was indicted December 4, 1992, and charged with stealing classified information. This made him the first computer hacker to be indicted under U.S. espionage laws. Poulsen denied the charges and was held without bail during the court proceedings. Poulsen was able to convince the judge that he was not guilty, and the charges against Poulsen were dismissed on March 18, 1996. However, Poulsen did have to serve five years and two months for crimes he committed while he was a fugitive from the law and for the phone hacking incidents. He was freed from jail on June 4, 1996, at which point he was placed on supervised release for three years. He was also banned from owning a computer for the first year of his release and banned from any Internet use for a year and a half.

Since he left prison, Poulsen's story has been the subject of the book *The Watchman—The Twisted Life and Crimes of Serial Hacker Kevin Poulsen* by Jonathan Littman. Poulsen has also become an editor for the periodical *SecurityFocus* and was then hired as a senior editor at *Wired News*. He is an investigative reporter (for example, he broke the story of sexual predators on MySpace).

Source: K. Poulsen, "MySpace Predator Caught by Code," *Wired*, October 16, 2006, http://archive.wired.com/science/discoveries/news/2006/10/71948.

In 1996, the group AcidAngel created the Global kOs ("chaos") to create online disorder. They made new hacker tools available online so that script kiddies, or those who have limited technical skill, could launch malware easily. Their denial-of-service tool was used to attack the websites of Rush Limbaugh, MTV, and the Ku Klux Klan. Another group formed at this time was the Level Seven Group (created in 1999).

On June 3, 1998, a group of hacktivists known as MilwOrm targeted the computers of India's primary nuclear facility, the Bhabha Atomic Research Center. The group, operating from the United Kingdom, the United States, Russia, and New Zealand, broke through the center's firewalls. They lifted five megabytes of classified files about India's last five nuclear tests, erased data from two servers, and posted antinuclear messages on the center's website. The implications of the hack were huge and caused major upheaval as other institutions heightened their security. Another international hacking group appeared in 1994, the Network Crack Program Hacker Group, which was formed in Zigong, China.

On January 1, 1999, the Legion of Underground announced that it would attack and disable the computer systems of the People's Republic of China and Iraq. Other hacker groups, including the Chaos Computer Club, immediately announced opposition to the idea. They announced that, "Declaring war against a country is the most irresponsible thing a hacker group could do. This has nothing to do with hacktivism or hacker ethics and is nothing a hacker could be proud of."[20] Their response stopped the Legion of Underground from following through with the planned attacks.

International

The problem of cybercrime was also growing and being recognized on the international scene throughout the 1990s. Terrorist groups and organized crime began to move into the realm of cyberspace. The G8 group of nations chose to give the issue more attention, resulting in the Convention on Cybercrime. This was the first international treaty designed to attack crimes committed via the computer and the Internet (see chapter 10).[21]

Cyberterrorism became more prevalent in the 1990s. In 1999, during the Kosovo conflict, computers at NATO were flooded with email bombs and targeted with denial-of-service attacks by hackers. In addition, businesses, organizations, and academic institutions received emails with viruses attached, and many websites were defaced (see chapter 7).

The 2000s

By the 2000s, the majority of people in the United States and other parts of the world used technology regularly. Many people's lives were influenced by computers in some way on a daily basis. Computers impacted business, education, health care, banking, and research. The nation's critical infrastructure relied on computers to exist. At the same time, cybercrime continued to rise, and large-scale global malware attacks continued by the use of specific targeting of end-user systems. Cybercriminals continued to use email and websites to deploy malware. Advanced persistent threats became a regular concern, because they posed a threat to the intellectual property and financial assets of companies and nations. New threats at this time focused on mobile operating systems, such as cell phones. As these networked devices became common, criminals were actively developing new technology aimed at exploiting them.[22]

New laws have been passed at the federal, state, and international levels to deter cybercrime, but they often lag behind emerging technology, and cybercriminals stay one step ahead of the legislation. Businesses and homes need to have security systems installed to prevent becoming the victims of an attack. In 2003, Microsoft went so far as to announce bounties for anyone who aided in capturing hackers, virus writers, and various other computer criminals. It was an interesting way to combat computer crime. This time, there were changes in social media, international activity, new crimes evolving, attacks on mobile devices, new viruses and worms, government response, hacking groups, and entertainment.

Social Media

Social networking sites became very popular and widely used methods to communicate with family, friends, and business contacts in the 2000s. This has led to increases in crimes such as cyberbullying and harassment.[23] One of those crimes happened in 2008, when Lori Drew, a mother of a teenage daughter, created a fake MySpace page as a way to bully another teenage girl who happened to be her daughter's rival. The target of Drew's attention, Megan Meier, committed suicide as a result of the things Drew posted on the account. Law enforcement sought to hold Drew accountable for her actions and for the death of Meier. Drew was charged with crimes under the Federal Computer Fraud and Abuse Statute, even though the law does not address cyberbullying. In September 2009, U.S. District Judge George Wu dismissed the case. This was one of many examples of how people were using social media for criminal purposes.

Another example happened in 2009, when Brian Hurt used Craigslist to hire a prostitute to come to his home. When she arrived at his house, he shot and killed her. This case brought to light the dangers of advertising on Craigslist and responding to an ad on the site. It also became clear that many ads are actually part of a fraud scheme, and that the erotic services section was simply a euphemism for prostitution.

International

During the 2000s, members of organized crime groups began using the Internet to commit crimes in more ways than ever before. They used the Internet for money laundering, selling illegal prescription drugs, or promoting prostitution and escort services. Organized crime groups and terrorist groups use the Internet to recruit and radicalize new members, seek donations, and post instructions for making bombs online.

An example of this happened in 2009, when Israeli hacker Ehud Tenenbaum was suspected of stealing about $10 million from different banks in the United States. What made it interesting was that Tenenbaum had been arrested in Canada the year before for stealing $1.5 million in the same way. This case was more evidence that cybercrime does not respect hard boundary lines, and that geographic borders do not matter.

New Crimes

Throughout the 2000s, cybercriminals continued to develop new ways to commit crimes on the Internet. One of those new crimes was phishing, and criminals became much more sophisticated in their phishing attempts. Instead of sending an email that led a victim to a fake bank website, the email link would instead take the user to the real bank's website. A pop-up window was inserted in front of the real website that asked the victim to log on. This way, the criminal would get the victim's account number and password.

In June 2002, law enforcement authorities in Russia arrested a man for allegedly being a cyber spy for the United States. They accused him of hacking into the computer system of the Russia's Federal Security Service to gathering secrets, which he allegedly then sent to officials at the CIA. While it is likely that computer-based espionage was going on long before 2002, this is one of the first publicized cases.

Cybercriminals were also using spyware more often to commit acts of theft. In 2005, hackers attempted to transfer $420 million from a bank in London. If successful, these criminals would have carried out the largest electronic bank theft in history. The criminals used spyware placed on computers in the office that placed keyloggers on the systems used by employees. This way, the criminals could get bank account information and passwords of all users. Law enforcement was able to stop the theft before it happened.

Mobile Attacks

The 2000s saw a tremendous growth in the use of cellular phones and other personal devices. Many employees began to use their own devices as part of their work, increasing the risk of cybercrime. An employee's personal device is often not protected by security systems, leaving the device accessible for criminals to install malware. People also lose their devices or have them stolen. If they contain sensitive data, others could easily read that information and use it to commit crimes.

In addition, those who own these devices often download apps that are infected with malware. This happened in March 2014, when a fake Netflix app was downloaded by many people. Once downloaded, it stole personal and credit card information from the user. It turns out that the malware was preinstalled on some Android phones and tablets that were shipped from different manufacturers.[24] Android devices seem to be more susceptible to attacks from cybercriminals, but cybercriminals attack other types of devices as well.[25]

Viruses and Worms

Many viruses and worms also appeared during this period. In May 2000, the ILOVEYOU virus, also referred to as the Love Letter virus, attacked millions of Windows computers. The virus was sent via an email message that had "ILOVEYOU" in the subject line. When the user opened the email, it sent itself to the first 50 names in the recipient's address book.

The Code Red worm appeared in July 2001. This virus, which relied on a flaw in the Microsoft operating system, spread quickly. Once installed, the virus allowed criminals to deface or remove websites. The virus even brought down the web page for the White House for a short time.

Other major and damaging computer viruses were employed in 2003. The first, identified in January 2003, was called the Slammer because it infected thousands of computers in the span of about three hours. This worm caused a significant amount of damage, including shutting down cash machines and delaying airline flights. This virus was critical because of the speed with which it spread and the extensive damage it caused. In May 2003, the Fizzer email worm sent out pornographic email spam. Even though Microsoft offered a $250,000 reward for information that would lead to the arrest of the creator, that person was not caught. Another virus that appeared in 2003 was the sobig virus. This virus used a multimodal approach to spreading, meaning that it relied on multiple mechanisms to spread from one machine to another. It was able to copy itself to any shared drives on a particular network, and then it emailed the virus to other addresses in the infected machines' address books.

In 2003, there were also the MiMail and Bagel viruses. Each of these spread via email. In the MimMil virus, email addresses were identified in the infected computer's address book and from any document on the infected machine's hard drive. The Bagel virus also scanned the infected hard drive looking for email addresses. The viruses were then sent to other email addresses, further spreading the malware

The Sasser worm was discovered in 2004. Written by a 17-year-old German youth, it attacked the British Coast Guard, Agence France-Presse, and Delta Airlines. It also affected universities, hospitals, and corporations. This worm was written to attack those using the Microsoft operating systems Windows XP or Windows 2000. The virus blocked satellite communications and disabled mapping systems, causing major companies to shut down for a short time.

Three cyberattacks were carried out in the 2000s that focused on Iran's nuclear infrastructure: Stuxnet, Duqu, and Flame. Stuxnet, a virus that was recognized in 2010, was created by the U.S. and Israeli governments and attacked the operating systems of nuclear facilities in Iran. The Stuxnet virus resulted in physical damage to about 20 percent of the Iranian centrifuges. The monitors watching over the equipment relied on their monitoring equipment and did not realize that their infrastructure had been infiltrated. Duqu got its name from the prefix of the files it creates: DQ. The virus was not widespread, but it gathered information that could be used to carry out attacks in the future. The Flame virus had the ability to record information with the help of the microphone on the PC, capture screenshots, log keystrokes, and send data to a host. The code could be updated remotely, so the commands could be updated easily. This was an early form of spyware.

Another virus, Gauss, was deployed in September 2011 and discovered in June 2012. This was a Trojan horse used against the banking industry that allowed criminals to steal personal information (specifically banking information). Gauss seemed to be more focused on Lebanon.

Government

On September 19, 2002, Clinton administration officials issued a draft of a new cybersecurity plan for the nation. One of the controversial provisions that was later removed was a proposal to require high-speed Internet providers to bundle firewall products alongside their products. President Clinton also removed a provision that would require a cybersecurity fund and a provision that would restrict the use of wireless networks until they could improve their security. In the end, many in the security field criticized the report because they believed many of the sections pertaining to escalating security that were omitted from the original document should have been left intact as a way to protect the nation's cyberstructure.[26]

In 2003, officials in the U.S. Department of Homeland Security reorganized its cyberdefense offices to create a National CyberSecurity Division. The new agency was given the responsibility to protect government computers from hackers. Oddly, only a few years later, in 2007, Secretary of Defense Robert Gates had his email account hacked. The attack was traced back to the People's Liberation Army in China. Because it was his unclassified email account, little damage was done. In 2014, computers at the White House were allegedly hacked by Russians, but again, little data was lost.

Hacking Groups

In 2001, the hacktivist group World of Hell was formed. It attacked the websites of many major corporations. Other hacking groups formed around this time were TeaMp0isoN, LulzRaft, LulzSec, Encrypters, and UGNazi.

In 2003, the hacktivist group Anonymous was formed. Its organization is very loose, and there is no formal membership list, rules, or leadership. Anonymous opposes government action that results in censorship of the Internet and uses its hacking skills to bring attention to its causes. When the group appears in public, the members wear Guy Fawkes masks to remain anonymous. In 2008, the members attacked Scientology. More recently, in 2014, they took over the websites of Ferguson, Missouri, because they disagreed with how the protesters were being treated. When the Ku Klux Klan threatened the protesters, Anonymous seized the Twitter accounts of the KKK. The group has also threatened to launch digital attacks against nations it believes fund the radical Islamic terror group ISIS. The campaign, it said, would be called Operation NO2ISIS. It plans to use distributed denial-of-service attacks against government websites.[27] Despite its involvement in a variety of causes, Anonymous does not advocate for violence. For instance, after the January 2015 attacks on Charlie Hebdo in France, Anonymous condemned the attacks, in which 11 people were killed.

Entertainment

In 2004, the general public became more aware of the problem of online predators. The *Dateline NBC* program "To Catch a Predator" began airing in 2004, making the public more aware that sexual predators were meeting young children online then meeting them in person for sexual reasons. There was some controversy when this show was aired. Critics argued that the program was entrapping offenders, but it also made parents aware of the dangers of allowing their children to use the Internet where they could meet pedophiles. The program informed the general public about how online predators operate. It remains a popularly watched television show.

Conclusion

Cybercrime has evolved since the inception of computers. Every decade has brought new crimes and new patterns to the field of cyberattacks. Some individuals have been influential in developing cybercrime. In the future, there should be no doubt that new cybercrimes will continue to emerge and old crimes will evolve into crimes yet unseen.

Review Questions

1. Which key events that occurred before the 1970s affected today's state of cybercrime?
2. Describe the events of the 1970s that helped to define cybercrime today.
3. What happened in the 1980s that was important for the history of cybercrime?
4. Name some key events and people that influenced cybercrime in the 1990s.
5. What events in the 2000s had an impact on cybercrime?

Key Terms

2600
414s
Mark Abene
Anonymous
ARPANet (Advanced Research Projects Agency Network)
Chaos Computer Club
Code Red Worm
Creeper
Cult of Dead Cows
John Draper
Vincent Louis Gelormine
Chris Goggans
ILOVEYOU Virus
Legion of Doom
Masters of Deception
Melissa Virus
Michelangelo Virus
Kevin Mitnick
Robert Morris
Ian Murphy
Phrak
Kevin Poulsen
Herbert Zinn

Notes

1. Eoghan Casey, *Digital Evidence and Computer Crime*, 3rd ed. (Boston: Academic Press, 2011).

2. Derek Manky, "Cybercrime as a Service: A Very Modern Business," *Computer Fraud and Security*, June 2013, 9–13.

3. Casey, *Digital Evidence and Computer Crime*.

4. Will Gragido, Daniel Molina, John Pirc, and Nick Selby, *Blackhatonomics* (New York: Syngress, 2012).

5. Bruce Sterling, *The Hacker Crackdown: Law and Disorder on the Electronic Frontier* (New York: Bantam, 1992).

6. Gragido et al., *Blackhatonomics*.

7. Michelle Slatalla and Joshua Quittner, "Gang War in Cyberspace," Wired 2.12, December 1994, http://www.wired.com/wired/archive/2.12/hacker.html.

8. Michelle Slatalla and Joshua Quittner, *Masters of Deception: The Gang That Ruled Cyberspace* (New York: HarperCollins, 1995).

9. Gragido et al., *Blackhatonomics*.

10. Julian Dibble, "The Prisoner: Phiber Optik Goes Directly to Jail," *Village Voice*, January 12, 1994, http://www.juliandibbell.com/texts/phiber.html.

11. Ibid.

12. Gragido et al., *Blackhatonomics*.

13. Casey, *Digital Evidence and Computer Crime*.

14. Casey, *Digital Evidence and Computer Crime*.

15. "Timeline: The US Government and Cybersecurity Technology," *The Washington Post*, available at http://www.washingtonpost.com/wp-dyn/articles /A50606-2002Jun26.html.

16. Ibid.

17. Ibid.

18. Ibid.

19. Casey, *Digital Evidence and Computer Crime*.

20. 2600 News, 1999, LOU cyberwar press release, http://www.2600.com /news/view/article/362.

21. Manky, "Cybercrime as a Service," 9–13.

22. Rafe Pilling, "Global Threats, Cyber-security Nightmares and How to Protect against Them," *Computer Fraud and Security*, September 2013, 14–18.

23. Casey, *Digital Evidence and Computer Crime*.

24. David Bailey, "The Difficulty of Securing Your Mobile Workforce," *Computer Fraud and Security*, September 2014, 19–20.

25. RSA, "The Current State of Cybercrime 2014," http://www.emc.com /collateral/white-paper/rsa-cyber-crime-report-0414.pdf.

26. "Timeline: The US Government and Cybersecurity."

27. Jasper Hamill, "Anonymous Hactivists Prepare for Strike against ISIS 'Supporters'," *Forbes*, June 27, 2014, http://www.forbes.com/sites/jasperhamill /2014/06/27/anonymous-hacktivists-prepare-for-strike-against-isis-supporters/.

CHAPTER THREE

Types and Frequency of Cybercrime

Introduction

AS TECHNOLOGY EVOLVES AND BECOMES MORE ADVANCED, new cybercrimes have emerged. There are now many different types of cybercrime that did not exist just a few years ago. Some of those crimes are new crimes, whereas others are new versions of traditional crimes. This chapter will review different categories of cybercrime and how computers can be used to commit crimes.

Categories

There are many types of cybercrimes and therefore many ways to categorize them. For example, the U.S. Department of Justice categorizes types of computer crime in three ways: (1) the computer as the target (attacking the computers of others by spreading viruses or a denial-of-service [DoS] attack or an attack on a website), (2) the computer as the weapon (using a computer to commit traditional crimes, such as fraud, illegal gambling, or online pornography), or (3) the computer as an accessory or a device that contains data incidental to the crime (using a computer as a method to maintain records on illegal or stolen information).[1]

The United Nations lists five categories of cybercrime: (1) financial (crimes that disrupt a business's ability to conduct e-commerce, such as viruses, cyberattacks or DoS attacks, or e-forgery), (2) piracy (copying copyrighted material), (3) hacking (the act of gaining unauthorized access to a computer system or network and in some cases making unauthorized use of this access), (4) cyberterrorism, and (5) online pornography.[2]

However, a more useful set of categories is based on the intended victim of the crime, and these three categories will be used in this chapter: (1) cybercrimes committed against people, (e.g., the transmission of child pornography or stalking or harassment using a computer), (2) cybercrimes against property, most likely the computer (e.g., a virus), and (3) cybercrimes against government (e.g., cyberterrorism).

Cybercrimes against People

Crimes committed via a computer or the Internet are sometimes intended to harm an individual person. These include sexting/pornography, identity theft, hacking, vice crimes (e.g., drugs, gambling, prostitution), harassment, cybertheft, fraud, dating scams, Federal Bureau of Investigation (FBI) scams, Internet piracy, and phishing. These are each described in more detail in the sections that follow.

Sex Offenses: Sexting, Child Pornography, and Sexual Predators

Many types of sex-related offenses have become much easier to commit with the advent of network technology. The growth of the Internet has provided a new outlet for those who create and distribute child pornography, for example. While these crimes have existed for many years, they have evolved and adapted to the Internet. New technologies, such as digital cameras, personal computers, software, and remote storage drives, have made it easier to produce images of children in sexual poses. The Internet also makes it easier to trade and distribute such images, and child pornography is widely distributed and readily available online in a global market. It is easier and cheaper to access than ever before. Moreover, there is now a perceived sense of autonomy because users are not forced to go through a dealer to purchase it.

One study of online child pornography found that nearly 1 of 10 people consume child pornography regularly. Though the study found that two-thirds of child pornography users were male, nonwhite males were more likely to report the use of Internet child pornography. The study also found that a higher number of females engaged in Internet child pornography than originally suspected.[3]

In most countries, child pornography is considered to be a form of child abuse, and the production, distribution, and possession of it is illegal. Many laws have been passed to criminalize the possession or distribution of online pornography that depicts children. According to such laws, the images do not have to involve obscene behavior but may include suggestive explicit content depicting any person under the age of 18 years. Furthermore, the image only needs to have been accessed, not necessarily saved on the offender's computer. In some images, the body may be an adult but the head is replaced by a child's to make the image appear to be that of a child.

The Internet also makes it easier for predators to meet potential victims. One of the most commonly encountered sex offenses on the Internet is soliciting minors for sex. Offenders are no longer limited to finding a victim in a small, geographic region. Instead, potential victims can be found anywhere around the world. Moreover, victims sometimes make it easier for offenders by posting personal information about themselves online, whether via online dating sites (e.g., personals.yahoo.com) or Facebook. Victims upload flattering pictures of themselves and list their age, hobbies, and job. Clearly, a predator can easily portray himself or herself as someone else by using a different name, age, gender, occupation, or physical description to be more attractive to a potential victim.[4] By hiding their true identity, predators appear less threatening to a victim.

Sexual predators often prowl the Internet, using chat rooms and other sites to meet vulnerable children, sometimes exchanging pictures or gifts. Their goal is to gain the victim's trust so the predator can convince the victim to meet for sexual purposes. The process by which a predator gains the trust of a potential victims is called "grooming." The predator seeks to find out more details about the child and establish a relationship. This may lead to face-to-face contact and sexual advances. The victim is persuaded to keep the conversation private so no one knows. Talking to a child to engage in sexual behavior is illegal in some places, so even if the predator and the child never meet, the predator may still be indicted for child sex abuse.

To assist those who seek to carry out a sex offense, there are now adult-child sex advocacy websites that provide predators with hints and tips. The boards have discussion groups and bulletin boards that provide offenders with techniques for committing these crimes. The boards sometimes post stories of criminal behaviors that can be imitated.[5] These can give some predators enough information to give them the confidence to carry out these acts.

The volume of child pornography production is particularly problematic. According to the Center for Missing and Exploited Children, the prevalence of child pornography has increased by 82.2 percent since 1994. Between 2004 and 2008, the Crimes Against Children Task Force found an increase of over 200 percent in online enticement of minors. Through the Child Victim Identification Program, over 1.3 million images of children online have been documented.[6]

Sexting

While child pornography is a traditional crime that has evolved to take advantage of new technology, a new sex-related crime has emerged in the digital age. "Sexting" refers to the practice of sending nude or seminude images of minors (youth under the age of 18 years) through cell phones to anyone else. The images can then be distributed through computers, web cameras, digital cameras, and cell phones. The age of the receiver typically does not matter, but the age of the victim is critical. Sexting can have serious implications for the youth involved, as they can be labeled as sex offenders for the remainder of their life. The images can also be used to create child pornography.[7]

Identity Theft

One of the most significant and fastest-growing forms of Internet crime is identity theft. According to the Department of Justice, identity theft refers to "all types of crime in which someone wrongfully obtains and uses another person's personal data in some way that involves fraud or deception, typically for economic gain."[8] This crime occurs when an offender steals personal information from a victim, such as a Social Security number, date of birth, home address, passwords, or driver's license number, and then uses that information to access a victim's bank accounts and/or makes charges on the victim's credit cards. The offender can also apply for bank loans or steal Social Security checks. In some cases, an offender applies for a passport or driver's license with his or her picture but the victim's name. If the offender is arrested, the victim is identified as the offender.

The crime of identity theft can be subdivided into four categories. The first is financial identity theft, when a criminal uses another person's name, Social Security number, or other personal information to steal funds from an account or otherwise obtain goods and services. The second category is criminal identity theft, which occurs when a person poses as another person when accused of a crime or apprehended for a crime. The third type of identity theft is identity cloning. This happens when a criminal uses another person's identifying information to assume that identity in daily life. The fourth is business/commercial identity theft, which involves using another's business name as a means to obtain credit.

To date, millions of people have had their personal information stolen and then used for illegal purposes. A criminal may be able to steal personal information through fake emails and websites. Victims may assume they are signing into their bank account website and use their login and password, but it is really a bogus site linked to an offender. Criminals also steal information through dumpster diving, which is rummaging through a person's trash to look for bills, documents, or papers with personal information. Skimming (stealing credit/debit card numbers by use of a special storage device when processing a card) and phishing (pretending to be a financial institution and sending spam to get people to give out information) are commonly used techniques to gather personal information. Some criminals divert billing statements by completing a change of address form, thus having mail delivered to a fake address. Of course, information can be stolen through traditional methods, such as stealing wallets, purses, or preapproved credit cards. Some criminals also use hacking techniques or spyware, Trojan horses, or hacking (described later). They can also "shoulder surf" by looking over someone's shoulder as they type in information at an ATM or a store checkout.

Many victims of identity theft are not aware that their information has been stolen. This means an offender has plenty of time to carry out crimes before the theft is reported. It also means police have a more difficult time finding the offender. The longer the time between a crime being committed and reported, the less evidence is available against an offender.

Victims of identity theft can have their credit rating ruined or be arrested for things they did not do. This could happen if an offender provides false identification to police, creating a criminal record or leaving outstanding arrest warrants for the person whose identity has been stolen. Victims can lose thousands of dollars from theft and often must also spend thousands of dollars to clear their name and record. Some victims have been unable to cash checks, open credit cards, or take out loans, and they end up with huge debts. In some cases, the offender is attempting to tarnish another person's reputation or put the blame for something on someone else.

According to the Theft and Assumption Deterrence Act of 1998, identity theft is a federal crime. In 2013, it is estimated that over 40 million people in the United States were victims of identity theft.[9]

Hacking

Hacking is unauthorized or illegal access to a computer system, and a hacker is a person who has the skills to gain unauthorized or illegal access to computers. At one time, the term "hacker" had a more positive connotation. These were people who enjoyed learning about the details of computer systems or knew about programming computers, and they broke into systems for the challenge of doing so.[10] This is often no longer the case. Many hackers are now known for the harm they cause to individuals, schools, governments, and businesses. They look for vulnerabilities in systems or for systems that are poorly protected or have poor security systems. That weakness can then be used to get inside the system. Once in the system, hackers can deface or change information to cause confusion or harm or steal a person's identity. They may seek to change the appearance of a website, avoid long-distance charges, or steal copyrighted software. Hackers can access classified information, install malware, or launch a DoS attack. They can overwhelm a system with requests so the system cannot cope with the demand and cannot handle requests from users, leading the computer system to shut down.

A related term is "cracker," which refers to a person who attempts to exploit flaws in a system for malicious purposes. The term was more relevant when "hacker" had a positive connotation. Then, "cracker" or a "black hat hacker" were terms for hackers who sought access to a computer system with the intent of causing harm or defacing a website. As "hacker" now refers to someone who intends harm, the distinction between the two is less relevant.

If a black hat hacker intends harm, a white hat hacker is a person who does not have any criminal intent and does not intend to commit any crimes. Instead white hat hackers look for potential gaps in security and, thus, learn how to protect systems better. They are also called "sneakers" or "tiger teams." Some companies have hired white hat hackers to hack into their systems and recommend ways to improve the security systems.

A third group of hackers are called "grey hat hackers." These individuals are somewhere in between black hat and white hat hackers. Sometimes they hack into computers to commit crime and other times do so with no intent of harm. They may search for weaknesses but only disclose those vulnerabilities to the system administrator under certain circumstances, often for monetary reward. They may make the gap known so they can protect themselves, or they may compel software makers to distribute software patches to fix any security problems.

A hacker's motivation for breaking into a system varies. Some hackers are curious or bored and see hacking as entertainment. Some see hacking as a challenge or may seek to point out possible security risks. Others may be seeking a feeling of power or peer recognition.[11] Most are seeking access to personal or financial information or accounts, though some are motivated by ideals. For example, some hackers believe that all information should be free and accessible to everyone and that there should be no secrets.

Other hackers are motivated by political reasons. They may seek to infiltrate the websites of competing political organizations. Some have tried to help those living under totalitarian regimes exchange information more freely. On the other hand, cyberterrorists attempt to cause damage for political reasons.

Hackers can be placed into one of four categories. The first and largest group comprises casual hackers, who tend to be less skilled and usually only commit nuisance crimes. But because they are less skilled, or may use tools purchased from the Internet, they make mistakes and can be easily caught. They are usually motivated by curiosity or by the thrill of breaking into a system. Oftentimes these hackers are referred to as "script kiddies."

The second group of hackers consists of political hackers, often called "cyberactivists." These hackers have specific targets and are pursuing a specific cause. The knowledge and skill of political hackers can vary, but they generally tend to deface websites.

The third type of hackers comprise organized crime hackers who seek a profit. They tend to focus on breaking into bank accounts, stealing credit card numbers, or stealing confidential information.[12] More complex hacking requires an extensive knowledge of computers. Organized crime hackers tend to focus on business computer systems, as it is not worth their time to break into an individual home computer. More often such hackers focus on systems that are likely to have data on many people, such as banks and businesses.

The fourth type of hacker, known as "phreakers," consists of those who hack telephone systems. They were more prevalent prior to the advent of cell phones.

Most computer systems today have some kind of a security system to prevent hackers from stealing their information. The security systems often include some type of firewall that protects a hacker from accessing their system. The firewall typically inspects any data that is being sent into or is leaving the company. If the data is clean, it will be allowed in. Skilled hackers can generally find any vulnerabilities or weaknesses in the network and get through the firewalls. Because of this many hackers refer to firewalls as "cottonwalls."

Hackers are commonly thought of as being males who like to work alone.[13] One study found that hackers tend to be young males and school dropouts in their mid-20s,[14] whereas another study found that hackers have a higher level of "moral disengagement" than other groups. They tend to believe it is acceptable to hack into computer systems if it does not result in any serious harm to others. Moreover, hackers tend to perceive their chances of being caught as fairly low. They participate in hacking behaviors because they believe the gains they receive will exceed any potential costs.[15] Other studies have found that hackers are a much more diverse group, ranging in age from teens to persons in their sixties.[16]

Other analyses show that while hackers do tend to be from different races and genders, most appear to be white males.[17] As a group they tend to be highly educated; many have a college degree, and about half have been married.[18] Many hackers are employed and have incomes that average between $50,000 and $57,000 a year.[19] Most had an interest in computers early in their lives and were bright students who showed the potential for academic success. Most hackers report that they are often not punished for their hacking behaviors. Instead, the victim often asks them to help to fix the security of the system.[20]

In addition to the characteristics hackers share in terms of demographics and interests, hackers also generally adhere to what has been termed the "hacker ethic." While not universal in terms of hacker subculture, it does help differentiate it from other technocentric groups. The hacker ethic consists of three primary beliefs. The first belief is that information wants to be free. In other words, any restriction on information is an affront to the hacker, which explains much of their interest in subverting secure systems to access information.

The second belief of the hacker ethic is a belief in the do-it-yourself, or DIY, mentality. Thus, hackers believe in a hands-on approach. In part, this explains why hackers are more likely to actively engage with technology, building computers as well as designing systems.[21]

Third, hackers generally believe in technological utopianism. This is the belief that technology is the primary solution to nearly every social problem. Nearly any issue faced, from the individual level through the societal level, is thought to have a technical solution. Moreover, they believe technology should be used to go around any particular issues that face the hacker—including restricted access.[22]

Two acts that are subcategories of hacking are cyber trespassing and cyber vandalism. Cyber trespass is when a hacker accesses another's computer or network without the permission of the owner but does not alter, misuse, or damage any of the data or the system itself. Cyber vandalism is accessing a computer or a network with the intent of causing damage or disrupting a website or data but not misusing it. An example is disrupting or stopping a computer system or posting obscene or incorrect data. This would cause the owner to shut down the website in order to repair it. In general, these attacks do not cause harm.

Session Hijacking

Session hijacking is a more technical method of computer hacking. It involves finding a legitimate remote connection, such as a professor using a VPN (Virtual Private Network) to connect to his or her office and literally hijacking that session. There are many ways to do this, each of which require a high level of computer hacking skills and knowledge of networks. For this reason, this type of attack is less common than others.

Password Cracking

Password cracking is when an offender is able to discern a user's password so that the offender can log on to a network as that user. There are different tools to discover passwords, all of which are available on the Internet. One, called a "sniffer," oversees all data that goes through a computer network and determines what the data is, the source of the data, and where it is being sent. Another tool is a password cracker, which is used to automate the process of breaking passwords.

An offender might use a dictionary attack, a brute-force attack, or a combination of both to crack passwords. In a brute-force attack a software tool simply tries every single combination of letters, numbers, and symbols until a password is found. A dictionary attack is possibly the quickest way to uncover a password. This method tries commonly used passwords, or passwords that are specifically related to a target. For example, if the person whose password you wish to crack loves flowers, passwords with words related to flowers can be put into a file. Then this file will be loaded into a cracking application and tried on user accounts. Because most passwords are simple, a dictionary attack is often successful at cracking passwords.

Hacktivists

Hacktivists are people who hack into a computer system for some kind of a political motive. They may do this to discredit those they view as their enemy, or they may seek to spread their own message. Once in a system, a hacktivist can use a DoS attack to bring down websites. Hacktivists may also be affiliated with religious groups and thus may not be interested in financial gain. One hacker attempted to embarrass Sarah Palin, the republican nominee for the vice presidency in 2008. By using a dictionary attack, David Kernell, a 20-year-old college student, was able to use her biographical information (zip code, date of birth, and place where she met her husband) to break into her email account. He then posted the illegally accessed emails online.

Vice Crimes

Many vice crimes are now committed online. Most of these offenses existed before the Internet, but they have evolved with advances in technology. Even though they are traditional crimes, offenders have found new ways to use the Internet to commit them. One such crime is the sale of illicit or prescription drugs. Though the sale of these drugs via the Internet is illegal except to a customer through a state-licensed pharmacy based in the United States, computer sites offering illegal or prescription drugs for low prices are widely available. Another form of vice on the Internet is online gambling, which is illegal in the United States because gambling service providers require electronic payment via credit cards, debit cards, or electronic fund transfers. Prostitution is another vice crime on the Internet; this is against the law because the process of accessing the Internet crosses state and national borders.

Harassment (Cyberstalking and Cyberbullying)

Cyberstalking and cyberbullying are traditional crimes that have evolved as Internet crimes. Cyberstalking is when an offender repeatedly tracks the location of a victim, either physically or online, and gives that person constant, unwanted attention, despite requests to stop. In some cases, the offender threatens to harm the victim or actually carries out those threats. A more complete definition of cyberstalking is found in Box 3.1.

Cyberstalkers and cyberbullies may post offensive messages on social networks or may continually telephone, email, or text a person who does not want that attention. Cyberstalkers and cyberbullies sometimes encourage others to harass their victim, order unwanted goods to be delivered to the victim, and generally cause their victim embarrassment. If not taken seriously, cyberstalking may lead to violence against the victim such as sexual assaults, or even death. A stalker may appear at a person's home or place of business uninvited or unwanted, may leave notes, messages, or objects for a victim, or may even vandalize the victim's property.

The majority of stalkers are men, and the majority of victims are women.[23] Research shows that women are more likely to be stalked online by men (67 percent) than by other women (24 percent). In addition, about 50 percent of cyberstalking victims who were able to identify their attackers (about 60 percent of all victims) reported that they had no previous

Box 3.1   U.S. Department of Justice Definition of Cyberstalking

"Although there is no universally accepted definition of cyberstalking, the term is used . . . to refer to the use of the Internet, email, or other electronic communications devices to stalk another person. Stalking generally involves harassing or threatening behavior that an individual engages in repeatedly, such as following a person, appearing at a person's home or place of business, making harassing phone calls, leaving written messages or objects, or vandalizing a person's property. Most stalking laws require that the perpetrator make a credible threat of violence against the victim; others include threats against the victim's immediate family; and still others require only that the alleged stalker's course of conduct constitute an implied threat."

Source: U.S. Department of Justice, Office of Justice Programs, Violence Against Women Act, May 2001, "Stalking and Domestic Violence: A Report to Congress," p. 1, NCJ 186157, https://www.ncjrs.gov/pdffiles1/ojp/186157.pdf.

relationship with the stalker. Interestingly, about a third of cyberstalking incidents involve more than one offender.[24]

Cyberbullying can lead to tragic consequences. In January 2010, 15-year-old Phoebe Prince committed suicide after being cyberbullied by her schoolmates. In September 2010, Rutgers student Tyler Clementi committed suicide after his roommate set up a secret webcam in their dorm room to stream video of Clementi kissing another man. He posted the message "Jumping off the gw bridge sorry" on Facebook before taking his life. In October 2006, 13-year-old Megan Meier from Missouri hanged herself after communicating online with a person she thought was a young man. Her new friend turned out to be a female classmate and her mother.

Most states have anti-stalking laws on the books, and many have expanded those to include stalking and bullying in cyberspace. Unfortunately, the definitions of many of the terms, including "harass," "threaten," and "intimidate," are vague and can mean many things. Thus, those terms vary a great deal from one jurisdiction to another. Most agree that if the words used in an email would be threatening if said in a face-to-face conversation, then it would be considered a threat.

Cybertheft

Cybertheft occurs when an offender uses a computer to steal another person's money, property, or other secrets. The secrets or property may then be sold to others. This category of crime includes embezzlement, unlawful appropriation of goods, espionage, identity theft, and piracy. An example is when an offender hacks into a bank's records and transfers money from someone's account into his or her own account. The offender is then able to withdraw the money. Offenders might also hack into a bank's security files to access account numbers, passwords, and PINs. They may hack into businesses to adjust accounts.

As more people turn to online shopping, there are more opportunities for online theft. The number of fraudulent websites has grown in recent years. For example, criminals may create websites that seem to be that of a major retail company. Users may think it is the real website and give their credit card number to the criminal. Other fake sites provide goods or a service but then quickly disappear once the money is collected. For example, a website may offer tickets to an event. Purchasers receive fake tickets or none at all. Or credit card data is stolen as it is sent to the company. Online companies try to prevent crimes by using encryption technology that scrambles personal information so that it cannot be stolen by hackers but crimes still happen.

Computer-based Fraud

In basic terms, fraud is a lie. If someone leads you on or allows you to believe something that is false to benefit them, they are lying and committing fraud. In many cases, fraud can result in a victim voluntarily giving money or property to another person who has misrepresented himself or herself or the service they are offering. The term "Internet fraud" refers to any type of fraud scheme that uses one or more online services—such as chat rooms, email, message boards, or websites—to present fraudulent solicitations to prospective victims, to conduct fraudulent transactions, or to transmit the proceeds of fraud to financial institutions or to others connected with the scheme. The term refers to acts such as investment offers, auction fraud, failure to send merchandise, sending a buyer a product that is less valuable than what was originally advertised, failure to deliver a purchased good in a timely manner or at all, or failure to disclose all relevant information about a product or terms of the sale. Some common types of Internet fraud include identity theft, purchase scams, counterfeit money orders, phishing for sensitive information, and click fraud, whereby false hits are generated for websites to gain advertising money.

A common example of computer fraud is the Nigerian or 419 scam ("419" refers to the section of Nigerian law that the scam violates). In this scam, a potential victim receives an unsolicited email asserting that the sender requires help in transferring a large sum of money out of Nigeria. There is typically some issue or problem prohibiting the sender from simply moving the money, and the sender asks the victim to provide a bank account number or some other information to help them move the money. Sometimes they ask the victim to send the fees for transferring the money to the victim's account. In exchange, the sender promises to give the receiver a portion of the money. The offender uses the bank account number or other information to steal money from the victim.[25]

Auto Auction Fraud

A new form of cybercrime involves the sale of automobiles. In these scams, someone will try to sell a car that they do not own or is not in their possession. They will place the car for sale at a price far below the car's true value, explaining that they must sell it because they are moving and cannot take the car with them, or are facing an emergency and need the money. Because of the urgency, the seller asks that the car be sold quickly. They ask the buyer to send a full or partial payment immediately, and once the payment is received, the offender takes the money and disappears. Many of the sales are from outside the United States, so the law enforcement jurisdiction is unclear, making investigation more difficult. According to the Internet Crime Complaint Center (IC3), there were 16,861 reports of vehicle scams in 2014, most coming from men. Total reported losses were $56,222,655.[26]

Dating Scams

Many cyber scams are related to people who seek a romantic partner online through a dating website or a social media outlet. Victims may believe they have met and are dating someone who is not who they seem to be. Often, the pair never physically meet but will converse online for many weeks or even months. The offender will ask for money, claiming to be in some emergency or suffering a tragedy, or maybe sick and need financial help. A victim may be willing to send money, because they have met their soulmate and are sure that eventually there will be a future relationship. Once the offender receives the money, they disappear.

In 2013, Internet Crime Complaint Center (IC3) reports that there were 6,412 people who filed complaints that they had been victims of a romance scam, with a total monetary loss of $81,796,169.[27]

FBI/Government Official Scam

In some new online scams, victims will receive an email that seems to be from a high-ranking government official such as the director of the FBI. In some cases, the official's name is included to make the email appear more authentic. The letter will demand payment for an outstanding bill or some other purpose. Because it seems official and threatening, many people who receive the note actually send money, which ends up in the hands of a criminal, not the FBI or other agency. In 2013, the IC3 reports that there were 9,169 complaints of this scam, with a loss of $6,348,881.[28]

Another version of this scam has been termed the "grandparent scam," in which an elderly person gets a message that a grandchild needs financial assistance. In some cases, the email may appear to be from the grandchild. The grandchild pleads for money because he or she has been the victim of a crime, often in a foreign country, and needs money to get medical help or to travel home. Most of the time, the child is home safe and sound.

File Sharing/Internet Piracy

File sharing is when someone provides files for other users to download over the Internet. This allows a person to share music and video files with other users without downloading the original files from the original website. This means people do not have to pay for the music or video. Similarly, digital piracy is the act of copying copyrighted digital material—including digital goods, software, documents, music, and video—for any reason other than backing up existing files, without obtaining permission from and providing compensation to the copyright holder.[29] Simply, it is the unauthorized electronic distribution and sale of copyrighted works over the Internet. File sharing and piracy are considered to be a form of online theft because the original artist or author (or other copyright owner) is not getting his or her percent of sales.

File sharing and digital piracy are rampant on the Internet. For many years, pirated software has been sold or made available online. More recently, pirated movies have been sold over the Internet. In these cases, the owner does not have a legal right to the good, but there is a high demand for stolen products on the Internet. The copied or stolen software, video, or book may be available free or for a very small cost, and the chances of being caught and punished for downloading a movie are extremely low. So users continue to download pirated products or share files with friends. One case of a person arrested for illegally downloading music is described in Box 3.2.

Box 3.2   A Case of Illegal Music Downloads

In 2005, Jammie Thomas-Rasset was accused of violating copyright laws after downloading 1,702 songs on the peer-to-peer platform Kazaa (although the plaintiffs were seeking damages on only 24 of them). She then shared the files with others.

In 2007, Thomas-Rasset appeared in federal court in Minnesota to face the charges against her. (The case was Capitol Records, et al. v. Thomas-Rasset, 2009, 11-2820.)

She claimed that she did not download any files, and that her computer was being controlled by someone else because of malware. After only five minutes of deliberation, the jury found her guilty and liable for the damages of over $9,000 for each of the 24 songs in question for a total of $222,000. Because of an error in the judge's instructions to the jury, the court vacated the decision and a second trial was held. In that trial, Thomas-Rasset was again found guilty of willful copyright infringement. This time, the judge ordered that she pay $1.92 million in damages to the record companies. This was the equivalent of $80,000 for each of the 24 songs she allegedly shared.

Sources: Steve Karnowski, "Jammie Thomas-Rasset Loses Supreme Court Appeal, Must Pay $222,000 for Illegal Downloads," Huff Post Tech, March 18, 2013, http://www.huffingtonpost.com/2013/03/18/jammie-thomas-rasset-supreme -court-illegal-downloading_n_2902093.html; Michael Bachmann, "Suing the Genie Back in the Bottle," in *Cyber Criminology: Exploring Internet Crimes and Criminal Behavior*, ed. K. Jaishankar (Boca Raton, FL: CRC Press, 2011), 155–172.

One way file sharing can be carried out is with the use of a BitTorrent. This breaks a large file, such as a movie, into many smaller files. The BitTorrent tells a computer how to put the smaller files together to create the larger one. The smaller files are found on many different computers. This way, no one can be held responsible for sharing an entire file with another user. With a BitTorrent, a user can download files from one computer and then upload parts of the same file to somebody else. One website that uses this method is Pirate Bay (see Box 3.3).

Another method for sharing files is the peer-to-peer (P2P) model, in which the files are stored on personal computers, and the owners share files with other users on the Internet. Users can link their computers with others' computers located anywhere in the world. File sharing on a P2P system differs from file trading because downloading files from a P2P

Box 3.3   Pirate Bay

In 2003, a website called Pirate Bay was created in Sweden. This is a site on which anyone can share files for music and videos. A user can search the Pirate Bay website and choose a product to download. The owners of Pirate Bay do not directly provide the video or music sought by the consumer. Instead, they provide a torrent file that can be thought of as instructions that help a computer assemble many small files into one. When a consumer purchases a movie from Pirate Bay, the movie is actually in small files located in many hosts that are sharing it at any given moment. The user's computer will find the small files and reassemble them to make the movie file complete. This is considered to be "distributed" file sharing, as no one contributes the entire final product.

In 2006, police raided the Pirate Bay website and temporarily shut it down. But it wasn't long before it was operating again. This time, the owners set up servers in different places, making it very difficult to completely shut it down again. The site also moved to cloud-hosting in two different countries. According to the owners, this makes it almost impossible for law enforcement to raid the site.

In 2009, law enforcement officials charged the founders of Pirate Bay with helping to break copyright laws. They were convicted and given sentences of one year in prison and fined $4.2 million. However, because their servers are located around the world, there are questions about who owns the company. The company may have been sold to a shell company in 2006.

Today, the Pirate Bay site exists, although it has periods where it is down and not accessible to users.

network does not require the user to upload the file, although in some cases that may be an option.[30]

Digital piracy has been illegal in the United States since the passage of the No Electronic Theft Act in 1997. This law made copyright infringement a federal offense. Whether or not the provider makes a profit, if he or she sells, trades, or provides another user with copyrighted material, the provider can be punished with a term of five years in prison and up to $250,000 in fines. Internationally, the World Intellectual Property Organization developed a number of treaties or agreements, including the Copyright Treaty, Performers and Producers of Phonograms Treaty, and

Databases Treaty, which are meant to halt the theft of copyrighted materials online.

Two professional interest groups, the Recording Industry Association of America (RIAA) and the Motion Picture Association of America, have spent large amounts of resources attempting to convince lawmakers in Washington to support new laws aimed at preventing file sharing. Some copyright owners have also paid companies to help challenge those who share material illegally. The RIAA was able to force music-sharing system Napster to close its operation based on the fact that the shared files were stored on a central computer. Since then, Napster has set up subscription-based legal file sharing for music files.

Many file-sharing sites are located outside the United States, in places where U.S. copyright laws are often not enforced. For example, the program Kazaa is owned by the Australian company Sharman Holdings, incorporated in Vanuatu and developed by two Dutch software engineers.

Phishing

Phishing is the process of sending emails to users in an attempt to steal their private information, which can then be used for other crimes. The victim receives an email that appears to be from a legitimate organization, such as a bank or a credit card company, that claims there is a problem with the victim's account or that the account needs to be verified. Typical subject lines are "problem with your account" or "verify your account." The victim is asked to supply personal information or follow a link to a website to provide personal information. The user is prompted to click on a link and log in to his or her account, which requires a user ID and password. Though the link appears to be from a legitimate financial institution, it is operated by an identity thief. When the victim enters his or her information to verify the account, the victim is also providing the offender with a username and password that can be used to log in to the real account and steal funds. The illegitimate websites are crafted so they appear to be legitimate. Some of the bogus sites appear to be the website of the Internal Revenue Service or even the FBI.[31]

An example of phishing occurred in 2006, when phishers targeted MySpace users, particularly young users. A message was sent to random MySpace users promising a free $500 Macy's gift card. In order to receive the card, the MySpace user had to supply various items of personal information, allowing the perpetrators to steal the member's identity. The scam also involved sending emails to the victim's MySpace friends while posing as the victim and posting comments on their profiles that recommended that the victim's friends also sign up for the free gift card.

Three types of phishing have been identified. With the first type, termed "generic phishing," an email is sent in a random fashion to multiple recipients—no one in particular. The sender hopes some of the recipients will believe the email is real and respond. Even though most recipients will ignore the message, some will likely unwittingly supply their information.

The second type of phishing is loosely targeted phishing, whereby a message might be sent to a group of people who have a particular characteristic or who belong to a specific group or a targeted community. For example, an email might be sent to older people or those who have young children. This increases the likelihood that a recipient will respond to the email and provide information.

The third type, termed "spear phishing," in which a message is sent to a particular set of users, for example those who work in a certain field or belong to a particular organization. Although these messages are sent to a smaller population than the other categories of phishing, the messages are specifically tailored to the recipients, thus lending more credibility to the message. In turn, this gives the phisher a higher chance of fooling potential victims. Spear phishing is being used more often as a way to hack into a company's computer system. Employees might receive emails that contain personal information, so they appear legitimate. When that employee opens the email or an attachment, malware is installed on their computers. In this case, the target is not the individual, per se, but the company.[32] An extreme form of this type of phishing is referred to as "whaling," because the messages are aimed specifically at a senior official or other influential individual, and therefore the scam is phishing for a big target.[33] Often, the emails appear to be from loved ones or close friends, claiming to be in an emergency situation or the victim of a crime and asking that money be sent to a location abroad.

Social Engineering

Social engineering is the process of trying to get personal information out of someone through personal contact. This scam begins with offenders gathering details about a victim (phone numbers, birth date) from social network sites like MySpace or Facebook, or a professional site such as LinkedIn. Then the offender might make a phone call to an office or business to get more personal information. This is not unlike simply conning a victim by using use social skills to get sensitive information from them.

In this type of scam, an offender may have the names of employees at a company, maybe even managers. They then call a secretary or receptionist, pretending to be a computer repair person or the company tech expert. Through the conversation, the offender will mention the names of managers or other employees, and then ask for a person's password. Because the caller seems to know so much about the company and the employees, the receptionist may believe the caller is real and provide the personal information. The offender can then use that information to access files.

The offender may then get unauthorized access to data that he or she has does not have permission to use or the authority to access. The reasons for the access could be benign, like a police officer who uses a criminal database to investigate a potential date. Other people want to access information simply because they are curious and want to know more about a person or a company. However, some may want to steal that information and use it to harm others or steal their identity. Or they may want to steal business plans or other secrets. Either way, it is illegal.

Cybercrimes against Property (Computer Vandalism)

Viruses

One commonly recognized type of malware is a virus. This term refers to any software that, once installed on a computer, self-replicates in order to disrupt how the computer works. A virus can affect network traffic or harm a computer by damaging system settings, deleting files or data, or disabling security systems. Some viruses can cause damage immediately upon being installed; others may lie dormant in a computer, concealed until something sets it into motion, such as a particular date.[34]

Viruses are spread through infected emails or malicious websites and can infect multiple computer systems. Simply opening an attachment or email or visiting a particular website installs the virus. In some cases, a virus may be present on a CD or disk and can infect another computer if shared. Once installed, some viruses can read the computer's address book and then send itself to all of the addresses.

One special kind of virus is a file infector. This type of virus attaches to program files, usually files with the extension of .COM or .EXE (although other types of files can be infected as well). When the infected program is opened, the virus is loaded onto the computer. Another special kind of virus is a system or boot-record infector. These viruses attach to the DOS boot sector on diskettes or the Master Boot Record on hard disks. Often, a user will receive the disk that contains a boot disk virus. When the operating system is running, files on the diskette can be read without triggering the boot disk virus, which means the user would not know the virus is present on the disk. One of the most common types of viruses are macro viruses. They tend to do little damage but usually infect the Microsoft Word program by inserting unwanted words or phrases into existing files.

If a computer system is infected with a virus, it can be costly to remove the virus and repair any damage to the computer. Thus, it can be difficult to define the true cost of a virus attack. The direct costs of a computer virus include cleaning the computers and network to remove the malicious code. Indirect costs include the business lost during the period a network is shut down to remove the virus and repair any damage.

Because of the potential for harm, it is illegal to create and distribute a computer virus in many places. Nonetheless, people continue to create them. In March 1999, the Melissa virus infected many computers. This early virus was not designed to cause harm but instead simply replicated so quickly that computer systems were overloaded, causing many companies to shut down their email system.

In May 2000, the ILOVEYOU virus affected computers worldwide. The virus was transmitted through an email attachment that, once opened, copied itself and sent the virus to everyone in a receiver's address book. In the companies attacked, the virus often started a sort of feedback loop. In which employees' email addresses might be copied multiple times, leading to thousands of email messages flooding the mail server, each with the virus, causing a slowdown of the network.

Bots

Bots are programs that are attached to a computer that allows a person to access and control that computer remotely. Bots can allow a controller to support illicit activity, including sending spam and phishing emails or installing additional malware. Bots can also allow criminals to steal money or personal information from a user. When many bots are under the control of one commander, it is referred to as a "botnet."[35] Similarly, when cybercriminals use bots to take control of many computers at one time they are referred to as "zombie" computers.

In November 2013, an app was available to Android users that appeared legitimate but turned out to be a bot. The iBanking Mobile Bot was offered for sale in a Russian-speaking underground community for $4,000–$5,000. The bot allowed a criminal to send commands to the infected computer. All text messages coming to the device were sent to the offender, who could send messages from the victim's phone to any number, without the owner's consent. The offender could intercept and listen to all incoming phone calls. All phone numbers could be stolen, and the location of the phone (and thus the user) could be traced. The bot could also access all images that were stored on the device.[36]

Cutwail, one of the largest and most notorious botnets, sends spam email that impersonates well-known online retailers, mobile phone companies, social networking sites and financial institutions. Cutwail has affected about 1.5 to 2 million individual computers and sends approximately 74 billion spam messages a day, the equivalent of 51 million messages every minute.

Trojan Horses

Like a virus, a Trojan horse is a type of malware that damages a computer. The name comes the mythological event in which Greek soldiers invaded the city of Troy by hiding inside a giant wooden horse. Once the horse was moved inside the city walls, the soldiers emerged to fight at a strategic time. Similarly, when a person receives a Trojan horse, it will appear to be a legitimate item the recipient wants or may find helpful, such as a picture or a software product. It can also be an attachment in an email message. When the file is opened, the Trojan horse installs itself on the computer. The Trojan horse will then either deliver a second program, such as a virus, worm, or other type of damaging program, or it will simply take some malicious action itself, such as allowing another person to gain control of the victim's computer. Trojan horses can also be used to deliver spyware to target machines. Because they are installed on the user's machine by the user, they are often not detected by an agency's security measures.[37]

In 1999, a Trojan horse provided an apparent upgrade to Internet Explorer, but when it was installed, the creator of the malware could take control of the computer, gaining access to the victim's personal files and information.

Worms

A worm is a type of malware that is similar to a virus. Some experts consider worms to be a different type of malware from a virus, while others consider worms to be a special type of a virus. Nonetheless, a worm is essentially a virus that can replicate itself without help from a person. The difference is that with a virus the user must take some action to activate the malware. For instance, a user must visit an infected website. If the user does not visit the website (or open an email attachment), then the virus is not activated and will not spread. Conversely, a worm does not require human action on the part of the recipient to activate the malicious code. Instead, a worm is able to travel on its own from computer to computer. Once a computer is infected the worm will seek out methods to copy itself, sometimes sending out thousands of copies to other users. For example, it might find shared network drives to copy itself to and then attempt to send itself to other computers on that network. Thus, the worm is able to spread through computer networks and the Internet by itself.[38] Once a computer is infected with a worm, the code may disrupt email and other operations. It can also access files, delete files, and/or damage the system's software and hardware.

It is not unusual for a computer to be infected with a worm that goes unnoticed for a long time. It may only be discovered when the worm has been replicated so often that the computer system is so bogged down that the computer ceases to work.

In September 2010, the Stuxnet worm was transmitted by use of Universal Serial Bus (USB) keys (portable memory devices). The virus infected computers at a secret nuclear power station (a nuclear fuel enrichment facility) in Iran. Because it was transmitted through USB keys, the worm also affected systems that were not connected to the Internet. Once attached to a computer, the worm reprogrammed the software that sent instructions to motors and coolers, in essence telling them to turn on or off. It is estimated that the Stuxnet worm destroyed 984 centrifuges.

Spyware

Spyware is any software or technology that secretly tracks a computer user's activity and gathers information about that person's computer use. Because it is done without the knowledge or consent of the user, it is termed "spyware." This type of malware tracks how a person uses a computer, including the websites visited and personal information, such as passwords, account information, mad corporate data. It may also track all keystrokes the user makes, or allow an offender to read a victim's email or text messages. It can also allow a criminal to track a person's location or listen to their phone calls. Not only can spyware be used to steal a person's identifying information but it can also cause advertisements to automatically be displayed on a computer. It can also damage a computer or cause it to slow down.

Information from the computer may be sent to the creator of the spyware in many ways. Sometimes there is a hidden file on the machine that the criminal can access. In other cases, the spyware sends data to an Internet Protocol (IP) address or email address at regular intervals. Clearly, victims are not aware that their computer is infected with spyware. Instead, the program hides in a computer for long periods, which gives the criminal time to gather information on the user.

Spyware that is used to track every keystroke a user makes is called a "keylogger." This means everything a person types is recorded, including every website address, all usernames and passwords, credentials, and account information. Another type of spyware takes screenshots of what is on a user's computer screen, which is then sent to the criminal.

The goal of using spyware is obtain the user's personal data from his or her computer and use it for other reasons. However, it does have some useful purposes. Parents may use spyware to monitor their children's computer usage. Employers may want to track how their employees are using their computers. Companies may want to know what websites a person visits so they know what types of ads to send to a particular user. This type of spyware is called "adware."

Because these technologies have some legitimate purposes, many companies create and market inexpensive spyware. Because it is so inexpensive and readily available, however, it is popular among cybercriminals. Spyware is becoming one of the most prevalent computer-security threats in today's world. In some cases, products designed for parents to monitor their children's computer use can be easily modified for other reasons. Moreover, spyware is easy to deliver to a user's computer. It may be delivered by use of a Trojan horse, for example, so that a person who downloads a free video game will also be downloading spyware. Or it can be loaded onto a machine when a user visits a website or opens an email attachment.

Logic Bomb

A logic bomb is a program that lies dormant (and thus undetected) in a computer system until a particular condition is met, such as a certain date arrives or a particular user logs onto the computer. A logic bomb may also be programmed to go off when the originator sends a message. When the specified criterion is met, the logic bomb activates and executes its code.

An example of a logic bomb is the case of Michael Lauffenburger, a consultant for defense contractor General Dynamics. In June 1992, Lauffenburger was arrested for introducing a logic bomb into the company's computer system that would delete data pertaining to a sensitive project. Lauffenburger released the logic bomb in the hopes that once the data was found missing, the company would need to rehire Lauffenberger as a consultant to fix the problem. However, an employee discovered the logic bomb before it was activated. Lauffenburger was charged with computer tampering and attempted fraud and was fined $5,000 with no jail time.

Another example of a logic bomb occurred in October 2008, at the Fannie Mae mortgage company. About that time, a logic bomb was discovered in the company's computer systems. The malware had been planted by a former contractor, Rajendrasinh Makwana, who had been fired as a consultant. The bomb, set to activate on January 31, 2009, would erase all data from the company's servers. When it was discovered, Makwana was indicted in a Maryland court for unauthorized computer access. As of this writing, the case has not been resolved.

Rootkit

A rootkit is a type of malware that attempts to "gain root" in a computer system. It refers to any program that attempts to hide malware (such as viruses, Trojan horses, worms, or logic bombs) that have been installed on a machine. For the most part, rootkits are fairly sophisticated pieces of software and usually require a criminal to have extensive knowledge of the target operating system in order to be successful. However, premade kits are available online so less skilled hackers can download the tools needed to carry out a rootkit.

Spam

Spam is the unwanted or unsolicited emails that are sent to thousands of users, sometimes anonymously. Spam can be used to promote or advertise products or to trick people into giving up personal information (phishing). They may offer free investment opportunities or sexual enhancement products. They are often carriers for computer worms, viruses, and other malware. A person who is behind this activity is called a "spammer."

For the sender, spam is economically viable. Users have no operating costs beyond the management of the mailing lists. Because of this, the volume of unsolicited emails has grown. But for the recipients, there may be significant costs to spam. If they have malware attached, the costs can be very high. The direct effects of spam include the consumption of computer and network resources as well as the cost in human time and attention of dismissing unwanted messages. In addition, spam has costs stemming from the kinds of spam messages sent, from the ways spammers send them, and from the race between spammers and those who try to stop or control spam. Because most spam is unwanted and can be very harmful, some email users have spam filters that attempt to block or delete the spam messages.

The European Union's Internal Market Commission estimated that in 2001 that "junk email" costs Internet users €10 billion per year worldwide. In addition to direct costs are the indirect costs borne by the victims—both those related to the spamming itself, and to other crimes that usually accompany it, such as financial theft, identity theft, data and intellectual property theft, virus and other malware infection, child pornography, fraud, and deceptive marketing.

Denial-of-Service Attack

A DoS attack occurs when a website has so many requests to view the site that it cannot deal with the demand, causing the site to slow down or prevent access. This means a legitimate user or organization is unable to use the services of a resource they would normally expect to have. In a distributed DoS attack, multiple compromised systems (a botnet) attack a single target.

While DoS attacks do not typically result in the loss of information, they can cause serious economic damage by slowing down or halting business until the computer systems can be cleaned up. In most cases, there is a loss of services such as email. A DoS attack may also destroy programming and files in computer systems. Sometimes DoS attacks have forced websites to become unavailable. Often, the computers involved in the attacks are doing so without the owner knowing. This could happen if a computer has been infected by a virus or has become a zombie computer under the control of a bot. In 2009, Facebook and Twitter were hit with a DoS that rendered them inoperable for several hours. It was later determined that the attack came from Russia.

It takes much less technical skill to carry out a DoS attack than other attacks, so they are more common. The goal of a DoS attack is to simply overload the target computer system so legitimate users are not able to access it. In some cases, a DoS attack is used as a means of extortion. Offenders may threaten to disrupt a business, possibly at an important time of the year, in exchange for money or another good. Because businesses do not want to take the chance of losing business days, they will pay the fee. This occurred in 2004, when the credit card authorization company Authorize .net received a message that indicated they needed to pay money, or their site would be hit with a DoS attack. The company did not to pay the money, and its site was attacked. It took months before the site was able to operate again.

Ransomware

A new scam has been hitting computer users in recent years. The targeted computer users receive a message saying that their files have been encrypted and if they want them back, they need to pay a ransom. The ransomware, sometimes called CryptoLocker, is often attached to an email that appears to be from a legitimate source, such as FedEx or UPS tracking notices. Once installed on a computer, the ransomware prevents a user from opening documents, records, and photographs. Victims who do not pay lose all of their files. Since the ransom is usually not very high (typically between $300 and $700), and because many people don't have backup files, they pay the ransom. Businesses often pay because it would cost more to have the ransomware removed. This is one way in which hackers can extort money from individuals and businesses.[39] Reports of ransomware like this grew by 500 percent from 2012 to 2013.[40]

Cybercrimes against Governments

Cyberterrorism

According to the FBI, cyberterrorism is any "premeditated, politically motivated attack against information, computer systems, computer programs, and data which results in violence against non-combatant targets by subnational groups or clandestine agents."[41] Cyberterrorism occurs when an individual or group hacks into a government website with the intent of causing terror, violence against persons or property, or enough harm to generate fear. Cyberterrorism can be distinguished from other acts of cybercrime by its severity. These acts are usually planned, are premeditated, and use computer technology to commit politically motivated violence against civilians. These are criminal acts that target national security data and top secret information or that disrupt the provision of services. They are designed to cause physical violence or extreme financial harm. Possible cyberterrorist targets include the banking industry, military installations, power plants, air traffic control centers, and water systems.

Terrorist groups also use the Internet to communicate with each other, spread information about their activities, and plan future attacks. They can also use the Internet to attack a particular target to spread panic and alarm, recruit new members, or seek donations.

In 2007, Michael Curtis Reynolds from Montana was part of a plot to blow up the Trans-Continental gas pipeline with help from Al Qaeda. He also had similar plots against an oil refinery in Wyoming and the

Trans-Alaska oil pipeline. He was arrested in 2005 as he was picking up a bag that contained $40,000 from an Al Qaeda contact. He was tried and convicted of charges related to cyberterrorist activities. He defended his actions by explaining that he was trying to catch terrorists. The court did not believe his story, and he was sentenced to 30 years in prison. A much more complete picture of the problem of cyberterrorism is given in chapter 7.

Cyberwarfare

Cyberwarfare, also known as cyberwar, is the ability to carry out large-scale attacks on computers, websites, and networks. Criminals do things like hijacking a satellite or phone network, hijacking computers and turning them into zombies that spread malicious code, or paralyzing a website by repeatedly trying to gain access through a DoS attack. Cyberwarfare is an attack on technology. Those on one side of an issue can hack or disrupt the computers of their opponent or enemy to gain an advantage. For example, one side could start a DoS attack so that armies will not be able to keep in touch with each other, or they can hack into a system and track what the enemy is doing or planning. They can also use the Internet to deface websites and post inaccurate or false information that embarrasses the other side. A detailed examination of cyberwar can be found in chapter 8.

Conclusion

The types of crimes being committed with the use of the Internet are expanding. Old crimes are evolving and new ones are being created. Whatever the type, cybercrime can cause a great amount of damage and harm to businesses, organizations, and individuals.

Not only has the potential for harm increased but the methods by which the harm can be caused have multiplied. Whether an attack uses a virus, worm, or other form of malware, the threats to private and public networks is high. Particularly worrisome in many regards is the increasing potential for cyberterrorism or cyberwar. Closer to home, issues of child pornography and identity theft remain complicated problems that are difficult to combat. No matter the circumstance, it is clear that cybercrime is still evolving, and remains difficult to deal with.

Review Questions

1. What are three categories of cybercrime?
2. Provide examples of cybercrimes committed against people.

3.   Describe cybercrimes against property.
4.   What are examples of cybercrimes against government?

Key Terms

Auto-auction fraud
BitTorrent
Black hat hacker
Bot
Brute force attack
Cracker
Cyberbullying
Cybercrimes against people
Cybercrimes against property
Cybercrimes against government
Cyber harassment
Cyberterrorism
Cyberwarfare
Denial of service (DoS)
Dictionary attack
FBI/government official scam
File sharing
Grey hat hacker
Hacking
Hacktivist
Identity theft
Internet piracy
Logic bomb
Nigerian (419) scam
P2P
Password cracking
Phishing
Phreaker
Ransomware
Rootkit
Session hacking
Sexting
Social engineering
Spam
Spyware
Trojan horse
Virus
White hat hacker
Worm

Notes

1. Bureau of Justice Statistics, U.S. Department of Justice, "Cybecrime," http://www.bjs.gov/index.cfm?ty=tp&tid=41#terms_def.

2. Ram Gopal, G. Lawrence Sanders, Sudip Bahattacharjee, Manish Agrawal, and Suzanne Wagner, "A Behavioral Model of Digital Music Piracy," *Journal of Organizational Computing and Electronic Commerce* 14 (2004): 89–105.

3. Kathryn C. Seigfried-Spellar, Richard W. Lovely, and Marcus K. Rogers, "Self-Reported Internet Child Pornography Consumers," in *Cyber Criminology: Exploring Internet Crimes and Criminal Behavior*, ed. K. Jaishankar (Boca Raton, FL: CRC Press, 2011), 65–77.

4. Kimberly Young, "Virtual Sex Offenders: A Clinical Perspective," in *Cyber Criminology: Exploring Internet Crimes and Criminal Behavior*, ed. K. Jaishankar (Boca Raton, FL: CRC Press, 2011), 53–64.

5. Rob D'Ovidio, Tyson Mitman, Imaani Jamillah El-Burki, and Wesley Shumar, "Adult-Child Sex Advocacy Websites as Learning Environments for Crime," in *Cyber Criminology: Exploring Internet Crimes and Criminal Behavior*, ed. K. Jaishankar (Boca Raton, FL: CRC Press, 2011), 103–126.

6. Center for Missing and Exploited Children, "Key Facts," 2015, http://www.missingkids.com/KeyFacts.

7. Kathy Martinez-Prather and Donna M. Vandiver, "Sexting among Teenagers in the US: A Retrospective Analysis of Identifying Motivating Factors, Potential Targets, and the Role of a Capable Guardian," *International Journal of Cyber Criminology* 8, no. 1 (2014): 21–35.

8. U.S. Department of Justice, "Identity Theft," http://www.justice.gov/criminal-fraud/identity-theft/identity-theft-and-identity-fraud.

9. McAfee Intel Security, "Net Losses: Estimating the Global Cost of Cybercrime," June 2014, http://www.mcafee.com/us/resources/reports/rp-economic-impact-cybercrime2.pdf.

10. Orly Turgeman-Goldschmidt, "Identity Construction among Hackers," in *Cyber Criminology: Exploring Internet Crimes and Criminal Behavior*, ed. K. Jaishankar (Boca Raton, FL: CRC Press, 2011), 31–51.

11. Paul A. Taylor, *Hackers* (London: Routledge, 1999).

12. Yves Lafrance, *Psychology: A Previous Security Tool*, SANS Institute, 2002, http://www.giac.org/paper/gsec/3754/psychology-precious-security-tool/105992; Masha Zager, "Who Are the Hackers?," Newsfactor Network, September 17, 2002.

13. Thomas J. Holt, "Lone Hacker or Group Cracks: Examining the Social Organization of Computer Hackers," in *Crimes of the Internet*, ed. Frank Schmallenger and Michael Pittaro (Upper Saddle River, NJ: Pearson 2009), 336–355.

14. Majid Yar, "Computer Hacking: Just Another Case of Juvenile Delinquency?," *Howard Journal of Criminal Justice* 44, no. 4 (2005): 387–399.

15. Randall Young, Lixuan Zhang, and Victor R. Prybutok, "Hacking into the Minds of Hackers," *Information Systems Management* 24, no. 4 (2007): 281–287.

16. Bernadette H. Schell, John L. Dodge, and Steve Moutsatsos, *The Hacking of America: Who's Doing It, Why and How* (Westport, CT: Quorum Books, 2002); Bernadette H. Schell and Thomas J. Holt, "A Profile of the Demographics, Psychological Predispositions, and Social/Behavioral Patterns of Computer Hacker Insiders and Outsiders," in *Corporate Hacking and Technology-Driven Crime: Social Dynamics and Implications*, ed. Thomas J. Holt and Bernadette H. Schell (Hershey, PA: IGI Global, 2010), 190–213; Kevin F. Steinmetz, "Becoming a Hacker: Demographic Characteristics and Developmental Factors," *Journal of Qualitative Criminal Justice and Criminology* 3, no 1 (2015): 31–60.

17. Michael Bachman, "Deciphering the Hacker Underground: First Quantitative Insights," in *Corporate Hacking and Technology-Driven Crime: Social Dynamics and Implications*, ed. Thomas J. Holt and Bernadette H. Schell (Hershey, PA: IGI Global, 2010), 105–126.

18. Bachman, "Deciphering the Hacker Underground"; Steinmetz, "Becoming a Hacker."

19. Schell et al., *The Hacking of America*; Schell and Holt, "A Profile of the Demographics, Psychological Predispositions"; Steinmetz, "Becoming a Hacker."

20. Zhengchuan Xu, Qing Hu, and Chenghong Zhang, "Why Computer Talents Become Computer Hackers," *Communications of the ACM* 56, no. 4 (2013): 64–74.

21. Kevin F. Steinmetz and Jurg Gerber, "The Greatest Crime Syndicate since the Gambinos: A Hacker Critique of Government, Law, and Law Enforcement," *Deviant Behavior* 35 (2014): 243–261.

22. Stephen Levy, *Hackers: Heroes of the Computer Revolution* (New York: Penguin Group, 1984).

23. Michael L. Pittaro, "Cyber Stalking: Typology, Etiology and Victims," in *Cyber Criminology: Exploring Internet Crimes and Criminal Behavior*, ed. K. Jaishankar (Boca Raton, FL: CRC Press, 2011), 277–297.

24. Danielle Keats Citron, *Hate Crimes in Cyberspace* (Cambridge, MA: Harvard University Press, 2014).

25. Department of Homeland Security, US-CERT, "Recognizing and Avoiding Email Scams," 2005, https://www.us-cert.gov/sites/default/files/publications/emailscams_0905.pdf.

26. FBI, Internet Crime Complaint Center, "2014 Internet Crime Report," 8, https://www.fbi.gov/news/news_blog/2014-ic3-annual-report.

27. FBI, Internet Crime Complaint Center, "2013 Internet Crime Report," 9.

28. Ibid.

29. Ram D. Gopal, G. Lawrence Sanders, Sudip Bahattacharjee, Mamish Agrawal, and Suzanne Wagner, "A Behavioral Model of Digital Music Piracy," *Journal of Organizational Computing and Electronic Commerce* 14 (2004): 89–105.

30. FBI, "Peer-to-Peer Scams," https://www.fbi.gov/scams-safety/peertopeer.

31. Department of Homeland Security, US-CERT, "Recognizing and Avoiding Email Scams," https://www.us-cert.gov/sites/default/files/publications/emailscams_0905.pdf.

32. Tracey Caldwell, "Spear-Phishing: How to Spot and Mitigate the Menace," *Computer Fraud and Security*, January 2013, 11–16.

33. Steven Furnell, "Still on the Hook: The Persistent Problem of Phishing," *Computer Fraud and Security*, October 2013, 7–12.

34. U.S. Department of Homeland Security, US-CERT, "Virus Basics," https://www.us-cert.gov/publications/virus-basics.

35. Jason Milletary, "Technical Trends in Phishing Attacks," US-CERT, https://www.us-cert.gov/sites/default/files/publications/phishing_trends0511.pdf,

36. RSA, "The Current State of Cybercrime 2014," http://www.emc.com/collateral/white-paper/rsa-cyber-crime-report-0414.pdf.

37. U.S. Department of Homeland Security, US-CERT, "Virus Basics."

38. Ibid.

39. Joyce M. Rosenberg, "Computer Users Face Hard Choice: Pay a Ransom or Lose Files," Associated Press, April 8, 2015; Sorin Mustaca, "Are Your IT Professionals Prepared for the Challenges to Come?," *Computer Fraud and Security*, March 2014, 18–20.

40. Symantec, "Internet Security Threat Report," 2014.

41. FBI, "Definitions of Terrorism in the US Code," http://www.fbi.gov/about-us/investigate/terrorism/terrorism-definition.

CHAPTER FOUR

Amount of Cybercrime

Introduction

MANY PEOPLE WHO STUDY CYBERCRIME OR SEEK TO prevent it desire to know how much cybercrime exists. This way, they can not only learn about new crimes that appear or evolve but also predict patterns or trends in cybercrime. That information could then be used to help mitigate or prevent further crime. Unfortunately, accurate statistics on the number of cyber events and the revenue loss caused by cybercriminals are simply not known. Although it is virtually impossible to be aware of exactly how much cybercrime has occurred in the United States or around the world, some agencies have attempted to estimate the number and patterns of cybercrime based on reported offenses. This chapter takes a close look at some of the estimates of computer crime to help understand the future of Internet crimes.

Why Is the Amount of Cybercrime Unknown?

We do not have precise information on the number of cybercrimes that have occurred for many reasons. First, most computer crimes remain unrecognized and therefore are not reported to officials. Sometimes a criminal hacks into a computer system but does no damage, or the damage is so small it is not identified. Pirated files may be shared among users without the knowledge of the original artist who thus cannot report the theft.

Even those who are aware that a crime occurred may not report it to authorities. They may be embarrassed that they fell for a phishing scam or feel foolish that they believed someone who told an outlandish story on a dating website. The victims may suffer only embarrassment and no financial harm, so they assume nothing can be done. Some victims may not understand that what occurred was a crime that could be reported. For example, a victim of cyberbullying may think the offender is just mean but does not consider the act to be a criminal offense. Many companies may be hesitant to report cybercrime incidents because they wish to avoid the negative publicity and possible loss of confidence by customers.[1]

Many victims of cybercrimes may think that even if they do report a crime, the criminal will probably not be caught and punished for the crime, so they opt to forgo filing a formal report. Many cybercriminals are very technologically savvy and have many tools to help them remain undetected. Instruments such as encryption devices make it difficult for law enforcement to track down the offender.

In some cases, there is a lack of clarity regarding the definition of the concepts involved. The meaning of the term "cyberbullying" may vary from one jurisdiction to another, for example. Furthermore, if a crime is a newly evolved offense, law enforcement may not know how to handle it. They may not know how to collect the required evidence needed to prosecute the offender. Thus, even if a victim attempts to report an offense, the confusion may prohibit an accurate reporting of events.

In some cases, a victim may not know whom to report the crime to. Is a cybercrime an issue for local police or for a federal agency such as the FBI? Who has jurisdiction over a crime when there are no boundaries per se?

Because so many crimes go unreported, the true amount of cybercrime is unknown and the damages that are caused by cybercriminals have been underestimated by the general population and experts in the field. Despite the difficulties, many agencies have attempted to track the number of crimes reported, though this is likely not an accurate portrayal of actual crimes.

Because of the difficulties inherent in counting cybercrimes, in 2004 the Computer Emergency Response Team/Coordination Center announced that it would stop publishing its annual report tracking the number of cyber intrusions reported each year. For many years, it had maintained a database of statistics regarding security incidents reported by businesses and individuals around the world. The agency chose to stop publishing the report because the cyberattack tools being used to commit cybercrimes had resulted in such a dramatic explosion of network attacks that traditional methods for tracking security incidents were now meaningless. The method used to count the number of offenses could not effectively assess the scope and effects of cyberattacks against computer systems.[2]

How Much Cybercrime Exists?

One way to look at the effects of cybercrime is to look at the costs. The FBI estimates that all types of computer crime in the United States cost the industry about $400 billion.[3] Other reports indicate that the global, annual economic loss due to malware attacks alone exceeds $13 billion.[4] Most studies, however, look at the number of cybercrimes reported. These are described in the sections that follow.

2010–2011 Computer Crime and Security Study

Instead of relying on reported incidents of cybercrime, the Computer Security Institute carried out its own survey of agencies and asked if they had ever experienced a cyberattack. The goal was to determine a more accurate picture of the number of cyber offenses. The Institute surveyed 5,412 security practitioners by traditional mail and email and asked questions about cybercrimes committed from July 2009 through July 2010. In total, 351 surveys were completed and returned.

Of the 351 who responded, almost half (49.8 percent) had not experienced a security incident in the previous year, 41.1 percent had experienced some type of cybersecurity incident, and 9.1 percent did not know. Of those who had experienced an attack, 21.6 percent reported that they were the victim of a targeted attack, 54.5 percent were not targeted, and 24 percent were unable to determine the type of attack.[5] This shows that under half of the security personnel admitted to an attack, but a significant portion (about 9 percent) did not know whether they had been attacked at all.

The results of the survey showed that malware was the most common type of attack, reported by 67.1 percent of respondents who experienced attacks. Only 8.7 percent of those respondents reported financial fraud incidents.

Few of the respondents were willing to share information about the financial losses the company had suffered as a result of the attack, but they did report that their losses were not due to cybercrime perpetrated by insiders. In fact, 59.1 percent did not believe their losses were because of malicious acts by insiders, but only 39.5 percent reported that none of their losses were because of nonmalicious insider actions. Table 4.1 shows the percent of cybercrimes by category.

The 2012 Norton Cybercrime Report

The Norton Cybercrime Report is based on an annual survey of officials in 24 countries about their experiences with cybercrime. The 2012 survey included officials from Australia, Brazil, Canada, China, Colombia, Denmark, France, Germany, India, Italy, Japan, Mexico, Netherlands, New Zealand, Poland, Russia, Saudi Arabia, Singapore, South Africa, Sweden, Turkey, United Arab Emirates, United Kingdom, and the United States.

Table 4.1   Types of Cybercrimes Reported*

Category	2005	2006	2007	2008	2009	2010
Malware infection	74%	65%	52%	50%	64%	67%
Bots/zombies			21	20	23	29
Password sniffing			10	9	17	12
Financial fraud	7	9	12	12	20	9
Denial-of-service attack	32	25	25	21	29	17
Website defacement	5	6	19	6	14	7
Insider abuse of Internet access or email (e.g., pornography, pirated software)	48	42	59	44	30	25
Unauthorized access or privilege escalation by insider					15	13
System penetration by outsider					14	11
Theft of or unauthorized access to personally identifiable information due to mobile device theft/loss				8	6	5
Theft of or unauthorized access to intellectual property due to mobile device theft/loss				4	6	5
Theft of or unauthorized access to personally identifiable information or protected health information due to all other causes				8	10	11
Theft of or unauthorized access to intellectual property due to all other causes				5	8	5

*Blank boxes indicate that the data pertaining to that category was not gathered that year.

Source: 2010/2011 Computer Crime and Security Survey; Computer Security Institute, p. 15, http://reports.informationweek.com/abstract/21/7377/Security/research-2010 -2011-csi-survey.html.

The agency conducted an online survey of 13,018 adults between the ages of 18 and 64 years.

The findings of the 2012 report showed that there were 556 million victims of cybercrime each year, or 18 victims per second. It estimated that there were 1.4 million cybercrime victims every day. The study put the average loss per victim at $197 when measured globally, but higher in the United States, at $290. In addition, the findings showed that the cost of consumer cybercrime is about $100 billion a year, though this figure may be low because so much cybercrime is unreported.

The Norton Cybercrime Report revealed some interesting patterns about cybercrime and social networks. Of the respondents, 15 percent had had their social network profiles hacked and said that another person had pretended to be them. About one in ten users of social websites reported that they had fallen for a scam or fake link on a social network.

Finally, this report found that the highest number of cybercrime victims were in Russia (92 percent), followed by China (84 percent) and South Africa (80 percent). Of the men who participated in the survey, 71 percent reported being a victim of cybercrime, whereas 63 percent of the women reported being a victim.[6]

The 2012 HP Cost of Cybercrime Study

HP also conducts an annual study of cybercrime, and the 2012 report found that both the number of cybercrime attacks and the costs related to them had increased for the third year in a row. This study looked at cybercrimes in the United States, the United Kingdom, Japan, Germany, and Australia. The results showed that the number of attacks had more than doubled since 2010, and the financial costs to businesses rose by nearly 40 percent. However, the rate of increase appeared to be slowing. Overall, there was an average of 102 successful cyberattacks each week. More than three quarters of these attacks involved malware, denial of service, stolen or hijacked devices, and malicious insiders.[7]

The 2013 Norton Cybercrime Report

The 2013 Norton Cybercrime Report, which had 13,022 respondents, showed that the number of online adults who had experienced cybercrime had decreased from 2012. There were 378 million victims of cybercrime, or about 12 victims per second. However, the average cost of cybercrime per victim had risen by 50 percent. In 2013, the average cost of a cybercrime was $298 (USD). Of the 2013 respondents, 64 percent of the men and 58 percent of the women reported being victims of cybercrime, a lower percentage than in the 2012 report.[8]

2013 Cost of Cybercrime Study: United States

In 2013, to find out about the costs companies have incurred as the result of a cyberattack the Ponemon Institute surveyed a representative sample of senior-level personnel from 60 organizations in various industry sectors. Most were located within the United States but some were multi-national corporations.

The research found that cyberattacks were fairly common for these companies. In total they experienced 122 successful attacks each week, or about two successful attacks per company per week. The average annual cost of cybercrime to these companies was $11.6 million per year, with a range of $1.3 million to $58 million. The 2012 study had shown an average annual cost of $8.9 million, so costs had increased 26 percent from 2012 to 2013. Table 4.2 shows the total cost of cybercrimes reported by companies in different countries. At $11.56 million the United States had the highest cost, and Australia had the lowest total average cost at $3.67 million.

The researchers found that

> US companies are much more likely to experience the most expensive types of cyber attacks, which are malicious code, denial of service and web-based incidents. Similarly, Australia is most likely to experience denial of service attacks. In contrast, German companies are least likely to experience malicious code and botnets. Japanese companies are least likely to experience stolen devices and malicious code attacks.[9]

Another finding was that all types of businesses were victims of cybercrime, regardless of their area, but some industries (i.e., financial, defense, and energy) had higher cybercrime costs than others (i.e., retail, hospitality, and consumer products). The cost of cybercrime was related to the size of the organization. Small organizations had a higher per capita cost

Table 4.2 Total Annual Cost of Cybercrime Experienced by 234 Companies in Six Countries

Country	Cost in Millions (USD)
Australia	$3.67
United Kingdom	$4.72
France	$5.19
Japan	$6.73
Germany	$7.56
United States	$11.56

Source: Ponemon Institute, *2013 Cost of Cyber Crime Study: United States*, October 2013, http://media.scmagazine.com/documents/54/2013_us_ccc_report_final_6-1_13455.pdf.

($1,564) than larger organizations ($371). Whatever the size of the organization, the cost of a cyberattack increased the longer it took to contain it. The average time it took to contain an attack was 32 days, with an average cost to the organizations of $1,035,769 during this time. The results indicated that malicious attacks by an insider can take more than 65 days to contain. When it came to external costs associated with a cyberattack, information theft had the highest cost, followed by disruption of business. The highest internal costs were for recovery and detection.

The survey also found that the costs of cyberattacks were mitigated by a strong security system. In fact, the companies that had a strong security system were better at detecting and containing cyberattacks. This meant that they had lower costs when a cyberattack did happen.[10]

2013 European Network and Information Security Agency

In 2013, the European Network and Information Security Agency, the European Union agency concerned with cybersecurity, published the report *ENISA Threat Landscape: Responding to the Evolving Threat Environment*, a meta-analysis of 120 separate reports published between 2011 and 2012 by different groups and agencies. The report reviews potential threats and threat agents and lists the top threats and emerging trends in today's advancing technology. Following are the 10 most critical threats identified[11]:

1. Drive-by exploits
2. Worms/Trojan horses
3. Code injection attacks
4. Exploit kits
5. Botnets
6. Denial-of-service attacks
7. Phishing
8. Compromising confidential information
9. Rogueware/scareware
10. Spam

The Verizon 2013 Data Breach Investigations Report

Verizon's annual *Data Breach Investigations Report* is regarded to be one of the most comprehensive analyses of the state of cybercrime and information security, in particular because Verizon partners with the U.S. Secret Service and Department of Homeland Security, the Dutch police's National High Tech Crime Unit, and the European Cybercrime Center, among others, to gather their data. The 2013 report analyzed 47,000 security incidents that occurred in 27 countries and 621 data breaches that were investigated by Verizon's RISK Team. The results showed that there was a wider range of data breaches and network attacks in 2013 than in previous years. Attacks against financial organizations represented 37 percent of the breaches reported, which was the largest industry sector in terms of the number of attacks. Three-quarters of the attacks were motivated by a desire for financial gain.

In 2013, state-sponsored hacking made up a larger portion of attacks than in previous reports. These attacks focused on stealing intellectual property and industrial/military secrets. Such incidents accounted for 19 percent of the breaches, a much higher number than the year before. Even small companies own intellectual property that may be of interest to a foreign nation.

Although many believe attacks by insiders are a serious concern to organizations, this idea was not supported by the data in Verizon's report. Instead, it showed that only 14 percent of the breaches were committed by people inside the organization. Most attacks came from people outside the organization. However, though the majority of security incidents involved outsiders, insiders were more likely to be successful.

When a security breach occurred, who was responsible? More than half of the attackers (55 percent) were members of organized crime groups, and 21 percent were state affiliated. About the same number either had unknown affiliations or were unaffiliated with any known groups. Only 1 percent were committed by former employees.

The Verizon data showed that only 2 percent of the breaches were caused by someone who could be labeled as a hacktivist. About a third of these hackers were from China and about the same number from Romania. The remaining hackers were from the United States, Bulgaria, and Russia.

Attacks involved hacking and malware, sometimes together, and stolen credentials. The report noted an increase in the use of phishing, which was used four times as frequently as in 2011. Another critical finding was the time needed for a breach to be discovered. Many breaches went undetected for months. Many attacks (84 percent) took only a few hours to compromise a system, and 69 percent required just a few hours (or less) to steal data. In about 15 percent of cases, the data was stolen in a matter of seconds. In about two-thirds of the cases reported, months (and occasionally years) passed before a breach was discovered. However, the time period was usually only a few days (41 percent), weeks (14 percent) or months (22 percent) to contain the problem.[12]

The 2013 and 2014 Internet Crime Reports by the IC3

The FBI's Internet Crime Complaint Center (IC3) issues a yearly report of the amount of cybercrime reported to law enforcement. Table 4.3 shows the number of complaints the IC3 receives about cybercrime and indicates that there has been some fluctuation in the number of cybercrimes reported since 2000. In 2014, the IC3 received 269,422 consumer complaints regarding cybercrime, with a total dollar loss of $800,492,073. The average dollar loss for victims reporting a loss was $6,472. Most attacks are reported in July, followed by August, as shown in Table 4.4. Most cybercrimes happen to males (52 percent), and most occur to those between the ages of 40 and 59. They are also more likely to occur in California and in the United States. This is shown in Tables 4.5 through 4.8. More information on the types of crimes reported and the value lost is shown in Table 4.9.

Table 4.3   Cybercrime Complaints Reported to the IC3 by Year

Year	No. of Complaints
2000	16,838
2001	50,412
2002	75,064
2003	124,449
2004	207,492
2005	231,493
2006	207,492
2007	206,884
2008	275,284
2009	336,655
2010	303,809
2011	314,246
2012	289,874
2013	262,813
2014	269,422

Source: Federal Bureau of Investigation, Internet Crime Complaint Center, *2014 Internet Crime Report*, 5, https://www.fbi.gov/news/news _blog/2014-ic3-annual-report Federal Bureau of Investigation, Internet Complaint Center, *2014 Internet Crime Report*, http://www .ic3.gov/media/annualreport/2014_IC3Report.pdf.

Table 4.4 Number of Cyberattacks Reported to the IC3 by Month

Month	No. of Reports
July	24,521
August	24,076
September	23,354
December	23,132
October	22,847
March	22,715
April	22,042
June	21,947
January	21,751
May	21,140
November	21,009
February	20,888

Source: Federal Bureau of Investigation, Internet Complaint Center, *2014 Internet Crime Report*, 8, http://www.ic3.gov/media/annualreport/2014 _IC3Report.pdf.

Table 4.5 Sex Difference in Cybercrime Victims

Sex	Count	Percentage
Male	140,229	52.05%
Female	129,193	47.95%

Source: Federal Bureau of Investigation, Internet Complaint Center, *2014 Internet Crime Report*, 9, http://www.ic3.gov/media/annualreport/2014_IC3Report.pdf.

Table 4.6 Age Range of Cybercrime Victims

Age Range	Total Complaints	Combined Losses
Under 20	8,796	$105,663,164
20–29	48,032	$65,763,954
30–39	54,780	$112,806,573
40–49	55,838	$159,914,612
50–59	55,459	$177,563,723
Over 60	39,908	$160,129,686
Total	262,813	$781,841,611

Source: Federal Bureau of Investigation, Internet Crime Complaint Center, *2014 Internet Crime Report*, https://www.fbi.gov/news/news_blog/2014-ic3-annual-report.

Table 4.7 Top Ten States for Cyberattacks

State Total	Percent of Cyberattacks
California	12.54%
Florida	7.56%
Texas	6.87%
New York	5.85%
Pennsylvania	3.30%
Illinois	3.14%
Virginia	2.88%
New Jersey	2.85%
Washington	2.59%
Ohio	2.48%

Source: Federal Bureau of Investigation, Internet Complaint Center, *2014 Internet Crime Report*, 9, http://www.ic3.gov/media/annualreport/2014_IC3Report.pdf.

Table 4.8 Countries Reporting the Most Cybercrime

Country	Percent
United States	91.54%
Canada	1.51%
United Kingdom	0.78%
India	0.76%
Australia	0.53%

Source: Federal Bureau of Investigation, Internet Complaint Center, *2014 Internet Crime Report*, 9, http://www.ic3.gov /media/annualreport/2014_IC3Report.pdf.

Table 4.9 Cybercrimes and Losses

Type of Crime	Number of Complaints	Total Losses Reported
Auto fraud	16,861	$56,222,655
Government impersonation email scam	8,713	$11,334,077
Intimidation/extortion scam	7,923	$16,346,239
Real estate fraud	9,955	$19,800,172
Confidence fraud/romance scam	5,883	$86,713,003

Source: Federal Bureau of Investigation, Internet Complaint Center, *2014 Internet Crime Report*, 42–43, http://www.ic3.gov/media/annualreport/2014_IC3Report.pdf.

The 2014 *US State of Cybercrime Report*

The 2014 *US State of Cybercrime Report* was the result of a survey of over 500 U.S. executives and security experts in both the public and private sectors. It was done to determine more about their cybersecurity policies and readiness to combat potential cyber threats.[13]

The results of this survey indicated that three of four respondents (77 percent) had detected a security breach event in the prior 12 months, and over a third (34 percent) of respondents reported that the number of security events detected had increased over the past year. Not surprisingly, over 59 percent of respondents reported that they were more concerned about cybersecurity issues this year than in the past.[14]

The average number of security incidents in 2013 was 135 per organization, though this figure is probably low because it does not include attacks that were not detected. While 14 percent of respondents reported that their losses due to cybercrime have increased in the past year, over two-thirds (67 percent) of those reporting a security incident were unable to estimate the financial costs. Among those that were able to provide an estimate, the average annual monetary loss was approximately $415,000.[15] Table 4.10 gives more detail about the types of attacks discovered by different types of companies.

Table 4.10   Cyberattacks by Business Sector

Industry Sector and Type of Attack	Percentage Reporting
Banking Industry	
No incidents	20%
Financial fraud	20%
Denial-of-service attacks	23%
Financial losses	23%
Customer records compromised or stolen	29%
Identity theft	36%
Government	
No incidents	16%
Unauthorized access/use of data, systems, networks	19%
Operating systems/files altered	19%
Denial-of-service attacks	22%
Identity theft	24%
Confidential records (trade secrets or intellectual property) compromised or stolen	24%

Health Care

Theft of electronic medical data	15%
No incidents	19%
Private or sensitive data unintentionally exposed	19%
Email or other applications unavailable	22%
Financial losses	22%
Customer records compromised or stolen	30%

Information and Telecom

Software applications altered	11%
No incidents	19%
Private or sensitive data unintentionally exposed	20%
Email or other applications unavailable	28%
Financial losses	28%
Customer records compromised or stolen	33%

Insurance

Financial losses	19%
Unauthorized access/use of data, systems, networks	19%
Financial fraud	19%
Customer records compromised or stolen	19%
Confidential records (trade secrets or intellectual property) compromised or stolen	29%
No incidents	38%

Source: PriceWaterhouseCoopers, *US Cybercrime: Rising Risks, Reduced Readiness,* June 2014, 8; http://www.pwc.com/en_US/us/increasing-it-effectiveness/publications/assets/2014-us-state-of-cybercrime.pdf.

The 2014 McAfee Report

The 2014 McAfee Report estimated that the annual cost of cybercrime to the global economy was over $400 billion, with conservative estimates at $375 billion and more liberal estimates at $575 billion in losses. When examined more closely, they found that the direct cost of cybercrime was only $875 million, but the recovery and opportunity costs reached $8.5 billion.[16] These costs included the expenses related to hundreds of millions of victims who had their personal information stolen and the effects on businesses, such as damage to the brand and other reputational losses as well as harm to customer relations and retention.[17]

The 2014 Identity Theft Resource Center Report

The Identity Theft Resource Center is an agency dedicated to helping victims of identity theft. It provides resources to victims so they can restore their personal records and names as quickly as possible at no cost. The group also provides prevention education and training as a way to prevent identity theft.

The agency issues a report each year that documents information on the number of identity thefts that occur. In 2014, the agency reported that the number of U.S. data breaches was 783. Of these, the highest number of breaches was reported by the medical/health care industry at 42.5 percent. The business sector reported the second highest at 33 percent, followed by the government/military sector at 11.7 percent, the education sector at 7.3 percent, and the banking/credit/financial sector at 5.5 percent.[18] Hacking was the primary cause of the majority of the breaches. Of course, all of these breaches can lead to the loss of personal data, leading to other crimes such as identity theft. More information on the number of breaches that occurred in each year is found in Table 4.11.

Conclusion

At this point, there is no accurate data on the amount of cybercrime that exists, but many organizations have attempted to estimate cybercrime patterns. The reports have slightly different results, but each show, generally

Table 4.11 Number of Computer Breaches

Year	Number of Breaches in the United States
2013	614
2012	471
2011	421
2010	662
2009	498
2008	656
2007	446
2006	321
2005	157

Source: Identity Theft Resource Center, "2011 ITRC Breach Report Key Findings," http://www.idtheftcenter.org/ITRC-Surveys-Studies/2011-data-breaches.html.

speaking, that cybercrime is occurring more frequently and is more costly to businesses and individuals. In the future, better data collection will help agencies and individuals understand more about the types of cybercrimes being committed, and use that information to block these crimes and the harm associated with them.

Review Questions

1. Why are cybercrimes not reported to law enforcement?
2. What agencies have conducted surveys about cybercrime and what have they found?
3. What different business sectors have been the victims of cybercrimes and to what extent?
4. Who is more likely to become a victim of cybercrime?

Key Terms

Computer Crime and Security Study
European Network and Information Security Agency
The HP Annual Cost of Cybercrime Study
Identity Theft Resource Center
Internet Crime Reports by the IC3, 2013 and 2014
McAfee Report
Norton Annual Cybercrime Report
U.S. State of Cybercrime Report
Verizon Data Breach Investigations Report

Notes

1. Clay Wilson, "Botnets, Cybercrime, and Cyberterrorism: Vulnerabilities and Policy Issues for Congress," in *Cybersecurity, Botnets, and Cyberterrorism*, ed. George V. Jacobson (New York: Nova Science Publishers, 2009), 1–35.

2. Ibid.

3. Ibid.

4. "Malware Report: The Economic Impact of Viruses, Spyware, Adware, Botnets and Other Malicious Code," Computer Economics, 2007, http://www.computereconomics.com/page.cfm?name=Malware%20Report.

5. Computer Security Institute, "2010/2011 Computer Crime and Security Survey," http://gatton.uky.edu/FACULTY/PAYNE/ACC324/CSISurvey2010.pdf.

6. Symantec, "2012 Norton Cybercrime Report," http://now-static.norton.com/now/en/pu/images/Promotions/2012/cybercrimeReport/2012_Norton_Cybercrime_Report_Master_FINAL_050912.pdf.

7. "Cybercrime Attacks Double in Three Years," *Computer Fraud and Security*, October 2012, 1, 3.

8. Norton, "2013 Norton Cybercrime Report," http://www.norton.com/2012 cybercrimereport.

9. Ponemon Institute, *2013 Cost of Cyber Crime Study: United States*, October 2013, http://media.scmagazine.com/documents/54/2013_us_ccc_report_final_6-1 _13455.pdf.

10. Ibid.

11. "ENISA Surveys Evolving Threat Landscape," *Computer Fraud and Security*, January 2013, 1–3.

12. "Data Breach Investigations Report: The Rise of State-Sponsored Attacks," *Computer Fraud and Security*, May 2013, 1–3.

13. PriceWaterhouseCoopers, *US Cybercrime: Rising Risks, Reduced Readiness*, June 2014, 8, http://www.pwc.com/en_US/us/increasing-it-effectiveness/publications /assets/2014-us-state-of-cybercrime.pdf.

14. Ibid.

15. Ibid.

16. Cyber Defcon, "The World's Community and the War on Cyber Crime— What About Italy," 2012, https://www.securitysummit.it/upload/file/Atti/22.03.12 _JARR%20ARMN.pdf.

17. McAfee Intel Security, *Net Losses: Estimating the Global Cost of Cybercrime*, June 2014, http://www.mcafee.com/us/resources/reports/rp-economic-impact -cybercrime2.pdf.

18. Identity Theft Resource Center, "Breach Report Hits Record High in 2014," http://www.idtheftcenter.org/ITRC-Surveys-Studies/2014databreaches.html.

CHAPTER FIVE

Law Enforcement

Introduction

LAW ENFORCEMENT AGENCIES FROM THE UNITED STATES AND other countries have put forth concerted efforts to thwart cybercriminals and reduce the potential damage from their crimes. Unfortunately, law enforcement agencies are often unable to track criminals and collect evidence that can be used against them. At this point, it can be relatively easy for cybercriminals to evade law enforcement. Nonetheless, many law enforcement groups at the national and international levels devote a significant amount of resources to cybercrime.

This chapter will discuss the difficulties law enforcement agencies face when tracking cybercriminals. It will also describe the law enforcement groups that address cybercrime and what their roles are. The final section of this chapter examines cyber forensics, or the investigation of cybercrime.

Why Cybercrime Is Difficult for Law Enforcement to Combat

The new crimes that have appeared, and continue to appear, as a result of advancements in technology fall into unknown areas for the law enforcement agencies responsible for identifying cybercriminals and gathering evidence against them. Crimes committed in cyberspace pose new challenges for law enforcement. When a cybercrime is detected, those who are responsible for the damages are often not identified, caught, or punished for their offenses. In fact, it is estimated that only 5 percent of cybercriminals are ever arrested or convicted because the anonymity associated with web activity makes them hard to catch, and the trail of evidence needed to link them to a cybercrime is hard to unravel.[1] Some of the many reasons why cybercrimes are hard for law enforcement to investigate are outlined in the sections that follow.

Cybercrimes Are Borderless

When a typical, that is, non-cybercrime occurs, it is defined by a geographic border or a line that separates jurisdictions. This can be a state boundary, a national boundary, or an international boundary. The jurisdiction in which a crime takes place helps delineate the rules that apply in each case, as different legal rules apply in different areas. Further, the jurisdictional boundaries define the offense and the agency that has the power to enforce any relevant laws and arrest an offender. The boundaries also help to define the rights of the defendant.

These easily identifiable boundaries do not exist when it comes to cybercrimes. Many computer crimes are transnational, meaning that they cross borders and jurisdictions. A cybercrime can be committed in one country toward a victim in another country, thousands of miles away. Because every nation is connected to the Internet, cybercriminals can commit offenses from anywhere, and victims can be from anywhere. Moreover, offenders can be very mobile, moving from one place to the next very quickly. Hackers can physically operate in one country, easily access data on computers located in a different continent, and then move to another location. The borderless nature of cybercrime also means that any nation can be targeted and its citizens victimized from anywhere in the world.

This makes it very difficult, if not impossible, for law enforcement to determine the country in which the crime was actually committed and then to locate the specific offender. If an offender is found, it may be unclear what agency should have jurisdiction to adjudicate the offense. Because of the confusion, many cybercriminals are not pursued, and if they are located, they may not be punished.

Even though criminals can cross borders, law enforcement is prohibited from operating in another jurisdiction. If officials seek to convict an offender, they may need to extradite that person, that is, they may want to transport an individual from the nation where they committed their acts to their country. Most U.S. extradition treaties require the offense to be a crime in the country in which it was committed and the country demanding the perpetrator. This stipulation can create a major obstacle for pursuing criminals.[2]

Cybercrimes Are Easy to Commit

Using the Internet to commit a crime does not require many resources and can be accomplished quickly, often by one person with a personal computer, sometimes as quickly as the time it takes to type a few words.

In addition, the number of potential victims is seemingly limitless. Many cybercrimes can be carried out from a person's home or office, or even in a location thousands of miles away from the victim's geographic location. These offenses can easily be committed anonymously or by pretending to be another person. All of this is compounded by the fact that more and more people are using computers every day.

Resources Are Lacking

It is not easy to establish the facts of an alleged cybercrime, and investigating computer offenses and punishing offenders requires a significant amount of resources. The costs associated with a cyber investigation can be extremely high, as these investigations may be lengthy. Most law enforcement agencies do not have adequate resources to track cybercriminals. But in addition to money, there is a need for trained investigators who possess knowledge of cybercrime. These investigators need to know how to conduct the investigation and gather evidence and must also be able to convince a jury and a judge that a crime took place and that the person accused of the crime committed the alleged act. The problem is that few people are trained to investigate cybercrime. A lack of trained officers means that few cybercriminals are fully investigated, let alone prosecuted.[3]

Large and powerful countries, such as the United States, China, Australia, and major European countries (Germany, France, and the United Kingdom) can afford to have specific services, police departments, or an agency within a police department that is responsible for prosecuting cybercrime. They are able to devote resources into developing intelligence about cybercrime. Unfortunately, smaller countries often have limited number of resources and are unable to do this.[4]

Offenders Are Transient

Today, computers are located everywhere and can be easily moved from one location to another. This poses problems for law enforcement because technologically sophisticated cybercriminals know how to hide their tracks and any evidence of their crimes. They may commit the crime (i.e., a phishing operation) only for a short time in one location before moving to a different place. They can even move the operation offshore where there are fewer regulations. They know what countries have lax laws or are less likely to investigate offenses. Thus, it may be difficult to identify the specific location of the offender when the offense was committed. Many cybercrimes begin in locations so remote that it is difficult for law enforcement to determine the country in which a crime was committed. By the time an offense is discovered, the offender has moved to another location and little evidence remains.

Laws and Policies Are Ineffective

Many governments have passed laws that outlaw cybercrime. However, many of these laws are not serious attempts to define specific cybercrimes or specify the punishment for that behavior. Fewer than one in five countries have passed laws that address new forms of cybercrimes. When anti-cybercrime laws are passed, they become outdated or obsolete in a short time.

Furthermore, new legislation is sometimes inconsistent with existing laws. An act may be illegal in one country but legal in another place, allowing criminals to move from place to place and remain unpunished for their acts. And since many laws that govern cybercrime are based on jurisdiction, they apply only in the country where the law was passed. Thus, when a cybercrime is committed, it is possible that many laws will apply to that crime, or that none will. Because these laws are ineffective or nonexistent, it is easy for criminals to evade law enforcement.

Damage Is Unclear or Unreported

Many cybercriminals are very good at hiding their crimes, and victims may not know they have been victimized or may not be aware of the full extent of the harm for many weeks or months. Thus, many cybercrimes are not reported to officials because a victim is unaware that an offense has occurred. Some victims may be embarrassed that they have become a victim, especially if they succumbed to a phishing email or fell for a scam. They are reluctant to report an offense because they feel partly to blame or think nothing can be done. Businesses are unwilling to report attacks because of potential liability concerns. The United States Computer Emergency Readiness Team (US-CERT) estimates that as much as 80 percent of all computer security incidents are unreported. Finally, it is sometimes difficult to determine the exact financial consequence of a cybercrime attack. If that is unknown or underestimated, a crime may go unreported.

Cultural Norms Differ

Another problem facing law enforcement are different cultural norms, that is, moral, political, or constitutional differences related to the Internet in different countries. An act that is considered to illegal or morally offensive in one country may be permissible and accepted in another. Pornography is one such example. In the United States, material that might be banned as pornographic in some countries is legal and protected under the First Amendment of the U.S. Constitution. Another cultural difference relates to the concept of free speech. Speech that may be allowed in some countries, such as the United States, may not be permitted in other countries. These cultural differences can create problems when it comes to cyberspace. Consequently, material that is legally posted online by an Internet user in one location may be violating a law in another location.[5] This makes it difficult for law enforcement, as confusion arises over what rules apply and who has jurisdiction.

Turf Wars Are Common

Sometimes turf wars break out between law enforcement agencies. Agencies may disagree over who has jurisdiction over cybercrime investigations. The FBI may believe it has jurisdiction when it comes to investigating cybercrimes, but other federal, state, and local agencies may make the same claim. The Secret Service, the U.S. Marshals Service, and agents from the Department of Homeland Security are all involved with investigating these crimes. They sometimes do not work cooperatively and hide information from each other.

Law Enforcement Agencies

Many law enforcement agencies battle cybercriminals. Local, state, and federal organizations attempt to enforce laws pertaining to cybercrime, and some international organizations work in cooperation to stop the harm caused by computer crimes. Some of these organizations and their activities are described in the sections that follow.

Department of Justice

Personnel within the Department of Justice are responsible for investigating and prosecuting those accused of intellectual property crimes, including those who have violated copyrighted materials, trademarks, and trade secrets. The different agencies within the Department of Justice that deal with cybercrimes are the Computer Crimes and Intellectual Property Section (CCIPS), the Computer Hacking/Intellectual Property (CHIP) Unit, the Intellectual Property Task Force, the International Criminal

Investigative Training Assistance Program, the National Security Cyber Specialists (NSCS), the Cybersecurity Unit, and the FBI.

Computer Crime and Intellectual Property Section

The CCIPS of the Department of Justice is a group of about 40 prosecutors who work within the Criminal Division of the Department of Justice. These attorneys focus solely on enforcing laws pertaining to computer crimes and intellectual property laws. Fourteen attorneys work exclusively on intellectual property cases. The CCIPS attorneys, in addition to litigating cases, provide advice and guidance to agents and prosecutors at any time of the day, any day of the week. They help resolve technology-related legal issues and give advice to prosecutors and investigators, both domestically and abroad, as a way to support a higher level of international cooperation.[6] As a result, the CCIPS attorneys have established strong relationships with international law enforcement groups.[7]

Computer Hacking/Intellectual Property

The CHIP Unit is a network of about 260 experienced federal prosecutors who have specialized training in cybercrime. All 93 U.S. attorneys' offices have a CHIP attorney, and 25 of them have CHIP Units with two to eight CHIP attorneys. The CHIP attorneys have four major areas of responsibility: (1) prosecuting computer crime and intellectual property offenses, (2) serving as the district's legal counsel on all matters relating to cybercrimes or the collection of digital evidence, (3) training prosecutors and law enforcement agents, and (4) conducting public and industry education and awareness programs regarding cybercrime.[8] Currently, CHIP Units are located in Alexandria, Virginia; Atlanta, Georgia; Boston, Massachusetts; Chicago, Illinois; Dallas and Austin, Texas; Kansas City, Missouri; Los Angeles, Sacramento, San Diego, and San Jose, California; Miami and Orlando, Florida; New York City and Brooklyn, New York; Seattle, Washington; Nashville, Tennessee; Pittsburgh and Philadelphia, Pennsylvania; Washington, DC; Baltimore, Maryland; Denver, Colorado; Detroit, Michigan; Newark, New Jersey; and New Haven, Connecticut.[9]

Intellectual Property Task Force

In February 2010, the Department of Justice and the U.S. Attorney General created the Intellectual Property Task Force to address crimes related to the theft of intellectual property. The task force is overseen by the deputy attorney general and includes senior officials from other agencies who play some role in enforcing laws related to intellectual property theft.[10] The task force provides grants to state and local law enforcement groups for additional training and technical assistance. Known as the Intellectual Property Crime Enforcement Program, this effort is geared toward improving the ability of state and local agencies to address intellectual property theft.[11]

In 2012, the program gave $2,457,310 in grants to 13 law enforcement agencies. As evidence of the task force's success, since the program began, agents have seized $203,317,052 in counterfeit merchandise, $14,994,741 in non-counterfeit merchandise, and $2,382,598 in currency. Moreover, approximately 1,400 people have been arrested for violating intellectual property laws, over 345 search warrants have been served, and 600 piracy/counterfeiting organizations have been disrupted or dismantled.[12]

The task force established three working groups. The Criminal Enforcement/Policy Working Group assesses the department's intellectual property enforcement policies, strategies, and successes as well as recommending policy changes. The Domestic and International Outreach and Education Working Group focuses on efforts for public outreach and education related to intellectual property issues and works with local, state, government, and international groups. The Civil Enforcement/Policy Working Group is charged with identifying possible opportunities for increased civil intellectual property enforcement.[13]

According to the task force's annual report in 2013, state and local law enforcement officials have seized $251,759,893 in counterfeit merchandise, $16,813,323 in other property, and $3,206,166 in currency, for a total seizure value of $271,779,383. They have also arrested 1,230 individuals for violating intellectual property laws, served 232 search warrants, and disrupted 381 piracy/counterfeiting organizations.[14]

The Intellectual Property Task Force also works with the International Organized Crime Intelligence and Operations Center to investigate intellectual property offenses committed by members of organized crime and continues to work with representatives of other countries to coordinate efforts. They also cooperate with CCIPS. A more complete picture of the prosecutions of cybercriminal can be found in Table 5.1.

International Criminal Investigative Training Assistance Program

The International Criminal Investigative Training Assistance Program is overseen by the Department of Justice. Recently, it hosted programs in Eastern Europe, focusing on combating cybercrime and improving cybersecurity. As an agency working internationally, it is managed by the Department of Justice but funded by the U.S. Department of State. In addition to its work relating to cybercrime, the agency also has a significant national security function, focusing on helping to develop other countries'

Table 5.1   Cybercrime Activities of U.S. Attorneys

District Totals	FY 2009	FY 2010	FY 2011	FY 2012	FY 2013
Investigative matters received by assistant U.S. attorneys	285	402	387	390	334
Defendants charged	235	259	215	254	213
Cases brought to court	173	177	168	178	163
Defendants sentenced	223	207	208	202	205
No prison term	126	121	102	95	96

Source: United States Department of Justice, *PRO IP Act Annual Report FY 2013*, 32, http://www.justice.gov/sites/default/files/dag/pages/attachments/2014/10/31/pro_ip_act_report_fy2013_doj_final.pdf.

capabilities to combat cyberattacks so that the Internet is more secure for all countries.

National Security Cyber Specialists

In 2012, the Department of Justice established the NSCS as a place for lawyers, investigators, and private-sector professionals who are working to combat cyberthefts to receive legal assistance. Each U.S. attorney's office has at least one representative to the NSCS network. That representative provides technical and specialized assistance to his or her colleagues within the U.S. attorney's offices and serves as a point of contact for the department's headquarters. All National Security Division components, CCIPS, and other relevant sections of the Criminal Division are members of the network. The NSCS network also disseminates information to those working in the field, trains prosecutors on investigating cybercrimes, and coordinates national security cyber investigations.[15] Within the National Security Division is the Counter Espionage Section, which has a division that houses experts on investigating and prosecuting state-sponsored cybercriminals, including those who may participate in the theft of intellectual property.

Cybersecurity Unit

In December 2014, the Department of Justice created a Cybersecurity Unit that would be housed within the CCIPS. The personnel in this new agency provide advice regarding computer fraud statutes. The unit is helping to create cybersecurity legislation that effectively protects the nation's computer networks and protects individuals from cyberattacks. The unit also participates in outreach to promote cybersecurity practices.[16]

FBI

The FBI directs the fight against cybercrime of all kinds in the United States. To do this, the FBI has established many different agencies and divisions, including the Cyber Division located at the FBI headquarters. The Cyber Division has created Cyber's Most Wanted List of dangerous cybercriminals who have committed serious offenses and caused significant damage by their crimes. Box 5.1 describes an FBI sting operation developed to investigate a cybercrime ring.

Cybersquads

In addition to the Cyber Division, the FBI has initiated cybersquads in each of its 56 field offices staffed by agents trained specifically in cybercrime. The squads work to guard against computer intrusions as well as theft of personal information and intellectual property. They also attack child pornography and online fraud.

Cyber Action Teams

The FBI's Cyber Action Teams are FBI agents who are available to travel to the site of a computer intrusion or hacking and help local law enforcement gather evidence that will identify and be used to prosecute the offenders. These agents are on the scene of an attack within 48 hours. This is critical because evidence of a cyberattack can disappear quickly. The teams were originally created by the FBI's Cyber Division in 2006 to "provide rapid incident response on major computer intrusions and cyber-related emergencies." Each group has about 50 agents in field offices around the country who are special agents or computer scientists; they have received advanced training in topics such as computer languages, forensic investigations, and malware analysis. To date, Cyber Action Teams have investigated hundreds of cybercrimes.[17]

Computer Crimes Task Forces

The FBI's Computer Crimes Task Forces are located at the local level in different places across the nation to provide resources to federal, state, and local law enforcement. The task forces focus on cybersecurity issues that affect local businesses and individuals and are staffed by officials from the local, state and national levels who respond quickly to cyber events by conducting investigations, maintaining positive relationships within the

Box 5.1   FBI Operations on Cybercrime

Operation Card Shop: In June 2010, the FBI initiated Operation Card Shop as a way to investigate cybercriminals known as "carders." These offenders sell stolen credit card information to those who use it to commit other crimes. Some of the suspects were members of the UGNazi hacking group, which claimed to be behind some high-profile attacks, including one on Twitter. As part of the investigation, the FBI established a fake website called the Carder Profit Forum, which was a site for cybercriminals to trade information on stolen identities, different types of malware and hacking tools, forged documents, and information on stolen credit cards. Throughout the operation, FBI agents monitored all conversations and recorded the IP (Internet Protocol) addresses of all users who entered the site. They were also able to identify persons whose cards may have been stolen.

In the end, the operation resulted in the arrests of 24 people, and the FBI reported that with those arrests, $205 million worth of fraudulent transactions were prevented.

Operation Ghost Click: This operation was a two-year investigation overseen by the FBI with the cooperation of international law enforcement groups. The quarry was a group of cybercriminals who had installed malware on 4 million computers in 100 countries. The malware allowed the criminals to manipulate Internet advertising by modifying a user's browser setting and redirecting a user to an advertising site. Through this, the offenders were able to make around $14 million in illicit fees. In some infected machines, the malware actually prevented antivirus software from updating, in essence allowing infected machines to be infected with additional malicious software. Most users were not aware that their computers had been infected, including NASA. At the end of the operation, FBI agents arrested six cybercriminals from Estonia who were later charged with running an Internet fraud ring.

Sources: FBI, "Operation Ghost Click: International Cyber Ring That Infected Millions of Computers Dismantled," November 9, 2011, http://www.fbi.gov /news/stories/2011/november/malware_110911; "FBI Sting Operation Results in 24 Arrests," *Computer Fraud and Security*, July 2012, 1, 3.

community, and sharing information on potential threats with companies.[18] The mission of the task forces states: "In support of the national effort to counter threats posed by terrorist, nation-state, and criminal cyber actors, each [Cyber Task Force] synchronizes domestic cyber threat investigations in the local community through information sharing, incident response, and joint enforcement and intelligence actions."[19]

The FBI has developed cooperative relationships with other federal agencies that play a role in cybersecurity, including the Department of Homeland Security and the Department of Defense (DoD) (in particular the Cyber Crime Center) through the National Cyber Investigative Task Forces.[20] These task forces were established in 2008 by the Comprehensive National Cybersecurity Initiative, which was a plan to create a foundation for a whole-government approach to protecting the nation from cybercrime. The National Cyber Investigative Task Forces, formed through a presidential directive, were given the responsibility of coordinating the activities of all federal agencies that deal with cybercrime in some fashion. The task forces coordinate and share information to provide an integrated approach to fighting cybercrime.

Though the task forces are developed and supported by the FBI, they encompass 19 intelligence agencies and law enforcement groups. The overall goal of the task forces is to predict future crimes and prevent future attacks. To do this, the FBI and other task force members work closely with companies that make computers. Together, they attempt to identify and fix potential vulnerabilities in computer systems so criminals cannot exploit them. They also attempt to make the Internet safer by tracking terrorists and spies and cooperate with international law enforcement agents to pursue cybercriminals and investigate cyberattacks.[21]

iGuardian

The FBI also initiated iGuardian, a secure information portal for those who work in critical industries (i.e., communications, defense, banking and finance, and energy) to report cyber intrusions and ensure the safety of the nation's critical infrastructure. Through this secure network, the FBI can distribute alerts and bulletins to these industries in addition to sharing key threat information. Companies are asked to submit information about intrusions to the FBI, including any malware infections, website defacements, or denial-of-service attacks. The FBI then informs others about those attacks and any related threats through CyWatch, its 24/7 cyber operations center, where agents analyze the information and determine any next steps. They may notify the Computer Crimes Task Forces for further investigation.[22]

Internet Crime Complaint Center

The Internet Crime Complaint Center (IC3), formerly known as the Internet Fraud Complaint Center, was formed as partnership between the FBI and the National White Collar Crime Center. The mission of IC3 is to "serve as a vehicle to receive, develop, and refer criminal complaints regarding the rapidly expanding arena of cybercrime."[23] The IC3 provides victims with a simple way to report suspected cybercrime and assists law enforcement at the federal, state, and local levels to investigate these offenses.

Another role of the IC3 is to conduct research on cybercrime. Since it began, IC3 has received complaints regarding many types of cybercrime, including online fraud, intellectual property rights, computer intrusions (hacking), economic espionage (theft of trade secrets), online extortion, international money laundering, identity theft, and others.[24]

A person or organization that has become the victim of a cybercrime can file a complaint with IC3, which keeps a database of illegal activity on the Internet. The analysts review the complaint and determine if the new complaint has similar patterns to previous ones. Complaints may be referred to state, local, tribal, or international law enforcement for further action. Personnel at IC3 continually analyze data to look for patterns, trends, and emerging new crimes and inform the public of their findings.[25]

Secret Service

The Comprehensive Crime Control Act of 1984 gave the Secret Service jurisdiction over cybercrime. When President George W. Bush signed the PATRIOT Act in 2001, one provision mandated that the Secret Service create electronic crimes task forces comprising agents from federal, state, and local law enforcement agencies; prosecutors; and representatives from private industry and academia. The goal is to prevent, detect, mitigate, and investigate cyberattacks. The Secret Service also created the Electronic Crimes Working Group to investigate cases that involve cybercrimes.[26] In 2009, the Secret Service established the European Electronic Crime Task Force, which is intended to prevent cybercrimes such as identity theft. Secret Service agents work alongside agents from European agencies at the headquarters based in Rome, Italy.[27]

Department of Homeland Security

After the terrorist attacks of September 11, 2001, the president and the rest of the U.S. government became focused on protecting the security of the country and enhancing its resilience to bounce back from acts of terror, including cyberattacks. The first National Infrastructure Protection Plan was introduced in 2006 under President Bush as a way to mitigate risk to the nation's critical infrastructure. The plan was revised in 2006 and again in 2009.

The Department of Homeland Security has become the lead agency for managing cyber threats in the United States through the Directorate for National Protection and Programs. This agency published a second edition of the *Quadrennial Homeland Security Review* in 2014 and set four strategic priorities to protect against a cyberattack[28]:

1. Strengthen the security and resilience of critical infrastructure
2. Secure the federal civilian government information technology enterprise
3. Advance law enforcement, incident response, and reporting capabilities
4. Strengthen the ecosystem

The 2003 National Strategy to Secure Cyberspace outlines the federal government's role in combating cybercrime. This plan is one component of the National Strategy for Homeland Security and is a complement to the National Strategy for the Physical Protection of Critical Infrastructure and Key Assets. The plan notes that securing cyberspace is difficult and will require a coordinated effort from many departments and agencies. According to the plan, it is the Department of Homeland Security's role to protect the nation's infrastructure. This can be best accomplished by establishing relationships between the federal government and private owners and operators of critical infrastructure (such as banks). This will allow for more information sharing, which will, in turn, result in a more unified and efficient strategy for protecting assets from cyberattacks.

In 2011, the secretary of homeland security met with representatives from multiple agencies and offices to identify events that would pose the greatest risk to the nation's security. Cyberattacks against data and against physical infrastructure are two such events.[29]

In 2013, President Barack Obama issued an updated version of the plan in Presidential Policy Directive 21, entitled Critical Infrastructure Security and Resilience. This plan outlines 16 critical infrastructure sectors that are overseen by a sector-specific agency. Each agency is responsible for creating a sector-specific plan that outlines a planned response in the case of an attack. The critical infrastructure sectors include communications and information technology. The security-specific agency for these sectors is the Department of Homeland Security.

The sector-specific plan for information technology was the first plan written by both the government and private sector. It identifies the nation's security goals and initiatives to meet those goals. It also focuses on cybercrime in different ways. For example, one of its critical functions is to provide products and services that are essential for protecting national and economic security. Specifically, these products would be needed to maintain or reconstitute a network after an attack. Another critical function is to provide incident management capabilities in the case of a cyber event. The sector provides technology that authenticates or ensures the identity of users as well as technology needed to protect computer systems. Goals include the development of coordination plans to ensure that the private and public sector could respond to, and recover from, threats and disruptions.[30]

The sector-specific plan for communications also focuses on cybersecurity. A terrorist attack or malicious attack could bring down the nation's communications systems, causing even greater damage. This sector works to ensure that the nation is able to detect and prevent possible attacks, and then respond to them as needed. One way to prepare for this is through a training exercise called Cyber Storm. The plan helps to identify procedures and relationships needed to address a cyber event and to help expand coordination of responses among different government officials.[31]

President Obama also issued Executive Order 13636, Improving Critical Infrastructure Cybersecurity. This order directs federal agencies to coordinate with those who own or operate critical infrastructure and work collaboratively to develop and implement risk-based approaches to cybersecurity.

Within the Immigration and Customs Enforcement Homeland Security Investigations is the National Intellectual Property Rights Coordination Center. This agency is concerned with the theft of intellectual property, among other things. To better enforce laws, the center works with 23 other agencies, including federal agencies (e.g., Customs and Border Protection, Postal Inspectors), international agencies (e.g., Europol, Interpol), and other governments (including Canada and Mexico). The group collects intelligence from private industry and law enforcement groups and then uses it to help coordinate law enforcement activities.[32] The center seizes pirated goods and other counterfeit products before they enter the economy and provides training for other law enforcement agencies. The center's activities have led to seizures of illegal property and the prosecution of offenders.

United States Computer Emergency Readiness Team

The personnel in the Department of Homeland Security's US-CERT oversee efforts to improve the nation's policies regarding cybersecurity.

US-CERT responds to cyber incidents and provides technical assistance to victims of cybercrime. It also notifies the public about potential security threats and vulnerabilities as well as partners with private-sector owners of critical infrastructure, members of academia, federal agencies, information sharing and analysis centers, state and local partners, and domestic and international organizations to enhance the nation's cybersecurity posture.[33]

Department of Defense

The DoD also works to protect the United States and its interests from cyberattacks. The DoD has three primary goals: (1) defend the department's networks, systems, and information; (2) defend the U.S. homeland and U.S. national interests against cyberattacks of significant consequence; and (3) support operational and contingency plans.[34] To reach these goals, the DoD shares information about cyber threats and attacks with other agencies and coordinates with them on cyber activities; the DoD builds bridges with the private sector and alliances and partnerships abroad.

The DoD released a strategy for attacking cybercrime in 2011, and then a revised edition on April 23, 2015. The strategy provides guidance for developing and implementing the DoD's Cyber Mission Force structure, which became functional in 2012 and comprises 6,200 cyber operators within 133 different teams. The teams support three missions: (1) defending the DoD's own computer networks, (2) protecting the U.S. homeland and U.S. vital interests against significant cyberattacks, and (3) providing full-spectrum cyber capabilities for military operations. Each team has members that represent different groups: the military, civilians, and contractors. Some of the groups include the Combat Mission Forces, or the Cyber Protection Forces; there is also a Cyber Protection Team that defends the network by discovering, detecting, analyzing, and mitigating threats and vulnerabilities.[35]

The new strategy emphasizes building and maintaining of international partnerships as a way to more effectively defend against future cyberattacks. The DoD will focus on the Middle East, the Asia Pacific region, and key NATO allies as areas to establish these partnerships.

However, an area of concern in the new strategy is the development of cyber capabilities across the military. Currently, these actions are largely uncoordinated, with each branch building its own cyber platforms and tools. This has resulted in a redundant system. Plans for a more unified approach are outlined in the revised strategy.[36]

The National Defense Authorization Act of 2014 required that a new office, the Office of the Principal Cyber Advisor, be created to advise the secretary of defense on cyber issues. The office will govern the development of DoD cyberspace policy.

International Law Enforcement

Law enforcement attempts to attack organized crime are also carried out by international agencies. Some countries have set up a section within the police force specifically to deal with digital or "in-game" crime, but not all countries have that capability.[37] For example, the U.K. government created a cybersecurity defense force, the Joint Cyber Reserve Unit, whose hundreds of information technology security specialists work with officials from the government and the military to protect critical infrastructure.

Interpol

The international police force Interpol was the first international organization to formally address computer crime and related legislation. At a 1979 conference in Paris the organization emphasized that computer crime is international. In December 1981, Interpol sponsored the first Interpol training seminar for investigators of computer crime in Paris.

Europol

On January 1, 2013, the European law enforcement group Europol founded the European Cybercrime Centre (EC3) to provide assistance to countries as they attempt to combat cybercrime. Europol also sought to improve mutual cooperation between countries within the European Union as a way to protect European citizens as they use the Internet.

In a September 2014 report, the *Internet Organized Crime Threat Assessment*, the EC3 asserted that cybercrime is increasingly being carried out by professionals and that organized gangs who intend harm are able to find highly skilled people who are willing to assist them in an ongoing arms race. The report also described how cybercriminals are using legitimate technologies and that traditional crimes are being enhanced by the use of emerging technologies.[38]

Also in September 2014, the EC3 created a new Joint Cybercrime Action Taskforce (J-CAT) to coordinate international investigations into online threats with the support of the FBI and the United Kingdom's National Crime Agency. The goal of J-CAT is to make joint and coordinated actions by international organizations against cybercrime more effective and to ultimately disrupt cybercrime. They group operates out of Europol's headquarters with assistance from experts and analysts from the European Cybercrime Centre.[39] After a six-month trial period, the J-CAT is currently under review.

Europol formed a cooperation agreement with the European Union's European Network and Information Security Agency to work closely with each other and exchange knowledge, skills, and information expertise as a way to fight cybercrime. They also provide training and raise awareness of cybercrime, all in an effort to safeguard network and information security.[40]

International Cyber Security Protection Alliance

The International Cyber Security Protection Alliance is a new consultation process designed to help governments, law enforcement agencies, and businesses combat cybercrime. Through Project 2020, the alliance analyzes current trends in cybercrime and attempts to predict how those crimes may evolve in the future using the expertise of law enforcement agencies, different organizations, and members of professional communities. The goal of Project 2020 is to raise awareness of cybercrime prevention programs among governments, businesses, and citizens.[41]

Strategic Alliance Cyber Crime Working Group

In 2008, the Strategic Alliance Cyber Crime Working Group was created when law enforcement agencies from five countries and three continents (the Australian Federal Police, the Royal Canadian Mounted Police, the New Zealand Police, the United Kingdom's Serious Organised Crime Agency, and the FBI) came together to fight cybercrime. Representatives of this subcommittee of the Strategic Alliance Group (a partnership between these nations dedicated to tackling larger global crime issues, particularly organized crime) discuss ways to share information and investigations on critical issues, carry out joint training programs, and support public awareness campaigns.[42]

Cyber Forensics

Police at the state, federal, and international levels must collect evidence of cyberattacks when they occur. The goal, of course, is to gather enough evidence against an offender so that charges can be brought. When criminals use computers to commit crimes, substantial digital evidence is usually left behind in the computers, which law enforcement can use as

Box 5.2   Examples of International Cooperation on Cybercrime

Because so much cybercrime transcends international boundaries, cooperation between law enforcement agencies in different countries is essential for the successful prosecution of cybercriminals. This collaboration between law enforcement agencies often goes unsung, however. Following are two recent accounts of cooperative efforts involving law enforcement from multiple countries working together to combat cybercrime.

Silk Road 2.0

Law enforcement agencies from across the globe took part in the investigation that led to the shutdown of over 400 illicit services, including the notorious black market website Silk Road. In addition to the website's being removed from public access, 17 people were arrested for enabling the site in various capacities. Over 40 investigators from 17 countries, including Bulgaria, the Czech Republic, Finland, France, Germany, Hungary, Ireland, Latvia, Lithuania, Luxembourg, the Netherlands, Romania, Spain, Sweden, Switzerland, the United Kingdom, and the United States, were involved in the operation. The investigation was based in Europol's Joint Cybercrime Action Taskforce headquarters in the Hague and was in operation for six months before the arrests were made. The investigation was made particularly difficult by the fact that users of the site used Tor anonymization to mask their identities online.[a]

Blackshades

Global cooperation was also used with the investigation into Blackshades, a remote-access Trojan. Investigators from units in Europe, Asia, and the United States worked to stop users of the malware, which allows operators to spy on unsuspecting victims through their webcams, log their keystrokes, encrypt files (which can then be used for extortion), or access the users' accounts and other private information. The software had been installed on more than 500,000 computers. The international effort to stop the malware led to the arrests of over 100 people involved in its creation or distribution. Perpetrators were arrested in the United Kingdom, the Netherlands, Belgium, Canada, Chile, Croatia, and Italy.[b]

[a]"Multinational Approach Brings Down Dark Net," *Computer Fraud and Security*, December 2014, 1, 3, www.computerfraudandsecurity.com.

[b]"International Police Operation Leads to 100 Arrests," *Computer Fraud and Security*, June 2014, 3, www.computerfraudandsecurity.com.

evidence against the offender. Fraud investigators and auditors can gather data that will identify the offender and trace his or her steps throughout the offense. For instance, digital traces left on a floppy disk the BTK serial killer sent to a television station led investigators to a computer in the church where the serial killer Dennis Lynn Rader was council president.

The process of collecting, analyzing, and presenting evidence of a cybercrime to the courts is called "cyber forensics." Forensics deals primarily with the recovery and subsequent analysis of evidence to prove that a crime occurred and the suspect carried it out. The evidence can take many forms, from fingerprints left on a computer to files on a hard drive or search patterns.[43] Other common terms include digital forensics, e-forensics, or computer forensics, but all refer to the study of digital data to look for evidence of a crime and a possible link between the offender, a victim, and a crime scene. Digital evidence can be gathered through a computer, laptop, cell phone, or other device.[44]

For many years, computer forensics investigations concentrated primarily on financial wrongdoing. These investigations were often overseen by federal law enforcement agencies such as the U.S. Internal Revenue Service Criminal Investigative Division or the FBI. When needed, organizations in the private sector would carry out their own investigations or rely on the help of large corporate auditors. More recently, forensic investigations have expanded well beyond financial misdeeds to include criminal behavior. Consequently, many other agencies participate in forensic investigations, including local police agencies or small private companies.[45]

An expert in cyber forensics will "collect and analyze data from computer systems, networks, wireless communications, and storage devices in a way that is admissible as evidence in a court of law."[46] The goal is to discover the truth about a known criminal act or to uncover evidence of a previously unreported or unknown act. Investigators look for any data stored or transmitted by the use of an electronic device that supports or refutes a theory that an offense occurred, how that offense occurred, and who committed it. It can also uncover critical elements of the offense, such as a person's intent, or provide an alibi or other legal defense.

Investigators are then able to use the information to develop possible leads, build a timeline, reconstruct the events, and check the accuracy of statements by the witness and offender. An investigator can also discover possible information concerning the relationship of individuals involved in crimes (both victim and offender) to show if they were connected in some way. Computers may contain information about the Internet activities of persons suspected of committing a crime (i.e., websites visited). Computer records can help establish how a crime was committed, when

Box 5.3 Trouble with Cyber Forensics: The Casey Anthony Trial

One of the many difficult elements in dealing with digital forensic evidence is the fact that many departments are unaware or not technically adept at presenting the information they find. This was the case in the murder trial of Casey Anthony, who was accused of murdering her daughter, Caylee Anthony. Among other problems with the prosecution, evidence that Casey Anthony had searched her computer for the following was never presented:

- At 2:49 p.m., after George Anthony said he had left for work and while Casey Anthony's cell phone was pinging the tower nearest the home, the Anthony family's desktop computer was activated by someone using a password-protected account Casey Anthony used.
- At 2:51 p.m., on a browser Casey Anthony primarily used, a Google search was conducted for the term "fool-proof suffocation," in which the last word was misspelled "suffication."
- Five seconds later, the user clicked on an article criticizing pro-suicide websites that include advice on "foolproof" ways to die. "Poison yourself and then follow it up with suffocation" by placing "a plastic bag over the head," the writer quoted others as advising.
- At 2:52 p.m., the browser recorded activity on MySpace, a website Casey Anthony used frequently and George Anthony did not.

While by itself this information may not have changed the outcome of the trial, it is likely that it would have figured heavily into the jury's deliberations. Because the evidence was never given to the prosecution by the sheriff's department involved in the investigation—they likely were unfamiliar with digital forensic evidence or evidence presentation—the jury never had a chance to consider it.

Source: Tony Pipitone, "Cops, Prosecutors Botched Casey Anthony Evidence," Click Orlando, November 28, 2012, http://www.clickorlando.com/news/Cops-prosecutors-botched-Casey-Anthony-evidence/17495808.

events occurred, where victims and suspects were, and with whom they communicated. For example, Robert Durall's web browser history showed that he had searched for such terms as "kill + spouse," "accident + deaths," "smothering," and "murder" prior to killing his wife. These searches were used to demonstrate premeditation and increase the charge to first-degree murder. Sometimes information stored on a computer is the only clue in an investigation.

Digital evidence can be useful in many types of criminal investigations, including traditional crimes like homicides, sex offenses, or drug trafficking as well as newer crimes like identity theft or theft of trade secrets. Computer evidence can be helpful in cyberstalking or cyberbullying cases to present evidence against the offender. In some cases, civil cases rely on digital evidence, such as cell phone texts. Today, electronic evidence is becoming a routine part of civil cases. Businesses rely on computer forensics if their computer system is breached and customers' personally identifiable information is stolen. When that occurs, the company must be prepared to present evidence to apprehend and prosecute the offenders.

The exact nature of a forensics investigation will depend on the particular facts of the case. The investigation will be determined by the fact of the case, the type of device used (i.e., cell phone, laptop, or other device), and the people involved (as well as their location).

Despite the importance of cyber investigations, not many people are able to carry out these tasks. Experts who are well trained in collecting and analyzing cyber evidence are rare. As a result, digital evidence is often overlooked in criminal cases. When not done by a trained professional, the data may be gathered incorrectly, stored improperly, or analyzed ineffectively. There is a growing demand from law enforcement and corporations for individuals who have the training and technical skills to perform forensic investigations. For this reason, training programs that provide certification in cyber forensics are becoming more common. These programs help to ensure that examiners have the necessary skills to perform these jobs effectively and meet standards needed to perform the job.[47] In addition, some local agencies hire private cybersecurity companies to conduct investigations as they do not have the training and specialized skills needed, and some states have task forces and high-tech crime labs to assist local agencies with cyber investigations.

Another problem is the lack of standardization and consistency in cyber forensics training across jurisdictions.[48] Individuals who are interested in cyber forensics have many options for training. Many certification programs are available, each of which has its own requirements. They vary as to the education and training needed, proficiency tests required, professional experience, and references. The different certifications include the following:

- The Digital Forensics Certification Board: Digital Forensic Certified Practitioner (http://www.dfcb.org)

- International Society of Forensics Computer Examiners: Certified Computer Examiner (http://www.isfce.com/)
- SANS Digital Forensics and Incident Response: Global Information Assurance Certification as a Certified Forensic Analysts (http://forensics.sans.org)
- International Association of Computer Investigative Specialists: Certifications for law enforcement (http://www.iacis.com)

These certification programs are clearly attempts to train individuals so they are capable of carrying out reliable and comprehensive forensic investigations. However, these programs are certified by each individual state. No national standards exist for training and/or certification of forensic investigators. Part of the problem is that the field of computer forensics is a relatively new field, and one that is rapidly changing. There is disagreement about what the licensing process or the procedures for certification should entail. Moreover, disagreements about the accreditation standards for computer forensics labs are also evident. Several programs have been established that focus on developing standards for labs. One is the American Society of Crime Lab Directors Forensics Lab Certification and Accreditation Program, which law enforcement agencies sometimes use to analyze DNA, fingerprint, or digital evidence. Another program is the International Organization for Standardization (ISO) 17025 Forensics Lab Certification and Accreditation, which has more of an international focus. Despite the efforts of these groups, the certification/accreditation process will continue to be a hotly debated topic for at least the immediate future.[49]

In the United States, a group of organizations have established the Council of Digital Forensic Specialists, a working group with the goal of creating a core body of knowledge in digital forensics. The council seeks to standardize cyber forensics training by bringing together digital forensic specialists and defining an essential body of knowledge. This, then, can be used to provide guidance to educational institutions that are developing certification programs in cyber forensics. The group is attempting to identify the minimal qualifications needed for cyber investigators and create a code of professional conduct for those in the field.

Training and certification for professionals is essential because courts depend on the evidence gathered by digital investigators when determining the outcome of a case. A forensic scientist's ability to gather and interpret evidence, and then present it in a courtroom can determine the outcome of a trial and influence the verdict. An investigator must be able to present conclusions in a clear, factual, honest, and objective way that is also easy for the jury to understand. The investigator must also be able to leave personal opinions out of the testimony.

In 2008, the American Academy of Forensic Sciences, the professional organization for forensics, created a new section on Digital and Multimedia Sciences, thereby recognizing the need for standardized practices in digital forensics.[50]

The FBI says that the first person who is likely to respond to a cybercrime will be a network administrator or support technician. This technician must be sure to preserve the state of the computer at the time of the incident. This can be done by making copies of any logs, damaged or altered files, and files or evidence left by the offender. The FBI notes that if the incident is ongoing, auditing or recording software should be activated as it may provide more evidence about the offense.

Any and all losses need to be identified. Losses can include the following:

- Labor cost spent in response and recovery
- Damaged equipment
- Stolen data (and reconstruction of it)
- Lost revenue (down time, having to give customers credit due to inconvenience).

Stages

A digital crime scene is not like the traditional crime scene of yesteryear. Every crime scene is different, but some basic steps must be taken for all forensic investigations. Following proper procedures during an investigation is critical. An investigator must secure the scene, maintain a detailed chain of evidence, and document everything. The typical stages in a digital investigation are described in the following sections.

Step One: Identification

Someone, ideally an examiner, needs to determine what devices could hold evidence and should be examined. This can include laptops, pagers, cell phones, cameras (digital and video), memory cards, flash drives, hard drives, CDs, and DVDs. It is now possible to use data from global positioning systems to prove where a person went and at what times, and many cars now have event data recorders that record a person's speed, braking, and other driving behavior. Devices that may be helpful to the investigation, or authorized by a warrant, should be collected or "bagged and tagged."

The first step of this process is to secure the area so that any potential evidence is not contaminated. It is essential that only those people who must be there to gather evidence are allowed at the scene. This is particularly difficult in digital investigations, as multiple investigators are often involved in digital investigations.

Step Two: Collection or Extraction

The process of gathering electronic evidence that could prove a crime or who committed it involves identifying and collecting artifacts that could be evidence. In cybercrime cases, these items are in a digital form, and the evidence needs to be copied so the original is intact and preserved it in its original format. The evidence must then be given to law enforcement and the prosecutor.

As with traditional evidence, it is important to document all activity, including everyone who was at the scene. Keeping a chain of custody is essential, perhaps even more so than in physical investigations, as tampering may be extremely hard to prove. Therefore, any evidence seized must be cataloged properly.

The collection of digital evidence can be challenging as electronic evidence is fragile. It can transcend borders easily and quickly; it can be easily altered, contaminated, damaged, or destroyed; and it can be time sensitive. Thus, investigators need to gather it as quickly as they can and preserve it in the original format.

The collection of forensic evidence in the United States is limited and controlled by legislation and by the U.S. Constitution. The Fourth Amendment limits how police can search for evidence and what evidence they can collect (or seize). Prior to carrying out a search for evidence, law enforcement must obtain a search warrant that describes the places that will be searched and the evidence to be collected. This can make identifying relevant evidence complicated, as it is often limited by the warrant issued by the court. Given the hidden nature of some digital evidence, there can be many complications to collecting evidence.

Step Three: Interpretation and Analysis

The evidence will be interpreted by an investigator and presented to police or prosecutors. This must be done fairly and honestly, must be based on the facts, and must be conducted in a manner that is admissible in court. The evidence must also be formatted in a way that a judge and jury will understand.

One agency that has provided guidance for law enforcement agencies that are involved in collecting digital evidence is the International Organization on Computer Evidence. First established in 1993, the group has provided a forum for law enforcement to discuss and exchange information regarding cyber forensics.

As is clear from the discussion in this chapter, computer forensics can be an extremely difficult challenge for law enforcement. As additional agencies are getting accredited or certified, law enforcement is gaining the knowledge and tools needed to accurately investigate digital crimes. Additionally, with more guidelines being presented by organizations like the International Organization on Computer Evidence, law enforcement agencies can institutionalize best practices and make digital investigations part of their normal course of events.

Conclusion

Law enforcement clearly has a large role to play when it comes to combating cybercrime. As the many government agencies and task forces suggest, all levels of government are increasingly attuned to the problems presented by cybercrime. Despite this, many agencies, because of size or lack of resources, are understaffed or otherwise unable to deal with the issues surrounding cybercrime. Because of this, other organizations have sprung up to assist in investigations or to provide outside guidelines for digital forensics.

Given the range of organizations involved, from local law enforcement to the DoD, as well as the lack of traditional jurisdictional boundaries, domestic and international cooperation has become essential. Recent arrests by international task forces in multiple countries show that this cooperation is increasing. Moreover, while there remains a long way to go in terms of law enforcement preparedness for cybercrime investigations, the trends of increasing certification and accreditation demonstrate that they are headed in the right direction.

Review Questions

1. Why is cybercrime a difficult crime for law enforcement to pursue?
2. What is the role of the FBI in fighting cybercrime?
3. Which agencies of the Department of Justice handle intellectual property offenses?
4. How does the Department of Homeland Security combat cybercrime?
5. What is cyber forensics and why is it important?

Key Terms

Computer Crimes and Intellectual Property Section (CCIPS)
Computer Hacking/Intellectual Property (CHIP) Unit
Cyber forensics

Department of Justice Intellectual Property Task Force
Europol
FBI Computer Crime Task Forces
FBI Cyber Action Team
FBI Cyber Division
FBI Cyber Squad
iGuardian
International Cyber Security Protection Alliance
Internet Crime Complaint Center (IC3)
Interpol
National Security Cyber Specialists (NSCS)
National Strategy to Secure Cyberspace
Strategic Alliance Cyber Crime Working Group
United States Computer Emergency Readiness Team (US-CERT)

Notes

1. Clay Wilson, "Botnets, Cybercrime and Cyberterrorism: Vulnerabilities and Policy Issues for Congress," in *Cybersecurity, Botnets and Cyberterrorism*, ed. George V. Jacobson (New York: Nova Science Publishers, 2009), 1–35.

2. Salil K. Mehra, "Law and Cybercrime in the United States Today," *American Journal of Comparative Law* 58 (2010): 659–685.

3. Will Gragido, Daniel Molina, John Pirc, and Nick Selby, *Blackhatonomics* (New York: Syngress, 2012).

4. "UK Launches Cyber-Security Reserves," *Computer Fraud and Security*, October 2013, 1–3.

5. David R. Johnson and David Post, "Law and Borders: The Rise of Law in Cyberspace," *Stanford Law Review* 48, no. 5 (May 1996): 1367–1402.

6. United States Department of Justice, *PRO IP Act: Annual Report FY 2012*, December 2012, http://www.justice.gov/dag/iptaskforce/proipact/doj-pro-ip-rpt2012.pdf.

7. United States Department of Justice, "Computer Crime and Intellectual Property Section," http://www.justice.gov/criminal/cybercrime/.

8. United States Department of Justice, *PRO IP Act: Annual Report, FY 2012*.

9. United States Department of Justice, *PRO IP Act: Annual Report, FY 2012*; United States Department of Justice, *PRO IP Act: Annual Report FY 2013*, http://www.justice.gov/sites/default/files/dag/pages/attachments/2014/10/31/pro_ip_act_report_fy2013_doj_final.pdf.

10. United States Department of Justice, *PRO IP Act: Annual Report, FY 2012*.

11. Ibid.

12. Ibid.

13. Ibid.

14. United States Department of Justice, *PRO IP Act Annual Report FY 2013*.

15. Ibid.

16. United States Department of Justice, "Cybersecurity Unit," http://www.justice.gov/criminal/cybercrime/about/cybersecurity-unit.html.

17. FBI, "The Cyber Action Team: Rapidly Responding to Major Computer Intrusions," March 4, 2015, http://www.fbi.gov/news/stories/2015/march/the-cyber-action-team.

18. FBI, "Cyber Task Forces: Building Alliances to Improve the Nation's Cybersecurity," https://www.fbi.gov/about-us/investigate/cyber/cyber-task-forces-building-alliances-to-improve-the-nations-cybersecurity-1.

19. Ibid.

20. FBI, "Computer Intrusions," http://www.fbi.gov/about-us/investigate/cyber/computer-intrusions.

21. FBI, "National Cyber Investigative Joint Task Force," http://www.fbi.gov/about-us/investigate/cyber/ncijtf.

22. FBI, "iGuardian," http://www.fbi.gov/stats-services/iguardian.

23. United States Department of Justice, "Reporting Computer Hacking, Fraud and Other Internet Related Crime," http://www.justice.gov/criminal/cybercrime/reporting.html; FBI, Internet Crime Complaint Center, *2013 Internet Crime Report*, https://www.ic3.gov/media/annualreport/2013_IC3Report.pdf; FBI, Internet Crime Complaint Center, "IC3 Mission Statement." http://www.ic3.gov/about/default.aspx.

24. FBI, Internet Crime Complaint Center, "About Us."

25. FBI, Internet Crime Complaint Center, *2013 Internet Crime Report*.

26. U.S. Secret Service, "Electronic Crimes Task Forces and Working Groups," http://www.dhs.gov/sites/default/files/publications/USSS%20Electronic%20Crimes%20Task%20Force.pdf.

27. Jennifer Clark, "U.S. and Europe Jointly Establish Cyber-Crime Task Force," *The Wall Street Journal*, June 30, 2009, http://www.wsj.com/articles/SB124632958157771629.

28. Department of Homeland Security, *2014 Quadrennial Homeland Security Review Report Fact Sheet*.

29. Department of Homeland Security, *The Strategic National Risk Assessment in Support of PPD 8: A Comprehensive Risk-Based Approach toward a Secure and Resilient Nation*, December 2011, http://www.dhs.gov/xlibrary/assets/rma-strategic-national-risk-assessment-ppd8.pdf.

30. Department of Homeland Security, *Information Technology Sector-Specific Plan*, 2010, http://www.dhs.gov/sites/default/files/publications/IT%20Sector%20Specific%20Plan%202010.pdf.

31. Department of Homeland Security, *Communications Sector-Specific Plan*, 2010, http://www.dhs.gov/xlibrary/assets/nipp-ssp-communications-2010.pdf.

32. United States Department of Justice, "Reporting Computer Hacking."

33. US-CERT, "About Us," https://www.us-cert.gov/about-us.

34. United States Department of Defense, *The DoD Cyber Strategy*, April 2015, http://www.defense.gov/home/features/2015/0415_cyber-strategy/Final_2015_DoD_CYBER_STRATEGY_for_web.pdf.

35. Ibid.

36. Center for Strategic and International Studies, "2015 DOD Cyber Strategy," April 24, 2015, http://csis.org/print/55352.

37. Grainne Kirwan and Andrew Power, *The Psychology of Cyber Crime: Concepts and Principles* (Hershey, PA: Information Science Reference, 2012).

38. "Cybercrime Becoming More Professional," *Computer Fraud and Security*, October 2014, 3.

39. "New European Task Force Will Tackle International Cybercrime," *Computer Fraud and Security*, September 2014, 1, 3.

40. "Europol and ENISA Team Up as Cybercrime-Fighting Duo," *Computer Fraud and Security*, July 2014, 3.

41. "Europol to Lead Anti-cybercrime Alliance," *Computer Fraud and Security*, August 2012, 1, 3.

42. FBI, "Cyber Solidarity: Five Nations, One Mission," http://www.fbi.gov/about-us/investigate/cyber/cyber-task-forces-building-alliances-to-improve.

43. Department of Homeland Security, US-CERT, "Computer Forensics," 2008, https://www.us-cert.gov/sites/default/files/publications/forensics.pdf.

44. Frederick Gallegos, "Computer Forensics: An Overview," *Information Systems Control Journal* 6 (2005): 13–16; Department of Homeland Security, US-CERT, "Computer Forensics," 2008.

45. Christopher L. T. Brown, *Computer Evidence: Collection and Preservation*, 2nd ed. (Boston, MA: Cengage, 2010).

46. Department of Homeland Security, US-CERT, "Computer Forensics," 2005.

47. Eoghan Casey, *Digital Evidence and Computer Crime*, 3rd ed. (Boston: Academic Press, 2011).

48. Department of Homeland Security, US-CERT, "Computer Forensics," 2008.

49. Brown, *Computer Evidence*.

50. Casey, *Digital Evidence and Computer Crime*.

CHAPTER SIX

Organized Cybercrime

Introduction

WHILE BOTH CYBERTERRORISTS AND NATION-STATES HAVE MADE significant use of the Internet to commit attacks, organized cybercriminals are perhaps the largest users of the Internet for criminal purposes. Because of the nature of cybercrime and the secretive nature of organized crime groups, it is difficult to ascertain precisely how much cybercrime is conducted by organized crime groups versus individual cybercriminals. Estimates of the amount of illegal activity resulting from organized criminal behavior range from 20 percent to 80 percent.[1] What is known, however, is that a potentially large number of illegal groups are operating online, some of them related directly to organized criminal enterprises in the physical world.

This chapter looks specifically at organized criminal activity that takes place online. It first examines the overall problem of organized crime on the Internet and then examines some specific organizational forms that organized cybercrime takes. It also examines some of the different types of groups involved in organized crime online. Finally, it looks in depth at some of the organized crime groups that have been active recently in order to contextualize the rest of the information.

Evolution of Organized Crime

Organized crime is certainly nothing new. However, the types of organizations that most people think of, groups like the Italian Mafia or 1930s-era gangs like those led by John Dillinger, have long given way to much more sophisticated organizations. Within the United States, the transformation has been twofold. Not only are groups more organizationally and economically complex, but they have also become transnational, in many cases.

This transformation of organized crime is not unique to the United States, however. Organized crime offers significant advantages over individual criminal activity, and globalization has made this type of criminal exchange more profitable than ever.

The reason for the transformation from simple, gang-like organizations consisting of a leader and followers to complex organizations with a division of labor and a hierarchical structure is fairly straightforward: simple organizations are inefficient at revenue generation.[2] This means that organizations interested in increasing revenue generation often gain levels of complexity.

This can be seen in the development of a wide range of organizations. Gangs like MS-13 and terrorist groups like Hezbollah have become multinational enterprises with well-developed hierarchies spanning multiple nations. Additionally, it is clear that some organizations are moving into the online environment as a another way to make money, though the extent of these operations is not yet clear.

Also unclear is the development of organized crime online. While it is obvious that many organizations are operating online, their structures and extent are not yet widely understood. Moreover, it is not known whether these organizations will develop along similar lines as did organizations that developed in the physical world, though we are starting to understand how complex such organizations can become in the online world.

The increasingly diverse organizational structures are not unique to organized criminal entities. Legitimate organizations are also taking advantage of the opportunities technology affords to diversify their structures. Terminology like "virtual organization" has come into wide usage to describe companies that do not hold to traditional organizational structures. Unsurprisingly, criminal organizations have undergone similar transformations to take advantage of the same elements that make diffusion and change appealing to legitimate companies.

As shown in the previous discussion, organized crime is a complex phenomenon. One question that arises in any discussion of organized crime is what specifically that phrase means. For purposes of this chapter, organized crime is examined on two fronts. One is more traditional and uses the definition of organized crime suggested by Susan Brenner: "A criminal organization is an organization that devotes the majority of its efforts to committing crimes for the primary purpose of generating wealth." While this covers most of what is generally thought of as organized crime, it is insufficient because of the nature of the Internet. Organizations like Anonymous and CyberVor do not follow the hierarchical organization of traditional organized crime. Moreover, while they engage in activities that are considered criminal, they do not necessarily do so for profit. This chapter also covers this second type of organization.

Organized Crime and the Internet

Organized crime has been a problem for law enforcement since time immemorial. Recently, however, the advent of new technology has enabled criminal organizations to move into the online environment. They take advantage of this technology for the same reasons most individuals and companies do: increased communication, faster money movement, and opportunities to expand into larger environments. Because of the growth of the Internet, the online organized crime community has grown very large—so much so that it is difficult to tell exactly how large it is.

Though it is impossible to know just how much cybercrime is driven by organized crime, the amount is thought to be a significant percentage of the total.[3] Additionally, because of the organized nature of this kind of cybercrime, the amount of damage that is inflicted on victims can be significant. As a particularly poignant example, it is thought that a significant part of the cyberwar Russia carried out against Georgia and Estonia was conducted, not directly by Russian agents but instead by elements within Russian organized crime.[4]

One issue that makes the study of organized cybercrime more difficult is the fact that there is often only a limited distinction between individuals and groups and, perhaps more importantly, between groups and nation-states. As in the example of Russia's cyberwar activities, there is often little difference between organized criminals and state-run hackers. This is especially true in places like Russia and China, where the state allows some intermixing of organized crime elements within their military or governmental structure. Richard Clarke and Robert Knake make this point in their book, *Cyber War*[5]:

> Organized crime is allowed to flourish because of its unacknowledged connection to the security services. Indeed, the distinction between organized criminal networks and the security services that control most Russian ministries and local governments is often blurry. Many close observers of Russia think that some senior government officials permit organized crime activity for a slice of the profits, or, as in the case of Estonia, for help with messy tasks. Think of Marlon Brando as the Godfather saying, "Someday. . . I will call upon you to do a service for me."

The following section examines different types of groups operating online. It uses a typology developed by McGuire that was applied to online cybercrime by Broadhurst and colleagues.[6] It consists of three basic organizational types, with two subtypes each, dependent upon the strength of ties within the groups. An explanation for each type is given, along with an example of groups that fall into those types.

Organizational Types

Type I

Type I groups operate almost completely online. This means that groups falling into this category are generally composed of autonomous individuals and do not necessarily have a structure in the same way that a traditional organized crime group might. Type I organizations can be broken down further into what McGuire terms *swarms* and *hubs*.

Swarms

Swarms are generally considered the least organized of the group types. They operate as "leaderless resistance." In other words, while group members may be operating on the same principles and be motivated by the same objectives, there is not a single individual or entity that controls any aspect of the organizations. In a sense, these groups are self-organizing. In many respects, swarms are one of the most difficult types of groups to combat, because individual members may not know one another, and there is no organization (properly speaking) to disrupt.

The best-known group that falls into the swarm typology is the hacker collective Anonymous. While not meeting the strict definition of an organized criminal group, primarily because of its disregard for gaining money, the group does conduct illegal, organized campaigns against different organizations, including governments. Because of its nature as a swarm, law enforcement has had a difficult time disrupting the collective. Additionally, because the group sometimes engages in activities that indirectly support law enforcement, many question whether the group should be targeted by law enforcement at all.

Anonymous is not the only group that fits the swarm model. Many other collectives follow a similar organizational pattern. Some of these groups are more directly in line with traditional organized crime, but the number is thought to be few because of the difficulty of dealing with a distributed network in terms of money and goods.

Hubs

Hubs are similar to swarms in that they exist nearly completely in the realm of the Internet. But unlike swarms, hubs coalesce around a core group of individuals who may be considered leaders. The hubs therefore often have a more clear command structure than do swarms. Organizations that are arranged as hubs take part in a significant amount of criminal activity, and some have become quite well known. The website Silk Road, an online bazaar where illegal wares ranging from drugs to assassins can be found, fits the hub organization definition.

Other organizations that follow the same type of structure include carders' markets, that is, markets where stolen credit cards are sold, and some purveyors of scareware (malware that tricks people into buying useless or harmful programs by scaring potential buyers). These types of organizations cannot use the swarm structure because of the difficulty of developing, distributing, and collecting money from the programs that are developed. Instead, a small group of developers may enlist others to help spread the malware, or they may sell it on a marketplace and allow others to distribute it for their own profit.[7]

Type II

Type II groups combine online and off-line criminal activity. Unlike swarms or hubs, which are nearly exclusive to the online environment, Type II organizations move back and forth between modalities, making them, in some respects, the most complicated form of organized criminal group. For this reason, Type II organizations are called "hybrids," and they can be subdivided into two types: clustered hybrids and extended hybrids.

Clustered Hybrids

Clustered hybrids resemble hubs in their structure. The main difference between a hub and a clustered hybrid is the clustered hybrid's ability to operate across multiple environments, whereas a hub is only operational online. A large number of groups follow this organizational model, and the groups engage in a variety of illicit activity, both online and off-line.

Some organized crime groups are beginning to operate as clustered hybrids, oftentimes participating in illegal markets for credit card data or other information that can be sold. The cards may be stolen online or physically, and the information sold in online carders' markets. They may also participate in other types of activities outside the realm of the criminal. As noted previously, many of the hackers participating from the Russian side of the Russian/Georgian conflict were likely run by the *mafiya*: Russian organized crime.

Because of this ability to operate across the online and real worlds, clustered hybrid organizations can be quite dangerous. One specific fear is that terrorist organizations will develop the capacity to engage in this kind of criminal activity, both for fund-raising and operational purposes. Indeed, some terrorist groups have been able to cause minor damage in the online environment. Hamas, for instance, during the 2008 war with Israel, defaced a significant number of Israeli websites. Given Hamas's ability to operate in both the physical and online environments, it could be classified as a clustered hybrid organization—though clearly it is not yet well developed in the online world.

Extended Hybrids

Extended hybrids, like clustered hybrids, operate seamlessly in both the online and physical environments. The major element separating them from the clustered hybrid structure is that they are more diffuse. In this respect, they resemble a swarm more than a hub, but they still have the operational element that allows them to work in both the online and physical words, making them a Type II, rather than a Type I, organization.

This operational group is perhaps most clearly exemplified by groups engaging in child pornography. Generation of such material occurs in the physical environment and then is exchanged in a variety of online forums. Some of these groups represent end-to-end control, and thus demonstrate the extended hybrid model. A small group of producers can control the online generation of content, but beyond this the diffusion of the illicit material is outside their control. They move between illegal activity in the real world and online but do not necessarily need any more time in one than the other.

Unlike clustered hybrids, the extended hybrid model also allows for subunits to form and operate nearly independently of the original organization. This allows for some control, but extended hybrid organizations remain much more autonomous than clustered hybrids.

Type III

Type III organizations are characterized by their ties to crime in the physical world. They may extend their criminal activity online, but the base of their operations is in the real world. For instance, a traditional organized crime group that operates illegal gambling facilities may start a website that also allows for illegal gambling. While this type has not necessarily developed very far yet, it has the potential to eventually become a large part of online criminal activity. Type III organizations have two subtypes: hierarchies and aggregates.

Hierarchies

Hierarchies can best be thought of as sharing the same organizational characteristics as more traditional groups. In fact, these kinds of groups, similar to the Italian Mafia and Japanese Yakuza, are typical of hierarchies. They essentially represent the movement of physical organized crime into the digital world. Often, they engage in similar crimes in both locations because of the expertise built up in the physical world. Recent examples of this type of group include the Gambino crime family, who moved into interstate sex trafficking, and organized crime groups that have set up in places like the Caribbean to take advantage of gray areas in laws regarding crimes like online gambling.

In some respects, hierarchies represent nascent hubs or clustered hybrid organizations. However, the crimes they engage in remain linked directly to the physical capacity of the organized crime group rather than moving across physical and virtual spaces. While there is some concern that these groups will continue to move into online spaces, the larger problems seem to revolve around newer organizations in the hub and swarm models.

Aggregates

Aggregate groups are the swarm of Type III groups. They have organizational capacity, but their use of technology is ad hoc. They may use computers or other types of network technology (e.g., cell phones) to organize specific events, but their use is not integrated in a meaningful way in the operations of the organized crime. In other words, technology is incidental to aggregates, not integral.

While this makes aggregates the least concerning type of organization in terms of cybercrime, this type of organized crime group presents potential problems. For instance, in the case of some instances of violence, like riots, networks have been used to get organizational affiliates to participate.[8] Figure 6.1 gives a picture of these organization types and subtypes.

Division of Labor

It is easy to see that with many of the subtypes of organization mentioned earlier, there is little actual direction. However, some of the more sophisticated organizations have a complex division of labor that is organized by individuals running the organization. This allows for extremely complex crimes to be organized. The FBI gives the following examples of 10 different "jobs" within complex schemes.[9]

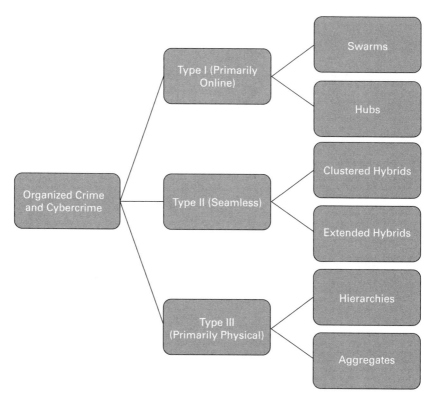

Figure 6.1   Organizational Types

1. Coders write the malicious software the organization uses in whatever criminal activity it is engaged in. It can consist of anything from malware to software for online gambling.
2. Distributors are responsible for trading and selling stolen data. Additionally, they are responsible for vouching for the quality of the data.
3. Technicians are responsible for the upkeep of the organization's network requirements. Server management, dealing with Internet service providers, and encryption are also the responsibility of an organization's technicians.
4. Hackers are responsible for breaching outside systems or exploiting vulnerabilities in networks. Usually this is done to gain information that can then be sold via the distributors, but it could also be used for other purposes.
5. Fraud specialists develop complex social engineering schemes, such as phishing schemes, spamming, and domain squatting.
6. Hosts provide the facilities that allow many other forms of criminal activity to take place. Often they provide servers, or other forms of digital space, through botnets and proxy networks.

7.   Cashers provide drop accounts and provide the information to other criminals—for a fee. They also typically control rings of the next specialization, cash couriers known as "money mules."

8.   Money mules are responsible for transferring the money from the illicit transactions, whatever their source, to third-party accounts and then into secure holdings.

9.   Tellers assist by transferring and laundering the money earned through digital currency services and between different currencies.

10. Executives of the organization determine what the targets are, recruit individuals, assign roles, and manage the distribution of the proceeds from whatever crimes are committed.

While not every instance of cybercrime, even those committed by organizations includes each of these types, the availability of individuals with the specializations mentioned here gives an idea of how complex cybercrimes can be.

It is also important to consider that while we tend to think of criminal organizations as singular, they also often work in networks with other organizations. This means that while one organization may possess many of the individual skills needed to successfully conduct organized cybercrime, any lack can be found by dealing with other organizations that have those capabilities. This adds even more complexity to an already complex area of cybercrime.[10]

Scope of Organized Cybercrime

Given the nature of cybercrime as an illegal activity and the fact that cybercrime is often most profitable when it remains undiscovered, the extent of organized cybercrime is difficult to ascertain. However, Group-IB, an organization that specializes in investigating cybercrime, recently tried to understand the extend of organized Internet crime in Russia.

Group-IB found that cybercriminals in Russia, both organizations and individuals, netted almost $2 billion, primarily through the sale of counterfeit products by spamming. Additional sources of revenue include other forms of fraud (e.g., phishing or bank fraud), internal markets (e.g., selling exploits to other criminals), and renting botnets for distributed denial-of-service attacks.[11]

While it is unclear how much of this revenue is generated by criminal organizations, given the increasing sophistication of many of the attacks and the interruption of many organizations, it is thought that a significant part is organizedcrime related. Additionally, many of these operations tend to function as service providers for individuals or other organizations, making the determination of who is part of an organized-crime syndicate difficult to understand.[12]

The Widening Capability of Organized Cybercrime

While many traditional organized crime groups understand that there is an opportunity, they lack the ability to successfully exploit the potential of online criminal activity. However, they realize that there are individuals (and other organizations) that may be hired to fill the need. In a 2006 report, the McAfee group stated, "Organised crime gangs may have less of the expertise and access needed to commit cybercrime but they have the financial clout to buy the right resources and operate at a highly professional level."[13]

In addition to the ability to buy the expertise they need, organized crime groups are beginning to recruit members with appropriate skills, sometimes directly out of technical programs in colleges and universities. The report states the following:

> In an echo of the KGB tactics employed during the Cold War to recruit operatives, organised crime gangs are increasingly using similar tactics to identify and entice bright young net-savvy undergraduates.
>
> Organised crime gangs are starting to actively recruit skilled young people into cybercrime. They are adopting KGB-style tactics to recruit high flying IT students and graduates and targeting computer society members, students of specialist computer skills schools and graduates of IT technology courses. . . .
>
> In some cases, organised crime gangs are going even further to sponsor eager would-be hackers and malware authors to attend information technology university courses to further their expertise. Criminals are also earmarking university students from other disciplines and supporting them financially through their studies with a view to them gaining employment with, and inside access to, target organisations and businesses.[14]

Moreover, in cases where there is a large profit to be made through illicit activity, there may be an increasing use of standard information technology business practices in order to help develop software used in the crimes.[15]

Widening Scope of Organized Cybercrime

One of the biggest concerns about the increasing scope and complexity of organized cybercrime is the possible connection this provides to drug trafficking—a historical stalwart of organized crime—and terrorism. Specifically, as the capabilities of organized criminal organizations increase in terms of their online capacity, they become more valuable to other groups, those outside the organized crime context, for carrying out operations. This, of course, further complicates an already complicated picture.

Given that organized criminals, whatever the shape the organization may take, have significant capabilities, the concern is that they will be used by other countries or organizations to cause harm. This can be seen in the Georgian/Russian conflict, but is perhaps more frightening in terms of terrorism.

Many terrorists groups, including Al Qaeda and ISIS, have clearly demonstrated that while they do not currently have the capacity to conduct cyberattacks, they wish to develop them. One way they could circumvent this process is by hiring organized crime groups to conduct operations for them. While this is discussed more in chapter 7, in many respects it is just as much an organized crime issue as one of cyberterrorism.

While capabilities and partnerships represent one element of organized cybercrimes' increasing scope, there is also the important element that organizations are becoming less tied to any physical proximity. Specifically, crime in cyberspace is freeing organizations from the constraints that more traditional organizations often have. This, in turn, is leading to entirely new forms of organizational development. Although the types mentioned earlier are a starting point for understanding what these new forms may look like, there are probably forms that have yet to develop. While traditional organized crime groups emphasize hierarchy, these new forms will likely be much more diffuse and networked. This could lead many organizations to become less organization-like, instead operating in what has been termed a "leaderless resistance" model in other contexts. If this transition from hierarchies to swarms, using the terminology from earlier in the chapter, persists, it could make combating organized criminal activity online much more difficult.

Organized Cybercrime Markets

One particular manifestation of the complexity of online organized crime is the development of marketplaces to facilitate these organizations; these marketplaces have themselves becomes sources of revenue for online organized cybercrime. The marketplaces have several functions, some specialize in selling stolen credit card and other sensitive data, while other markets focus on selling the exploits that allow for the theft. In both cases the markets present unique extensions of the organized crime system online as they can represent hubs in networks of organized cybercrime or may be organizations themselves.

A recent RAND study looking at online criminal markets had this to say: "The hacker market—once a varied landscape of discrete, ad hoc networks of individuals initially motivated by little more than ego and notoriety— has emerged as a playground of financially driven, highly organized, and sophisticated groups."[16]

Even more interesting in terms of these criminal marketplaces is the organizational form they usually take. According to the United Nations report on cybercrime:

> The market as a whole is not a single criminal group enterprise. Rather, it can be characterized as a "social network of individuals engaged in orga- nized criminal activity." Certain individuals and small groups—such as the original programmers of malware, and botnet C&C owners—may rep- resent key points within the market, around which other individuals, swarms, and hubs turn. Based on law enforcement investigations and ar- rests to date, those responsible for creating and managing key components of the market, such as botnets, appear to act in comparatively small groups or individually.[17]

Also interesting is the fact that many of these marketplace controllers, when there is a group at all, have been together only short periods of time, usually less than a year.[18]

The ability to remain small but produce a large market extends to those participating in the market in other ways. Often these marketplaces are accessed by a large number of users, but the relationships the market cre- ates may be ephemeral, lasting only for short durations, sometimes just the length of the transaction. However, some transactions, particularly transactions like renting botnets for spamming operations or distributed denial-of-service attacks, may create links that last a longer period.

Another interesting element of the marketplaces is the range of prices that services accommodate. Depending on the service desired, prices range from as low as $80 for a malware-prepped server to as high as $4,000 or more for zero-day exploits or a Zeus kit, which is essentially a do-it-yourself malware system.[19] These prices are sustained because they can result in huge revenue generations for the organizations or individuals that adopt them.

Organized Cybercrime Groups

Much of what we know about online organized crime is because of what has been learned from organizations that have been disrupted. In the following section, some of these groups, and the operations they were involved with, are examined for the type of model they represent in terms of their organized crime functions and structures.

Unlimited Operation

Unlimited Operations was the name of a cyberattack conducted by a group of individuals with significant ties to organized crime. The attack got its name because of the potential for unlimited returns in terms of the money stolen during the crime. While the attack was disrupted, the amount of money stolen in the operation topped $45 million; at one point the group stole more than $2.8 million in less than 24 hours.

The Unlimited Operations attacks focused on hacking into credit card processors' systems and removing limits from credit cards. Once this is done, and the hackers have access to credit card numbers, the amount of money they can withdraw using the cards is virtually unlimited. According to the Justice Department, the attacks had three key characteristics[20]:

1. The surgical precision of the hackers carrying out the attack
2. The global nature of the cybercrime organization
3. The speed and coordination with which the organization executes its operations on the ground

One of the most interesting aspects of Unlimited Operations was the sophisticated nature of the organization required to carry it out. Not only was there a complex division of labor, but aside from the eight people charged by the Department of Justice, a number of lower-level members were required to successfully carry out the operations. Specifically, the organization needed people to actually withdraw cash from ATMs in order to transfer the money from electronic to physical form. According to the Department of Justice[21]:

> The cybercrime organization cashes in, by distributing the hacked prepaid debit card numbers to trusted associates around the world—the two cyber-attacks charged in this case allegedly involved 26 countries. These associates operate cells or teams of "cashers," who encode magnetic stripe cards, such as gift cards, with the compromised card data. When the cybercrime organization distributes the personal identification numbers (PINs) for the hacked accounts, the casher cells spring into action, immediately withdrawing cash from ATMs across the globe. Meanwhile, the cybercrime organization maintains access to the computer networks of the credit card processors they have hacked in order to monitor the withdrawals. At the end of an

operation, when the cards are finally shut down, the casher cells launder the proceeds, often investing the operation's proceeds in luxury goods, and kick money back up to the cybercrime organization's leaders.

In other words, without a relatively hierarchical organizational structure and a complex division of labor among those participating in the crime, Unlimited Operations could not have been carried out.

While it is unclear how frequently frauds like Unlimited Operations happen, the huge amount of money involved in the operation, and the possibility that more opportunities like it exist, no doubt drives the development of additional organized crime groups online or pushes traditional organized crime groups to participate in cybercrime.

Carberp

Carberp is a piece of malware that focuses on gathering banking information from users by introducing a Trojan horse onto their computers. The Carberp malware has undergone an evolution, and at least three versions of the software have been released, despite the arrest of several of the original developers. While the total amount of money stolen by the software is unknown (it is possible that not all users realize they have had money stolen), at least $2 million has been illegally moved from individual accounts to the groups' accounts and taken out of ATMs.

While Carberp is interesting for a variety of reasons, one of the most interesting aspects of the malware is its development and what this suggests about the organization(s) using it. The program was originally developed by a small, tight-knit group of developers. They were the only users for several years, before they started to sell it to other cybercriminals and organizations. In 2013, eight of the operators of Carberp were arrested, including the two brothers who led the small group responsible for development.

What is interesting is that these arrests did little to stop the development of Carberp. Not only has the program continued to be developed, now in at least three versions as mentioned earlier, but it was most recently combined with another program to give it added functionality. Moreover, during this continuous development of the malware, it has been associated with at least three other organizations, and in some cases these groups worked together on additional development.

In fact, while the first group was directly associated with the developer of the malware, the second group worked in parallel with the first to improve the program, despite there being no direct connection with the original developer. The third group used Carberp as a way to upgrade from using a previous botnet called Origami Hodprot.

As the botnet grew, the group's operations became increasingly organised and members of the group were highly coordinated. They had command-and-control servers in several European countries and the United States, and attacked Russian as well as foreign banks. In December 2012, members from the Carberp team posted messages on underground Russian cybercrime forums, offering a new version of Carberp for rent. At US$40,000 per month, this was one of the most expensive kits thus far advertised.[22]

Again, what is interesting about Carberp is the level of organization that the fraud requires. There are individuals operating at most of the divisions of labor mentioned by the FBI. But rather than simply being a complex organization, Carberp shows how a fraud can actually lead to the development of more complex organizations and can begin to link those organizations together.

Internet Feds/LulzSec

The Internet Feds were a loosely organized group of hackers who engaged in what could be considered "gray hat" hacking against a variety of targets. Originally members of Anonymous, the members of the Internet Feds shared interests in a variety of issues and used their computer skills to steal private information to post publically and to deface websites with which they disagreed. Over time, the Internet Feds evolved into Lulz Security (LulzSec for short). The group conducted similar offenses until one of the members was indicted and implicated several others as part of a plea bargain.

One of the most interesting things about the group is the fact that they did not engage in classic criminal activity. That is, they did not steal money for personal gain. Rather, they engaged in classic hacking activity—as the group itself put it, they did it for the Lulz.

This fact has led many to argue that the group was not a criminal organization but rather a group of hacktivists, an argument regularly applied to Anonymous, from which Internet Feds and LulzSec derived. However, despite the fact that the groups did not engage in the same type of criminal activity that the groups mentioned earlier did, they did regularly deface websites and break into servers to steal information. These, for better or worse, are the analogues of the traditional crimes of vandalism and trespassing, along with theft, despite their digital nature.

As these groups broke away from (insofar as that is possible) Anonymous, they shared a similar structure. They closely match the swarm organizational subtype mentioned earlier. In this case, it was a very small group of individuals who were acting together to perpetrate relatively benign crimes. However, the fact that a small, nonhierarchical group was able to hack into Sony Pictures and release private information, as well as allegedly take down the CIA's website, suggests possibilities for this type of loosely organized group.

The Myth of Organized Cybercrime

One issue with the different structures that organized crime online has taken is whether or not some of the forms still constitute organized crime in the traditional sense usually meant by the term, or if it represents an entirely new phenomenon. Some argue that the narrative of organized cybercrime has been driven less by the actual development of the groups but rather by our societal perception of how we *think* they have developed. Foremost among these thinkers is David S. Wall, who argues that we are conditioned to think of online "organized crime" as something along the lines of "cyberpunk meets *The Godfather*."[23]

Wall argues that this is likely an incorrect view, but we cling to it because of the cultural touchstones we use to think about all cybercrime. Further, Wall suggests that organized crime online, to the extent that it exists, is becoming increasingly distributed and unorganized. In other words, rather than having a structure at all, organized crime is becoming "wikified." This idea suggests that groups are following a wiki model of organization, known as distributed online collaboration.

This model, whereby participants come and go at will and contribute what they wish to any given illegal endeavor, is somewhat antithetical to the general idea of organized crime. While in some ways it resembles the swarm model mentioned earlier, some believe it is unlikely that this represents any real kind of organization at all.

Conclusion

Organized cybercrime is a particularly troublesome area of crime in the digital era. Not only is it complex but the forms it takes suggest that it may eventually link with other forms of cybercrime, like cyberterrorism or cyberwarfare, to become even more problematic. While organized crime is nothing new, its movement from the physical world into the online world has been fraught with questions. With up to 80 percent of all major cybercrime now being committed by organizations, it is clear that the problem is not going away soon.

This means understanding the organizations, especially their structures and types, is essential for combating them. As discussed in this chapter, there are three primary types of organizations, those that operate online primarily, those that operate seamlessly between the online and physical worlds, and those that operate primarily in the physical world who use networks as a tool. Within these are six subtypes, ranging from a disorganized swarm of like-minded individuals to a hierarchical group with well-defined divisions of labor.

While many groups have sprung up on the Internet, and others have moved from the physical world online, three groups that are worth mentioning are the groups responsible for the Unlimited Operations, the Carberp botnet, and LulzSec. While these groups are perhaps not unique, they represent different degrees of organization from what is possible with organized cybercrime. What the future holds for the development of organized cybercrime is unclear, but it will likely involve the evolution of further markets and a flattening of traditional organizational types.

Review Questions

1. What constitutes a criminal organization?
2. What forms can a cybercrime organization take?
3. What are the characteristics of markets for cybercriminals?
4. What was Unlimited Operations and what were some of the characteristics of the organization that ran it?
5. What was LulzSec and does it represent an organized crime group?

Key Words

Aggregates
Carberp
Cashers
Clustered hybrids
Coders
Distributors
Executives
Extended hybrids
Fraud specialists
Hackers
Hierarchies
Hosts

Hubs
LulzSec
Money Mules
Organized Crime
Swarms
Technicians
Tellers
Type I online criminal organization
Type II online criminal organization
Type III online criminal organization
Unlimited Operations

Notes

1. United Nations Office on Drugs and Crime, "Comprehensive Study on Cybercrime," https://www.unodc.org/documents/organized-crime/cybercrime /CYBERCRIME_STUDY_210213.pdf.

2. Susan Brenner, "Organized Cybercrime? How Cyberspace May Affect the Organization of Criminal Relationships," *North Carolina Journal of Law and Technology*, 4 (2002): 1–50.

3. Group-IB, *"Threat Intelligence Report,"* http://report2013.group-ib.com.

4. Mark Rutherford, "Report: Russian Mob Aided Cyberattacks on Georgia," CNET, 2009, http://www.cnet.com/news/report-russian-mob-aided-cyberattacks -on-georgia/.

5. Richard A. Clarke and Robert Knake, *Cyber War: The Next Threat to National Security and What to Do About It* (New York: HarperCollins. Kindle Edition, 2010), 16.

6. Roderic Broadhurst, Peter Grabosky, Mamoun Alazab, and Steve Chon, "Organizations and Cybercrime: An Analysis of the Nature of Groups Engaged in Cybercrime," *International Journal of Cybercriminology* 8 (2014): 1–20.

7. Lilian Ablon, Martin C. Libicki, and Andrea A. Golay, "Markets for Cybercrime Tools and Stolen Data," RAND, 2014, http://www.rand.org/content /dam/rand/pubs/research_reports/RR600/RR610/RAND_RR610.pdf.

8. Ben Cubby and Amy McNeilage, "Police Investigate Rioters' Text Messages," *Sidney Morning Herald Online*, September 17, 2012, http://www.smh.com.au /nsw/police-investigate-rioters-text-messages-20120916-260mk.html.

9. Broadhurst et al., "Organizations and Cybercrime."

10. Steven R. Chabinsky, "The Cyber Threat: Who's Doing What to Whom?" Speech at the GovSec/FOSE Conference, Washington, DC, March 23, 2010, https://www.fbi.gov/news/speeches/the-cyber-threat-whos-doing-what-to-whom.

11. Group-IB, *Threat Intelligence Report*.

12. Clay Wilson, *Botnets, Cybercrime, and Cyberterrorism: Vulnerabilities and Policy Issues for Congress*, Congressional Research Service Report RL33114, 2008, https://www.fas.org/sgp/crs/terror/RL32114.pdf.

13. McAfee, *McAfee Virtual Criminology Report: Organized Crime and the Internet*, 2006, http://i.i.cbsi.com/cnwk.1d/html/itp/mcafee_ww_virtual_criminology _FINAL.pdf.

14. Ibid.

15. Clay Wilson, "Botnets, Cybercrime, and Cyberterrorism."

16. Ablon et al., "Markets for Cybercrime Tools and Stolen Data."

17. United Nations Office on Drugs and Crime, *Comprehensive Study on Cybercrime*, 2013, https://www.unodc.org/documents/organized-crime/cybercrime /CYBERCRIME_STUDY_210213.pdf.

18. Ibid.

19. Gregg Keizer, "Hackers Lock Zeus Crimeware Kit with Windows-like Anti-piracy Tech," *Computerworld,* March 15, 2010, http://www.computerworld.com /article/2516413/microsoft-windows/hackers-lock-zeus-crimeware-kit-with -windows-like-anti-piracy-tech.html.

20. U.S. Attorney's Office, "Eight Members of New York Cell of Cybercrime Organization Indicted in $45 million Cybercrime Campaign," May 9, 2013, http://www.justice.gov/usao-edny/pr/eight-members-new-york-cell-cybercrime -organization-indicted-45-million-cybercrime.

21. Ibid.

22. Broadhurst et al., "Organizations and Cybercrime."

23. David S. Wall, "Cybercrime and the Culture of Fear: Social Science Fiction(s) and the Production of Knowledge about Cybercrime," *Information, Communication & Society* 11 (2011): 861–884.

CHAPTER SEVEN

Cyberterrorism and Terrorists Online

Introduction

THE THREAT OF CYBERTERRORISM IS A HOTLY CONTESTED TOPIC. While most agree that cyberterrorism poses a significant issue for the United States, the exact nature of that threat remains unclear. In part, this stems from confusion about what constitutes cyberterrorism. Given the historical difficulty of defining terrorism, this should not come as a surprise, though the lack of understanding could be a significant problem in terms of countering cyberterrorism. This chapter examines the issue of cyberterrorism, specifically looking at efforts to define the threat and efforts to counter it. In addition, it looks at the ways terrorists use the Internet to further their goals, including financing, planning, and perhaps most importantly, recruiting.

Defining Cyberterrorism

The Problem with Terrorism

Despite being a topic of study for over 50 years, the term "terrorism" still does not have a settled-upon definition. While there are many reasons for this, the political nature of the term, the negative connotation it carries, and the constant variation in usage have all added to the problem of reaching consensus on what specific elements constitute terrorism.[1] This "definitional issue," as it has come to be called, is particularly problematic because of the practical implications of differing definitions.

Notably, there is not even agreement on whether a definition of terrorism is necessary. For instance, while some people, such as Sir Jeremy Greenstock (the former British ambassador to the United Nations [UN]), argue that "terrorism smells like terrorism," and others have argued that "you know it when you see it," former president of Lebanon Emile Lahoud and respected scholars such as Boaz Ganor argue that a precise definition is needed because we need to understand what exactly is being combated.[2] This argument over the need for a definition is also relatively old, though there seems to be a growing consensus that there does, in fact, need to be criteria by which acts of terrorism can be judged as such.

The problem of defining what exactly is meant by the term "terrorism" has become particularly acute after the attacks of September 11, 2001.[3] Efforts to combat terrorism internationally are, in part, dependent on different countries' definitions of terrorism, as organizing bodies such as the UN have yet to reach consensus on the specifics of what terrorism is.[4] This lack of international consensus, largely driven by different countries' political agendas, makes combating terrorism difficult as, in some cases, the countries involved in defining terrorism are actively engaged in promoting it.

Cyberterrorism

The lack of a specific definition for terrorism is compounded in the specific case of cyberterrorism. Issues that deal with "cyber" tend to be misunderstood by the public and misreported by the press.[5] Moreover, issues dealing with threats to national security in the context of "cyber" are often political—much like terrorism overall—compounding the issues of defining what specifically constitutes cyberterrorism.[6]

Unlike the more general term "terrorism," however, there are even arguments as to whether or not cyberterrorism constitutes a real problem.[7] Most agree that the *potential* for cyberterrorism presents a threat, but there have been few, if any, instances that would be considered *cyberterrorism* by most scholars.[8] This potential threat, but lack of actual attack, has created a situation where fear thrives, but there is little actual information on what exactly a cyberterrorist attack would or could accomplish. In many respects, it resembles the focus on terrorist use of weapons of mass destruction, which occupied much of the scholarship on terrorism before the 9/11 attacks.

Even considering the threat of cyberterrorism to be real does not necessarily improve the situation. As with all types of cybercrime, there are significant issues when it comes to jurisdiction, but in many ways these are exacerbated when you add the political element that is the lynchpin of definitions of modern terrorism.

This misunderstanding of terminology, while seemingly inconsequential, has real effects. One problem is the targeting of groups that are not terrorist organizations or a particularly large threat to national security under the guise of counter-cyberterrorism. While hacker collectives like

Anonymous present potential problems, their characterization as cyberterrorist organizations is antithetical to how the organizations see themselves and how they generally operate.⁹ In other words, the current problem can be seen as a paradox: We cannot define cybercrime, but if we do not define it, we cannot hope to adequately combat it.

Realistically, all of this definitional angst has meant that cyberterrorism has come to mean anything terrorists do using the Internet and other networked technology to further their goals, though in reality, cyberterrorism should involve actual attacks and damage. This lack of focus within the definition makes it difficult to differentiate it from other forms of cybercrime, as the primary distinguishing characteristic is the attacker's motivation, something that is often unknown in the case of cyber-related events. Additionally, it has become increasingly difficult to distinguish between Internet activism, hacktivism, and cyberterrorism, as the motivations and outcomes of many of the actors participating in each are the same, even if the overall goals of the organizations are different.¹⁰

Box 7.1   Definitions of Cyberterrorism

The term "cyberterrorism" was first introduced in the 1980s by Barry Collin, but scholars have yet to determine an agreed-upon definition for the term. Terms like "cyberterrorism," "cyberattack," "hacktivism," "information warfare," "online activism," and "cybercrime" are frequently used incorrectly, and often interchangeably, leading to confusion among the public. While scholars may disagree on a specific definition for cyberterrorism, most have settled on a variation of the following definition used by Dorothy Denning in congressional testimony in 2000:

> Cyberterrorism is the convergence of terrorism and cyberspace. It is generally understood to mean unlawful attacks and threats of attack against computers, networks, and the information stored therein when done to intimidate or coerce a government or its people in furtherance of political or social objectives. Further, to qualify as cyberterrorism, an attack should result in violence against persons or property, or at least cause enough harm to generate fear. Attacks that lead to death or bodily injury, explosions, plane crashes, water contamination, or severe economic loss would be examples. Serious attacks against critical infrastructures could be acts of cyberterrorism, depending on their

impact. Attacks that disrupt nonessential services or that are mainly a costly nuisance would not.[a]

Another scholar, Mark Pollitt, defined the term as the "premeditated, politically motivated attack against information, computer systems, and data which result in violence against non-combatant targets by subnational groups."[b]

This range of definitions used by scholars has made the study of cyberterrorism, like the study of cybercrime in general, difficult. Further, because there are unclear boundaries between hacktivism, information warfare, and cyberterrorism specifically (all three are politically motivated and can cause fear), it makes counter-cyberterrorism a difficult pursuit.

In terms of federal law, there is no specific statute that defines cybercrime, though any act on a computer meant to further an act of terrorism would be captured under several existing pieces of federal legislation, particularly 18 USC § 2332b: Acts of Terrorism Transcending National Boundaries (1996). Additional federal legislation may apply to cyberterrorism as well, in particular counter-cyberterrorism, but much of what applies depends on the definition one adopts.

[a]Dorothy Denning, "Statement of Dorothy E. Denning," May 23, 2000, http://ftp.fas.org/irp/congress/2000_hr/00-05-23denning.htm.

[b]Mark M. Pollitt, "A Cyberterrorism Fact or Fancy?," Proceedings of the 20th National Information Systems Security Conference, 1997, pp. 285–289.

Terrorist Use of "Cyber"

Despite the aforementioned consternation over the actual threat of cyberterrorism as commonly conceived, there has been a great deal of documented use of technology by terrorists—much of it computer based, and much of it involving networks.[11] Recent news stories have focused on terrorist recruitment strategies through traditional websites and social media, like Twitter.[12] Additionally, terrorist organizations have developed significant funding capabilities through use of the Internet,[13] and they have used computers in various ways to help plan attacks.[14]

The UN Office on Drugs and Crime has identified a functional approach to understanding how terrorists use the Internet that consists of six categories: propaganda (including recruitment, radicalization, and incitement to terrorism), financing, training, planning, execution, and cyberattacks.[15] The following sections use this outline as a way to explore terrorist use of the Internet and, subsequently, cyberterrorism.

Terrorist Propaganda

Terrorist use of the Internet for propaganda purposes is nothing new. Bruce Hoffman acknowledged that propaganda was central to the terrorist enterprise; without it, the rationale for any attacks is lost on those whom the terrorist wishes to influence.[16] Propaganda by modern terrorist groups is often carried out primarily through means of the Internet. The actual form of the communication can take different shapes. Terrorists often use multimedia communications posted on the World Wide Web or distribute links via social media to provide ideological justification, practical instruction, and other promotion of terrorist actions. The communications propagated by terrorists can take any number of forms, ranging from simple written communications to highly developed and slickly produced video games.

The propaganda distributed online by terrorist organizations can have different objectives, and individual communications oftentimes have different audiences. Terrorists often claim responsibility for attacks, attempt to recruit followers or militarize those followers who are otherwise supportive, or incite those who are already militarized to attack.

While there is a distinction between propaganda and legitimate political discourse, the line between the two is often fine. Given the importance of protecting people's right to free speech, especially in the relatively unregulated area of the Internet, stopping propaganda by terrorist organizations has proven extremely difficult. This very fact, plus the additional ability to provide direct communication to the audience of their choice without interpretation by other organizations (e.g., CNN, Fox News), makes the Internet an ideal place for terrorists to distribute their message.

Financing

In addition to distributing propaganda, terrorists also regularly use the Internet for fund-raising. While terrorist organizations use a large number of specific approaches to raise funds online, these approaches fall into four primary categories: direct solicitation, e-commerce, exploitation of online payment tools, and fund-raising through charitable organizations.[17] Each tool can be used individually or in combination to create a comprehensive fund-raising system for terrorist organizations.

Box 7.2 Online Terrorist Recruitment

While there are many disturbing elements when it comes to terrorist use of the Internet for propaganda, perhaps the most concerning is recruitment. Recent stories in *Time* and *Newsweek* have focused on the Internet, and in particular social media platforms like Twitter, as methods by which terrorist groups engage and further radicalize potential members and, in some cases, convince them to leave home and join the groups.

In one of the most striking cases of online recruitment, three teenage girls from London, Shamima Begum (age 15), Kadiza Sultana (age 16), and an unnamed 15-year-old took a Turkish Airlines flight to Istanbul and crossed the Syrian border to join the Islamic State terrorist group. While the specific motivations of the young women are not known, they were directly recruited by the Islamic State through social media.

A recent study suggested that while there has been much focus on women recruits who become jihadi brides (women who marry jihadis to support them while they fight), many women recruited from Western countries become fighters themselves. Up to 550 women from Western countries have been recruited by the Islamic State to fight. Interestingly, the report stated that many of the women become active in producing propaganda for the organization— primarily for additional recruitment.

One way countries have been countering terrorism online is through counterpropaganda. By releasing information to combat the information terrorists are posting, the hope is to dissuade those who would be interesting in following a terrorist group. As a strategy, it is not new; the United States has carried out similar operations for at least 50 years. However, targeting individuals in the online environment has provided interesting challenges for those who seek to counter terrorist propaganda.

Source: P. Mosendz, "Report: 550 Western Women Fighting for ISIS, They're More Than Jihadi Brides," *Newsweek*, June 28, 2015, http://www.newsweek .com/550-western-women-inside-isis-are-more-jihadi-brides-337052.

Direct solicitation is the use of websites, forums, email, and other types of targeted communications to request financial support directly. Once contacted, individuals can give money directly to the organization through a variety of means. Online direct payment systems like PayPal are common, though other systems, such as bitcoin, are becoming more common.[18] Websites used to directly solicit funds are also often used in e-commerce for organizations, sometimes even offering merchandise with organizational affiliations.[19]

The exploitation of online payment tools has become another common method of fund-raising for terrorist groups. Specifically, groups use tactics ranging from identity theft to intellectual property crimes to illegally obtain funds or launder money. These methods are sometimes large scale; in at one least one case over 1,400 individual credit cards were used to generate over $1.5 million dollars for Al Qaeda.[20]

Terrorist organizations also use legitimate charities to funnel money into their pockets. Groups such as Al Qaeda and Hezbollah have regularly used this tactic, sometimes establishing false charities as a front for fundraising and sometimes infiltrating a legitimate charity but diverting funds to the terrorist group.[21] The terrorist organizations use online donations to those organizations to fund terrorist operations or other activities helpful to the group. This is particularly difficult to combat because it is often unclear whether those individuals donating to the charities know about the terrorist group's involvement.

Training

Given the recent international focus on disrupting terrorist organizations, physical training camps, once prevalent, are becoming harder for terrorist groups to sustain. Because of this pressure, more groups are turning to the Internet as an alternative location to train their members. The type of training terrorist groups are able to provide online takes a variety of forms. Video and audio manuals for carrying out attacks or building weapons have become relatively common. The instructions produced can be quite detailed, and often include information not just on how to carry out attacks but also on counterintelligence operations and advanced surveillance techniques. Some manuals have even gone as far as to suggest which cities might be the best targets for terrorists interested in carrying out attacks.[22]

Planning

Given the increasingly networked world in which we live, it is perhaps unsurprising that nearly every successfully prosecuted case of terrorism in

Box 7.3   The Holy Land Foundation

Once considered the largest Muslim charity in the United States, the Holy Land Foundation for Relief and Development was founded to funnel money to the terrorist organization Hamas. In 2009 it was forced to close permanently. Five of the charity's founders were found guilty of 108 counts of providing material support to terrorists and sentenced to between 15 and 65 years in prison.

The organization itself was tied to the Muslim Brotherhood and was originally set up as a front group for Hamas fund-raising. Before its assets were frozen, the Holy Land Foundation had raised approximately $57 million, much of which went directly to Hamas.

In 2008, one of the Holy Land Foundation's partners, the technology company InfoCom, was also implicated. Among other things, InfoCom was responsible for the upkeep of the Holy Land Foundation's website.

Source: Federal Bureau of Investigation, "No Cash for Terror: Convictions Returned in Holy Land Case," November 25, 2008, https://www.fbi.gov/news/stories/2008/november/hlf112508.

the United States has involved electronic communications among those engaging in the terrorism. One of the most common uses of networked communication among terrorists is for planning a specific attack. This can include preparatory communications meant to assist in the actual collaboration between terrorists or public technology to assist in planning the terrorist attack.

One example of preparatory communication is the online "dead drop." This is a technique terrorists use to email one another while leaving a minimal digital trail. It works by using a common email account, where a person writes but does not send an email; instead, it is left in the draft folder of the email account. Another person with the password to the email account can then access it, open the draft folder, and read the email without ever having to actually send an email. Online systems are also available that can be used to anonymize communications, making them extremely difficult or impossible to track.

Use of publicly available information to plan attacks is another way terrorists can use online tools and technology to help plan attacks. Terrorists can use systems like Google Maps and Google Earth to help plan attacks

Box 7.4   Terrorist Use of the Internet for Planning

One of the ways terrorists have used the Internet to assist in their operation is through planning. Often this use is hard to detect, because terrorists have become savvy regarding the places and ways they can use tools to plan for their attacks. For instance, the 9/11 hijackers used emails to coordinate much of their action. It was hard to track this activity because they used public places to send emails and used large, public email systems.

When Abu Zubaydah, one of the 9/11 masterminds, was arrested thousands of emails to other Al Qaeda operatives were discovered. The frequency of the messages coincided with the development of the attacks, and the number peaked in August, just before the attacks were underway.

Al Qaeda is certainly not the only group that has used the Internet to plan. Hamas, a Palestinian organization listed as a terrorist group by the U.S. government, has used chat rooms to plan and coordinate attacks against Israel as well as other activities throughout the region. Incidentally, Hamas also maintains a robust web presence to assist with fund-raising and propaganda.

Sometimes the messages sent between terrorists use complex coding known as steganography. This involves hiding messages within images on a digital file. Many times however, the messages involve very simple codes, for example, attacks might be called "birthdays," or other common phrases. Mohamed Atta, one of the 9/11 hijackers, sent a message shortly before the operation that read, "The semester begins in three more weeks. We've obtained 19 confirmations for studies in the faculty of law, the faculty of urban planning, the faculty of fine arts, and the faculty of engineering."

With the increasing capabilities of programs online, the ability of terrorists to use such programs for planning also increases. The features of programs like Google Maps allow terrorists to conduct relatively detailed surveillance without having to go to the physical target at all. Moreover, the development of email systems designed to obscure the sender has made their communication more difficult to track.

In short, terrorist use of the Internet for planning purposes is problematic. The very development of the technology that assists the rest of us in planning our day can assist terrorists in planning their attacks.

because of the comprehensive information they provide on building locations, approaches, and other aspects. Information on individuals can sometimes be found on websites and social media, like Twitter and Facebook, which can then be used to improve planning for an event.

Execution

One of the hallmarks of terrorism is that the fear generated is what drives the change the terrorist group is looking for. That means there does not necessarily need to be an attack in order to generate fear and, therefore, commit terrorism. In this fear generation, the Internet serves as a fertile way for terrorists to create change without actually causing any physical damage. Threats of violence, communication among individuals during the course of an event, and purchase of items needed all constitute methods of assistance terrorists use in executing an attack.

Cyberattacks

While cyberattacks by terrorists have been rare, they remain a significant threat. Cyberterrorism attacks can include a variety of types of actions intended to disrupt the operation of computer systems, infrastructure (online or otherwise), or service provision. Types of attacks include hacking, propagation of malware or viruses (or worms), and malware or other methods that can disrupt digital and physical systems. Because of this, the division line between criminal behavior (such as online vandalism) and cyberterrorism is often hard to determine.

Efforts to Combat Cyberterrorism

Just as the growth of the Internet has provided new opportunities for criminals and cyberterrorists, it has also provided new means for law enforcement and other agencies to combat terrorism online.[23] With groups making their messages more public and using networked communications for planning and executing cyberattacks, additional opportunities are presented to gather intelligence and occasionally interdict terrorists before they are able to carry out an attack.[24]

Given the fact that cyber issues are almost always multijurisdictional, and often international in the case of cyberterrorism, there are a large number of agencies involved in countering cyberterrorism. In the following sections, these agencies, and their approaches to countering cyberterrorism, are examined.

Box 7.5 Terrorist Use of Social Media

Wherever you look in media outlets that focus on technology, it is likely they are talking about social media. Social media refers to programs or platforms that allow people to create content and share in the context of online communities. These characteristics allow for a huge range of possibilities in terms of human connection. Unfortunately, these very same features make social media attractive for terrorists to use.

Terrorist use of social media has become an increasing problem. While many groups have had websites for over a decade, the more recent advent of social media has presented new challenges. For one, there is no mediation between the terrorist organizations and those they are attempting to influence. Another issue is that, while social media outlets like Facebook and Twitter are attempting to combat them, it is relatively easy for an organization to simply start another account if they have been banned from a site.

Social media features direct access and easy creation, which make social media sites a popular method of recruitment and dissemination of propaganda. Groups like Al-Shabaab, a Somali terrorist group, and, more recently, ISIS have established a large presence on the social media platform Twitter. The U.S. military, which also maintains a presence on Twitter, has even occasionally communicated directly with the Taliban via the social network, in at least one case trading insults.

With the growing importance of social media, it is likely that terrorists' use of the platforms will grow as well. With new social media apps like Snapchat becoming popular, and designed to create content that lasts only a few seconds, the uses of social media by terrorists might become increasingly complex—and increasingly hard to combat.

Online Counterterrorism Strategy

The guiding strategy for all counterterrorism within the United States is the National Strategy for Counterterrorism.[25] The current strategy document, released in 2011, says surprisingly little about cyberterrorism considering the amount of press the topic gets. In terms of the use of the Internet by terrorists, the document focuses on countering the ideology of Al Qaeda and other related extremists within the context of the online world.

Scholars have identified other areas in which online counterterrorism operations can be used, however. Dorothy Denning, one of the premier scholars on cybercrime and terrorist groups online, classifies four strategic areas in which online counterterrorism can be effective: intelligence collection, denial, subversion, and engagement.[26]

Intelligence Collection

While referencing Al Qaeda specifically, Denning's reference to intelligence collection is viable across most terrorist groups operating on the Internet. Intelligence collection involves careful monitoring of the places on the Internet where terrorists congregate. This can be Internet forums, message exchanges, and, more recently, social media sites where there is communication between terrorists. The information harvested from these sites can be useful to law enforcement in a variety of ways. First, it may lead to a direct interdiction against a group to prevent an attack. Second, it may also lead to information about the group's organizational structure or individual identities within the group, which can help with long-term planning in combating a specific organization. Finally, as has been the case in recent years, the information gathered can be used to help convict people of terrorism or providing support for terrorist organizations.[27]

Denial

While intelligence collection can be essential to stopping terrorist organizations from operating on the Internet, another strategy for addressing terrorists online is denying them access to the Internet. This can be done by closing email accounts, shutting down websites, closing Internet forums where terrorists congregate, and removing extremist or violent content from websites not directly affiliated with the organizations.

This strategy has several potential effects that support counterterrorism online. By denying terrorists the ability to access the Internet, it is hoped that their access to potential recruits is similarly denied. Moreover, without the ability to communicate, denial can potentially provide disrupt planning between terrorists or limit their ability to get materials.

Unsurprisingly, given that most of these sites are either mirrored in multiple locations or are easily reestablished, denying terrorists Internet access has limited effectiveness. Additionally, and perhaps more problematically, there is the issue of infringing on people's free speech rights, as many of the videos and messages, as problematic as they are, are allowable under free-speech laws. Despite these challenges, however, there are cases where this strategy has been effective.[28]

Subversion

Subversion is the third strategy Denning mentions, and it focuses on gaining access to forums run by terrorist organizations, gaining the trust of the members, and providing disinformation to the group in order to stop operations or undermine leadership. This strategy is very difficult to carry out, as the operations can be discovered or backfire on the groups implementing them. Moreover, the coordination required across groups engaging in this type of counter-cyberterrorism is extensive, so that multiple organizations are not undermining one another's work. However, the strategy has been successfully used by law enforcement and others as a way of sowing discord among groups.[29]

Engagement

The fourth strategy suggested by Denning harks back to the beginning of the section, where individuals or organizations converse directly with the terrorists or potential terrorist recruits, trying to challenge the perceptions of the individuals engaging. There can be several goals when engaging with terrorists. One is outright deradicalization, or changing beliefs such that they no longer represent the radical perspective put forth by terrorists. Another goal can be demilitarization, where the individual may still be radical in his or her beliefs, but not willing to act violently to support those beliefs or support those who do.

There are significant challenges to the success of this strategy. First, the terrorists strongly hold the beliefs motivating them, so changing their mind through online engagement is very difficult. Even those who are still being recruited may be difficult to reach in terms of changing their beliefs or behavior. Further complicating the matter is that many of those who engage with terrorists or recruits do not have the standing within that community to be taken seriously. Some programs have tried to address this by using Muslim scholars and clerics, and while there is some suggestion of success with these programs, it is difficult to know whether that success was short or long term.

Actors

One of the interesting parts of counter-cyberterrorism is that there is little limitation on who can engage in it. While there is clearly heavy involvement by law enforcement organizations and the military, there are also individuals who engage in online counterterrorism; some online hacking groups have even decided to engage with groups like ISIS.

Individuals

One of the most disruptive (in the good sense of the term) characteristics of the Internet is the diffusion of access. In terms of cyberterrorism, this diffusion has meant the possibility that individuals can engage in acts of online terror, but it also means that individuals have the ability to go online and participate in their own counter-cyberterrorism. While there are many stories of individuals doing this, one of the most interesting is that of former Montana judge Shannen Rossmiller.

Posing as an Al Qaeda operative, Rossmiller goes onto forums and attempts to "recruit" individuals through email and other methods. When she has built up enough information, she turns it over to the Federal Bureau of Investigation (FBI) for further investigation and prosecution. According to Rossmiller, she has helped in over 60 cases, at least two of them domestic. In 2004, she testified against Specialist Ryan G. Anderson, a National Guard tank crew member who was plotting to conduct a terrorist attack in the United States. Anderson received a sentence of life in prison.[30] Another individual who has engaged in a similar method of investigation is Rita Katz, who has been engaged in what she has characterized as "terrorist hunting" for over a decade; her experiences are chronicled in the book *Terrorist Hunter*, which was published anonymously, though Katz was later revealed to be the author.[31]

While the opportunity for individuals to engage in this kind of investigation is interesting, it is also potentially problematic. Individuals can accidentally work at cross-purposes with law enforcement or otherwise interrupt ongoing investigations. Moreover, it is unclear what kind of risk is facing those who engage in this kind of investigation. In the case of Rossmiller, local entities have had to expend time and funds to provide some protection to her family.[32] Thus, despite the success of people like Rossmiller and Katz, it is unclear how effective this type of individual investigation is overall, and many believe law enforcement organizations are much more effective in the long run.

Private Groups

Along with individuals who have begun to investigate terrorists and terrorist organizations, a number of private organizations have sprung up to engage in online counterterrorist operations, ranging from intelligence gathering to actual counterterrorist operations over the Internet. These are primarily geared toward open-source intelligence gathering, though some organizations may go farther and engage in additional investigations by joining forums and undertaking other methods of subterfuge. Some of the more prominent groups are covered in the sections that follow.

SITE Monitoring Service

The Search for International Terrorist Entities (SITE) Intelligence Group, now called SITE Monitoring Service, is an organization established by the aforementioned Rita Katz in 2002. SITE provides online monitoring of terrorist activity for the government and individuals as well as training in online monitoring.[33] SITE uses infiltration techniques to view online activity by organizations and individuals associated with terrorism and gathers information to pass on to the government or other entities. The organization collects a variety of information, including claims of responsibility for attacks, video and audio messages, training manuals, and other digital media.

International Institute for Counterterrorism

The International Institute for Counterterrorism is dedicated to combating terrorism across all domains, including digitally. Founded in 1996, the think tank provides a variety of services across many issues dealing with terrorism. Like SITE, the group's primary function is collecting and disseminating intelligence, primarily gathered from online sources like jihadist websites and forums.[34]

Law Enforcement

Given the difficulty of defining cyberterrorism, and the similarity between other types of cybercrime and the online activity of terrorist groups, there are few agencies within the government that focus on cyberterrorism specifically, though there are specific initiatives by some agencies to combat it. The international situation is similar, with much being done in terms of coordination among different countries, but few specific initiatives dedicated to online counterterrorism. The sections below explore those programs that do focus directly on cyberterrorism and the use of the Internet by terrorists domestically and internationally.

It is worth noting that many commentators note the inadequate legal and organizational framework for combating terrorism in an online environment and cyberterrorism.[35]

Domestic

As mentioned earlier, many of the same agencies that address cybercrime more generally address issues of cyberterrorism and the use of the Internet by terrorists. The three main agencies responsible for combating online terrorism and cyberterrorism in the United States are the FBI, the Department of Homeland Security (DHS), and the Department of Defense

Box 7.6   Anonymous and Online Counterterrorism

One of the most interesting approaches to counterterrorism online (including cyberterrorism) has been taken by the hacker group Anonymous. Their campaign, #OpISIS, is a coordinated effort to expose members of terrorist organizations by infiltrating their online sites, accessing personal information about members and supporters of ISIS, and publishing that data for investigators and other interested parties.

To that end, the group recently published a hacking guide to assist others who want to expose ISIS members and fight the organization online. In a statement by the group, they offer three steps to finding members of ISIS on Twitter[a]:

1—Locating an Islamic State Twitter account.

If you are new to this locating an Islamic State Twitter account can prove to be difficult however after locating your first account you will be able to find thousands more following these steps. ISIS Twitter users are being aggressively hunted by Ghost Security and are called out for suspension on a regular basis. To locate an ISIS account on Twitter search the hash tags #GhostSec or #OpISIS and you will find your first Islamic State Twitter account.

2—I have located my first Islamic State Twitter account.

Now that you have located your first Islamic State Twitter account you will be able to collect many more and form a vast network of information. With the account you initially located review all of their following and followers collecting Twitter account names as you move forward. When you are collecting account names you must retrieve their Twitter ID by visiting the following website http://gettwitterid .com. If you do not collect the account ID they can easily change their account name to evade you as they commonly do once detected. As you are collecting ISIS Twitter accounts check each bio and their tweets for website URLS and collect the information. With the data you have compiled visit http://pastebin.com and publish a paste of your findings and remember to save the Pastebin link.

3—I have a Pastebin link of Islamic State Twitter accounts and URLS.

Now that you have collected this information you can take action against them by reporting your findings to Ghost Security. If your Pastebin link contains Islamic State Twitter accounts you can tweet your link making sure to use the hash tag #CtrlSec so their operatives can collect your information and terminate the accounts. If you have located Islamic State website URLS visit http://ghostsec.org and submit your Pastebin link so their operatives can collect your information and disable the websites.

What is perhaps most interesting about this tactic is it combines the group and invidual approaches to online counterterrorism. Additionally, while there is no real way to determine the scope of #OPISIS, it is thought to be one of Anonymous's largest operations to date.

ªAnonymous, 2015, http://pastebin.com/UWWyaPRX.

(DoD), though a variety of other agencies play supporting roles. Rather than examining the agencies, which are covered in chapter 5, the sections that follow focus on several security initiatives that have a direct impact on countering cyberterrorism and terrorism online.

Comprehensive National Cybersecurity Initiative

The Comprehensive National Cybersecurity Initiative (CNCI) was started by President George W. Bush in 2008 with Presidential Directive 54/ Homeland Security Presidential Directive 23. The initiative includes multiple agencies; DHS and other agencies work within its framework. The Cyberspace Policy Review initiated under President Barack Obama in 2009 updated the CNCI to help it evolve to meet the changing challenges presented by cyberterrorists and others who threaten the country. The CNCI has three major goals: establish a front line of defense against today's immediate threats, defend against the full spectrum of threats, and strengthen the future cybersecurity environment. To accomplish these goals, the CNCI identified 12 initiatives:

1. Manage the Federal Enterprise Network as a single network enterprise with trusted Internet connections.
2. Deploy an intrusion detection system of sensors across the Federal Enterprise.
3. Pursue deployment of intrusion preventions systems across the Federal Enterprise.
4. Coordinate and redirect research and development (R&D) efforts.
5. Connect current cyber ops centers to enhance situational awareness.
6. Develop and implement a government-wide cyber counterintelligence (CI) plan.
7. Increase the security of our classified networks.
8. Expand cyber education.

9. Define and develop enduring "leap-ahead" technology, strategies, and programs.
10. Define and develop enduring deterrence strategies and programs.
11. Develop a multi-pronged approach for global supply chain risk management.
12. Define the federal role for extending cybersecurity into critical infrastructure domains.

While clearly not only directed at cyberterrorism and online terrorist activities, the CNCI plays the coordinating role for the federal response to cyber issues, including cyberterrorism.

Cyberterrorism Defense Initiative
The Cyberterrorism Defense Initiative is a training program jointly run by the Federal Emergency Management Agency, which is part of DHS, and the University of Arkansas Criminal Justice Institute. The initiative is directed primarily at organizations that have a role in the nation's critical infrastructure. The program, which offers classes in comprehensive cyberterrorism defense and cyberterrorism first response, is unique in its explicit focus on cyberterrorism incidents. It clearly falls into the initiative to expand education in cyber issues under the CNCI.[36]

Department of Defense Cyber Strategy
The DoD has developed a cyber strategy to combat the threat of cyberattacks against the country or the department itself. It consists of four primary missions: build the capacity to conduct cyberspace operations; defend DoD networks; defend the homeland against significant cyber incidents; and, provide cyber support for military operations. To further these goals, the DoD has created a variety of response teams. As of this writing, there are 13 National Mission Teams, responsible for defending the United States against cyberattacks; 68 Cyber Protection Teams, responsible for protecting DoD networks; 27 Combat Mission Teams, which provide operations support to combatant commands; and 25 Support Teams that work with the Combat Mission and National Mission Teams.

While the cyber strategy is not explicitly focused on cyberterrorism, it clearly has a role to play in defending the United States against cyberattacks, including cyberterrorism carried out by substate actors for political purposes.[37]

Task Forces
The CNCI and the DoD cyber strategy represent larger-picture attempts to deal with cyberterrorism and the threat of terrorist groups operating

online, but a variety of task forces are also working on specific investigations. The National Cyber Investigative Joint Task Force (NCIJTF) was established under the auspices of the CNCI and developed to coordinate cyber threat investigations. Led by the FBI, the NCIJTF is designed to enhance collaboration among federal law enforcement and intelligence agencies. While not exclusively focused on cyberterrorism, cyberterrorism investigation and prevention are part of the NCIJTF's mission.

In addition to the nationally scoped NCIJTF, the FBI also participates with local partners with its Cyber Task Forces. Established in all 56 FBI field offices, the Cyber Task Forces are there to assist with cyber investigations and intelligence collection.[38]

International

While a great deal is being done at the national level, international partnerships have also developed specifically to address the threat of cyberterrorism and the use of the Internet by terrorists. The following sections examine several of these organizations and partnerships.

UN Working Group on Countering the Use of the Internet for Terrorist Purposes

While not involved directly in online counterterrorism or counter-cyberterrorism operations, the UN Working Group on Countering the Use of the Internet for Terrorist Purposes represents one of the widest-reaching coordination efforts among countries to combat terrorism online. According to the UN[39]:

> The Working Group aims to identify and bring together stakeholders and partners on the issue of abuse of the Internet for terrorist purposes, including through radicalization, recruitment, training, operational planning, fundraising and other means. In conjunction with Member States, the Working Group aims to explore ways in which terrorists use the Internet, quantify the threat that this poses and examine options for addressing it at national, regional and global levels, including what role the United Nations might play, without compromising human rights, fundamental values and the open nature of the Internet itself.

Even with the effort of the work group, it is extremely difficult to coordinate as not all countries are prepared to deal with online threats.[40] Addressing this lack of capacity is another one of the work group's goals, which will help countries fight terrorist use of the Internet in their own jurisdictions.

International Multilateral Partnership Against Cyber Threats

The International Multilateral Partnership Against Cyber Threats (IM-PACT) is a global partnership working in concert with the International Telecommunication Union to help improve cybersecurity for countries as well as for other actors in the international system. Formed as a private–public partnership, IMPACT's goal is to provide a space for collaboration not just among countries but also among private entities. Among IMPACT's partners are corporations that develop cybersecurity software like Symantec and Trend Lab.[41]

In addition to general collaboration, IMPACT also runs the Global Response Center (GRC), an advanced lab focused on helping to identify and deal with network threats. Modeled on the Centers for Disease Control and Prevention, the GRC helps to put technical measures in place to deal with real-time cybersecurity threats—including cyberterrorism incidents. Beyond the GRC, IMPACT also works to develop new research on cyber threats, including cyberterrorism, and provide training for countries and other entities dealing with a variety of online threats.[42]

Individual Country Efforts

Beyond partnerships, there are any number of individual efforts by countries around the world to combat cyberterrorism and terrorist use of the Internet. According to NATO, at least 60 countries have developed national strategies to deal with cyberterrorism and other cyber threats.[43] The Dutch counterterrorism strategy is perhaps exemplary in this regard[44]:

> The National Cyber Security Strategy (NCSS), which was submitted to the Dutch House of Representatives in February 2011, is an important resource in this respect [cyberterrorism]. The Dutch government wants this strategy to lead to more effective cooperation with other parties on security and reliability of an open and free digital society. Among other things the strategy provides for the setting up of a Cyber Security Council in which all the relevant parties at strategic levels can make agreements on the elaboration and implementation of the strategy. A National Cyber Security Centre is also to be set up to bring together expertise on threats and incidents and how to deal with them . . . although a threat can be a consequence of Internet use by terrorists, it is also the case that Internet can play a useful role in counterterrorism. After all it constitutes a powerful source of information for staying up-to-date on the activities and intentions of terrorist groups.

Conclusion

Cyberterrorism is a difficult topic, in part because of the difficulty of defining what cyberterrorism is. If taken to be the use of the Internet by subnational groups to create significant damage for political purposes, it seems to be a rare occurrence. If, on the other hand, it references any element of terrorism that uses the Internet to further its cause, cyberterrorism is rampant.

While it is unclear how much of a direct threat cyberterrorism poses, the continuing use of the Internet by terrorist organizations is troubling. Whether it is recruitment, propaganda, or planning or executing attacks online, terrorists' use of technology, specifically networked technology, is growing. Though there have been significant efforts to combat this from individuals, the U.S. government, and the international community, it is likely to remain a challenge for the foreseeable future. Additionally, with the increasing technical capability of some terrorist organizations, it is likely that we will face the increasing use of cyberterrorism to directly damage governments.

Review Questions

1. What is the main problem with defining terrorism? How does it relate to cyberterrorism?
2. How big a threat is cyberterrorism? Why is there so much focus on the topic?
3. How do terrorist groups use the Internet to further their goals?
4. What are some of the domestic efforts to combat terrorism online and cyberterrorism?
5. What actors are active in combating terrorism online?
6. What are some international efforts to combat terrorism online and cyberterrorism?

Key Terms

Cyberattack
Cyber Task Forces (CTF)
Cyberterrorism
Denial
Engagement
Execution
Financing
IMPACT
Intelligence collection
International Institute for Counterterrorism
National Cyber Investigative Joint Task Force (NCIJTF)
National Cybersecurity Initiative
National Strategy for Counterterrorism
Propaganda

Notes

1. Walter Lacquer, *The New Terrorism: Fanaticism and the Arms of Mass Destruction* (New York: Oxford University Press, 2000).

2. John Collins, "Terrorism," in *Collateral Language: A User's Guide to America's New War*, ed. John Collins and Ross Glover (New York: NYU Press, 2002); Al Jazeera, "Beirut Wants 'Terrorism' Defined," January 13, 2004, http://www.aljazeera.com/archive/2004/01/200841010738460226.html; Boaz Ganor, "Defining Terrorism: Is One Man's Terrorist Another Man's Freedom Fighter?," *Police Practice and Research* 3 (2002): 287–304.

3. Boaz Ganor, "Defining Terrorism."

4. Ben Saul, "Definition of 'Terrorism' in the UN Security Council: 1985–2004," *Chinese Journal of International Law* 4 (2005): 141–166; Alex Schmid, "Terrorism—The Definitional Problem," *Case Western Reserve Journal of International Law* 36 (2004): 375–419.

5. David S. Wall, "Cybercrime, Media and Insecurity: The Shaping of Public Perceptions of Cybercrime," *International Review of Law Computers and Technology* 22 (2008): 45–63.

6. Myriam D. Cavelty, *Cyber-security and Threat Politics: US Efforts to Secure the Information Age* (New York: Routledge, 2007).

7. Gabriel Weimann, *Cyberterrorism: How Real Is the Threat?*, United States Institute for Peace Special Report No. 119, 2004, http://www.usip.org/sites/default/files/sr119.pdf.

8. Gabriel Weimann, "Cyberterrorism: The Sum of All Fears?," *Studies in Conflict and Terrorism* 28 (2005): 129–149.

9. Dorothy E. Denning, "Statement of Dorothy E. Denning," May 23, 2000, http://ftp.fas.org/irp/congress/2000_hr/00-05-23denning.htm.

10. Dorothy E. Denning, "Activism, Hacktivism, and Cyberterrorism: The Internet as a Tool for Influencing Foreign Policy," *Networks and Netwars: The Future of Terror, Crime, and Militancy* 239 (2001): 288.

11. Eben Kaplan, *Backgrounder: Terrorists and the Internet*, Council on Foreign Relations, 2008, http://www.cfr.org/terrorism-and-technology/terrorists-internet/p10005.

12. Nick P. Walsh, "Syrian Jihadists Using Twitter to Recruit Foreign Fighters," CNN June 4, 2014, available at http://www.cnn.com/2014/06/03/world/meast/syria-defector-recruits-westerners/.

13. Michael Jacobson, "Terrorist Financing on the Internet," *Counterterrorism Center Sentinel* 2 (2009): 17–20.

14. United Nations Office on Drugs and Crime, *The Use of the Internet for Terrorist Purposes* (New York: United Nations, 2013).

15. Ibid.

16. Bruce Hoffman, "The Use of the Internet by Islamic Extremists. Testimony Presented to the House Permanent Select Committee on Intelligence," May 4, 2006, http://www.rand.org/content/dam/rand/pubs/testimonies/2006/RAND_CT262-1.pdf.

17. United Nations Office on Drugs and Crime, *The Use of the Internet for Terrorist Purposes*.

18. Tim Fernholz, "Terrorism Finance Trackers Worry ISIS Already Using Bitcoin," *Defense One*, 2015, http://www.defenseone.com/threats/2015/02/terrorism-finance-trackers-worry-isis-already-using-bitcoin/105345/.

19. Joseph Dana, "The Jihadi Gift Shop," *Slate*, August 8, 2014, http://www.slate.com/articles/news_and_politics/roads/2014/08/need_an_isis_hoodie_the_world_s_most_notorious_terrorist_group_has_a_gift.html.

20. United Nations Office on Drugs and Crime, *The Use of the Internet for Terrorist Purposes*.

21. Maura Conway, "Terrorist 'Use' of the Internet and Fighting Back," *Information & Security* 19 (2006): 12–14; David Gilbert, "Anonymous #OpIsis: Hacktivists Publish How-to Guide for Identifying Islamic State Accounts on Twitter," *International Business Times*, April 14, 2015, http://www.ibtimes.co.uk/anonymous-opisis-hacktivists-publish-how-guide-identifying-islamic-state-twitter-accounts-1496378.

22. United Nations Office on Drugs and Crime, *The Use of the Internet for Terrorist Purposes*.

23. Ibid.

24. Dorothy E. Denning, "Terror's Web: How the Internet Is Transforming Terrorism," in *Handbook of Internet Crime*, ed. Yvonne Jewkes and Majid Yar (Portland, OR: Willan Publishing, 2009), 194–213.

25. White House, "National Strategy for Counterterrorism," 2011, https://www.whitehouse.gov/sites/default/files/counterterrorism_strategy.pdf.

26. Dorothy E. Denning, "Terror's Web."

27. Wesley Yang, "The Terrorist Search Engine," *New York Magazine*, December 2010, http://nymag.com/news/features/69920/.

28. Dorothy E. Denning, "Terror's Web."

29. Ibid.

30. Blane Harden, "In Montana, Casting a Web for Terrorists," *Washington Post*, June 4, 2006, http://www.washingtonpost.com/wp-dyn/content/article/2006/06/03/AR2006060300530.html.

31. Anonymous [Rita Katz], *Terrorist Hunter: The Extraordinary Story of a Woman Who Went Undercover to Infiltrate the Radical Islamic Groups Operating in America* (New York: Ecco, 2003).

32. Harden, "In Montana, Casting a Web for Terrorists."

33. CITE Monitoring, "Services," 2015, http://ent.siteintelgroup.com/Corporate/services.html.

34. International Institute for Counter-Terrorism, "Cyber Desk," 2015, http://www.ict.org.il/Articles.aspx?WordID=99.

35. John W. Brennan, *United States Counter Terrorism, Cyber Law and Policy, Enabling or Disabling?* (Carlisle, PA: US Army War College, 2012), http://nsfp.web.unc.edu/files/2012/09/Brennan_UNITED-STATES-COUNTER-TERRORISM-CYBER-LAW-AND-POLICY.pdf.

36. "Cyberterrorism Defense Initiative," FEMA, http://cyberterrorismcenter.org/index.html.

37. Department of Defense, "Cyber Strategy," 2015, http://www.defense.gov/home/features/2015/0415_cyber-strategy/.

38. Steven R. Chabinsky, "Statement Before the Senate Judiciary Committee, Subcommittee on Terrorism and Homeland Security, Washington, DC," November 17, 2009, http://www.fbi.gov/news/testimony/preventing-terrorist-attacks-and-protecting-privacy-rights-in-cyberspace.

39. United Nations, "Working Group on Countering the Use of the Internet for Terrorist Purposes," 2015, http://www.un.org/en/terrorism/ctitf/wg_countering internet.shtml.

40. United Nations, "Counterterrorism Strategy," 2006, http://www.un.org/en/terrorism/strategy-counter-terrorism.shtml.

41. IMPACT, "Mission & Vision," 2015, http://www.impact-alliance.org/services/grc-introduction.html.

42. IMPACT, "Services and Solutions Offered: GDC," 2015, http://www.impact-alliance.org/services/grc-introduction.html.

43. NATO, "Cyber Security Strategy Documents," 2015, https://ccdcoe.org/strategies-policies.html.

44. The Netherlands, *National Counterterrorism Strategy 2011-2015,* https://english.nctv.nl/Images/nationale-ct-strategie-2011-2015-uk_tcm92-369807.pdf.

CHAPTER EIGHT

Cyberwar

Introduction

AS WITH CYBERTERRORISM, AND CYBERCRIME MORE GENERALLY, there is a lot of confusion surrounding the term "cyberwar." Some have argued that it does not exist, except as an extension of regular warfare; others have argued that is it the future of all warfare. More recently, with the conflict between Russia and Georgia involving extensive use of cyberattacks, the conversation around cyberwar has shifted into how we can best prepare for this type of conflict in the future. This chapter explores the concept of cyberwar, first by examining different approaches to the topic. It then moves to the different types of cyberwar and the advent of netwar. Finally, it looks at several recent instances of cyberwar, particularly the conflict between Russia and Georgia, and attempts to draw some conclusions about what cyberwar will mean in the future.

Cyberwar or Just More War?

As with all things "cyber," the terminology surrounding the concept of cyberwar is contested. But even more than the terminology, the idea of what constitutes cyberwar is one that has been recently rekindled. Though the term has been used since at least 1993,[1] whether or not cyberwar constitutes a separate, new phenomenon, or simply the movement of generalized warfare to a different battlefield, is unclear. Both positions are discussed in this section.

Cyberwar Is a New Phenomenon

Among the first proponents of the concept of cyberwar were John Arquilla and David Ronfeldt. In their landmark article "Cyberwar is Coming!"

they suggest that cyberwar would fundamentally alter the paradigm of warfare[2]:

> We anticipate that cyberwar, like war in Clausewitz's view, may be a "chameleon." It will be adaptable to varying contexts; it will not represent or impose a single, structured approach. Cyberwar may be fought offensively and defensively, at the strategic or tactical levels. It will span the gamut of intensity—from conflicts waged by heavy mechanized forces across wide theaters, to counterinsurgencies where "the mobility of the boot" may be the prime means of maneuver.

Arquilla and Rondfeldt see cyberwar as a major break from past methods of warfare. Even the battlefield, they argue, changes meaning in the face of cyberwar, as do the ideas of attack and defeat.

Although Arquilla and Rondfeldt's article was published in 1993, many proponents still argue that cyberwar is in fact a new type of warfare. Most of these arguments are based on elements like the increasing tie-ins between civilian and military networks or the unmapped terrain of the Internet as battlefield. Charles Schneier, a fellow at Harvard's Berkman Center and board member of the Electronic Frontier Foundation, listed 10 elements that make cyberwar unique:

- The Internet is an artificial environment that can be shaped in part according to national security requirements.
- The blinding proliferation of technology and hacker tools makes it impossible to be familiar with all of them.
- The proximity of adversaries is determined by connectivity and bandwidth, not terrestrial geography.
- Software updates and network reconfigurations change cyberbattle space unpredictably and without warning.
- Contrary to our historical understanding of war, cyberconflict favors the attacker.
- Cyberattacks are flexible enough to be effective for propaganda, espionage, and the destruction of critical infrastructure.
- The difficulty of obtaining reliable cyberattack attribution lessens the credibility of deterrence, prosecution, and retaliation.
- The "quiet" nature of cyberconflict means a significant battle could take place with only the direct participants knowing about it.
- The dearth of expertise and evidence can make victory, defeat, and battle damage a highly subjective undertaking.
- There are few moral inhibitions to cyberattacks, because they relate primarily to the use and abuse of data and computer code. So far, there is little perceived human suffering.[3]

Cyberwar Is NOT War

One of the interesting elements of the conversation about whether cyberwar is unique, is the idea that perhaps cyberwar, as popularly conceived, is not actually a war at all. Thomas Rid, in his book *Cyber War Will Not Take Place*, argues that because cyberwar is unlikely to result in casualties, it is not properly termed warfare at all.[4] Rather, the various attacks should be called what they are: vandalism, espionage, or subversion. By framing it this way, Rid hopes to move the debate away from the military sphere, which he believes is causing undue risk for warfare to actually arise because of cyberattacks—because if we term them war, then when they happen we are engaged in warfare.

In any event, it should be noted that Rid does not downplay the risk of cyberattacks. He emphasizes that the difference between the cyberattacks we have experienced and those that many suggest might happen means we have to make sure we have appropriate security in place. However, Rid holds that terming the attacks "cyberwar" ultimately presents more of a risk than the attacks themselves. What is perhaps most interesting about this approach is the fact that it highlights the novelty of cyberwar, whether or not we term it that.[5]

Cyberwar Is Just More War

While everyone agrees that cyberwar presents novel challenges, not everyone agrees that cyberwar is actually a truly new phenomenon. Erik Gartzke argues in "The Myth of Cyberwar" that though cyberwar presents no new individual threats, this is no different in many respects from a new kind of weapon being introduced to war.[6] This is important because, despite the novelty of the weapon, the objectives of war have not changed. Moreover, the fact that cyberwar has novel elements, some that can be destructive, in no way suggests that it will supplant physical warfare as currently experienced.

This view has significant implications for perspectives on cyberwar because while it does not downplay the necessity to look at cyber operations as an element of warfare, it does suggest that moving completely to focus on cyberwar to the detriment of other modes of war would be a profound mistake.

Another way to evaluate how cyberwar is connected to modern warfare is to look at the so-called domains of warfare. Traditionally, these are air, land, sea, and space. The U.S. military now sees cyberwar as the fifth domain of warfare[7] and has set up the United States Cyber Command (USCYBERCOM) as a subdivision of U.S. Strategic Command with specific supervision over cyber operations. Approaching cyberwar as a fifth domain emphasizes its links to other forms of warfare and reemphasizes the fact that cyberwar cannot supplant normal warfare.

What Is Cyberwar?

Given that there is quite a bit of debate about how cyberwar should be treated and the domain of the Internet as a battlefield, it is important to ask: What actually constitutes cyberwar? One definition, offered by the RAND Corporation, states that cyberwar is "the actions by a nation-state or international organization to attack and attempt to damage another nation's computers or information networks through, for example, computer viruses or denial-of-service attacks."[8] Another definition suggests that cyberwar is limited to attacks that cause physical destruction.

While the adoption of a specific definition seems like semantics, it is perhaps more important when it comes to cyberwar than any other cyber issue. This is because there are significant implications if a country engages in what is considered cyberwar. If, for instance, attacks from China against the United States were classified as an act of cyberwar, there are a variety of possible repercussions, all of which have significant impacts in the physical world. One particularly bad outcome could be the invocation of Article 5 of the NATO Charter, which could involve a significant part of Europe in a war with China, along with the United States.[9]

Another significant problem with the term "cyberwar" is the application of the laws of war in an online environment. Ideas like damage, sovereignty, combatants, and, perhaps more importantly, proportionality are unclear when it comes to cyberwarfare, making the application of the laws difficult.[10]

Because there are such problematic elements when it comes to defining cyberwar, many countries and international organizations, including NATO, have been reluctant to do so.[11] For the purposes of this chapter, cyberwar is an act of violence or sabotage committed by a nation-state for political or military purposes, primarily, though not exclusively, in the context of regular warfare. There are at least three levels of cyberwar, which are discussed in the next section.

Kinds and Levels of Cyberwar

Despite the fact that cyberwar is unlikely to supersede traditional warfare, that does not mean it is not essential to combat. One way to examine

Box 8.1   The Sum of All Fears

While we have yet to experience a large cyber event in the United States, it does not mean that fears of such an event occurring are unfounded. One of the best articulations of a worst-case scenario is in the book *Cyber War: The Next Threat to National Security and What to Do about It* by Richard Clarke and Robert Knake. They describe a scenario where multiple systems of infrastructure are attacked at once by an unknown adversary, leading to a great deal of chaos and likely thousands of deaths. In the scenario, you are a White House official:

> Unaware of what is happening across the river at the Pentagon, the Undersecretary of Homeland Security has called the White House, urgently needing to speak to you. FEMA, the Federal Emergency Management Agency, has told him that two of its regional offices, in Philadelphia and in Denton, Texas, have reported large refinery fires and explosions in Philadelphia and Houston, as well as lethal clouds of chlorine gas being released from several chemical plants in New Jersey and Delaware. He adds that the U.S. Computer Emergency Response Team in Pittsburgh is being deluged with reports of systems failing, but he hasn't had time to get the details yet.
>
> Before you can ask the Senior Duty Officer where the President is, another officer thrusts a phone at you. It's the Deputy Secretary of Transportation. "Are we under attack?" she asks. When you ask why, she ticks off what has happened. The Federal Aviation Administration's National Air Traffic Control Center in Herndon, Virginia, has experienced a total collapse of its systems. The alternate center in Leesburg is in a complete panic because it and several other regional centers cannot see what aircraft are aloft and are trying to manually identify and separate hundreds of aircraft. Brickyard, the Indianapolis Center, has already reported a midair collision of two 737s. "I thought it was just an FAA crisis, but then the train wrecks started happening . . ." she explains. The Federal Railroad Administration has been told of major freight derailments in Long Beach, Norfolk, Chicago, and Kansas City.[a]

The authors go on to describe other problems being experienced, including attacks on the Federal Reserve Bank, public rail systems, and the White House itself.

While this scenario is certainly extreme, individual components are no doubt possible. Indeed, in the book Clarke and Knake go on to discuss many known vulnerabilities that we face today, including back doors China installed in software the United States purchased from them for our power grid.

Despite this threat, however, many believe Clarke and Knake's scenario is unlikely. There are good reasons adversaries would not wish to attack our networks to the extent illustrated—particularly because they also benefit from the same networks. Nonetheless, Clarke and Knake argue that unless we beef up our security in the near future, scenarios like this one may become a reality.

[a]Richard A. Clarke and Robert Knake, *Cyber War: The Next Threat to National Security and What to Do about It* (New York: HarperCollins. Kindle Edition, 2010), 65.

how to combat cyberwar is by looking at the different ways cyberwarfare can be carried out. Shimeall and colleagues argue that there are three levels of cyberwar, each of which has its own obstacles to combat: cyberwar as an adjunct to military operations, limited cyberwar, and unrestricted cyberwar.[12]

Cyberwar as an Adjunct to Military Operations

In the context of modern warfare, controlling information or interfering with your adversary's available information can be decisive. While there are many ways to achieve information superiority or dominance in the context of battle, some methods of cyberattack can provide an advantage. Just as a missile can destroy radar or make other battlefield elements inoperable, cyberattacks can provide the same type of denial of capability. As an adjunct to military operations, this type of cyberwar focuses nearly exclusively on military targets or the systems related most directly to supporting them.

There is a sense that, in some ways, this kind of cyberwar can function as a great equalizer on the battlefield between nations. This is because information dominance does not require the same kind of investment as dominance in one of the other domains of battle (e.g., air superiority). Thus, in terms of information dominance, smaller countries can compete with countries with much larger military apparatus. This has spurred smaller countries, especially those with less reliance on networked interactions, to view information-based attacks as a potential method to compete with more conventionally dominant militaries.

Limited Cyberwar

Limited cyberwar is focused on the actual network connections and processes, rather than any physical consequences from those actions. In other words, degrading information capabilities is the goal, not necessarily achieving the equipment inoperability that is the goal of cyberwar as an adjunct to military operations. In short, the information infrastructure is the only target of attacks—all of which are based on the information infrastructure itself.

This kind of attack can be accomplished by a variety of methods. Large-scale denial-of-service attacks or malware installed directly to an adversary's network could decrease the level of service and force an enemy into alternative means of operations—perhaps exposing additional vulnerabilities. According to Shimeall and colleagues, this could "force the enemy to question the quality of information available to make decisions. . .the infrastructure could be perverted to attack itself—either via the implantation of multiple pieces of malicious software, or via deliberate actions that exploit weakness."[13]

This type of cyberwar has many applications. While limited warfare could easily be used as part of a campaign adjunct to military operations, a limited cyberwar could also have economic impacts. Moreover, if done during a tense period of time between nations, a limited cyberwar could have significant diplomatic repercussions.

Unrestricted Cyberwar

Unlike cyberwar in support of military operations or limited cyberwar, unrestricted cyberwar draws no distinction between civilian targets and battlefields. Moreover, and perhaps the most distinguishing characteristic, is that unrestricted cyberwar will have physical consequences—including casualties. While these could be caused by a variety of cyberattacks, tactics like direct assaults on energy infrastructure and secondary targets like the air-traffic control system are likely among them. In particular, a nation's critical infrastructure would almost certainly be the focus of many attacks.[14]

Perhaps even more damaging than the physical destruction potentially caused by unrestricted cyberwar is the economic damage. Because there is no distinction between civilian and military targets in this type of cyberwar, there is a high potential for attacks that are specifically designed to hurt the economic community of the country attacked. This, coupled with the potential physical impact of attacks against infrastructure, give an idea of the potential this kind of cyberwar has for impacting a country.

In fact, this type of unrestricted cyberwar has been termed a "Digital Pearl Harbor."[15] The implications in using this terminology are clear. Not only would an unrestricted cyberwar have devastating consequences in terms of civilian and military contexts, but it would also likely come as a surprise.

The World's First Cyberwars?

The United States has not faced cyberwar of the kinds mentioned, though it does regularly face cyberattacks from both nation-state and non-state actors (upward of 70,000 a year, in fact),[16] but that does not mean cyberwars have been absent from the world stage. In particular, situations arising while Estonia and Georgia were fighting with Russia have raised the profile of cyberwar in recent years.[17] While the attacks have never been conclusively determined to be the work of the Russian government, it is widely believed that while the *mafiya* or other non-state groups carried out the attacks, they were under the direction of the Russian government, or at the very least received tacit approval.[18] In the following sections, the situations in Estonia and Georgia are detailed.

Estonia and Russia: 2007

In April 2007, the Estonian government made a controversial decision to move a large, Soviet-era statue known as the *Bronze Soldier of Tallinn*. In particular, Estonia's Russian residents were upset about the move, as was the Russian government. The government also planned to relocate some war graves.[19]

On April 27, in the midst of this debate, a large-scale cyberattack was launched against Estonian interests. The attack lasted for over three weeks. The variety of targets ranged from Estonian nationalist party websites to the country's financial websites. Though there is some disagreement about the nature of the attacks, they had wide-reaching, though generally low-impact, effects on Estonia's digital capabilities. In particular, part of Estonia's banking system was shut down during the attacks, impacting the country financially. Other targets included the telecommunications infrastructure and government websites.[20]

The attacks against Estonia were of various types. Large-scale distributed denial-of-service attacks, likely done with rented botnets, were used to prevent access to sites all over the country. In addition to the access prevention, some websites were specifically defaced by those opposing the move of the statue.[21]

There have been a series of investigations into the attack on Estonia, because it represents one possible manifestation of cyberwarfare. NATO, of which Estonia is a member, was concerned enough to create a Cooperative Cyber Defense Center of Excellence in the country after the conflict, and a number of military scenarios have been based on the attacks on Estonia.[22] The criminal investigation into the attacks was stymied by the Russian authorities, who claim that the investigation was not covered under a mutual aid treaty with Estonia.[23] Russia has claimed that it had nothing to do with the attacks against Estonia.

The cyber conflict between Estonia and Russia represents a type of limited cyberwar that could become more common in the future. In particular, the use of non-state organizations that carry out state-oriented goals could increase. While the attacks against Estonia were problematic, they were small, considering the potential impact of cyberwar on a country.

Georgia and Russia: 2008

While the attacks against Estonia were, in many respects, just larger-scale versions of the types of attacks generally experienced by governments daily, the conflict between Georgia and Russia in 2008 was different on several levels.[24] Not only were the attacks more significant, but, more importantly, they were coordinated with a military campaign by the Russian government. This coordination, and the resulting issues it caused for Georgia in terms of its national defense, represent the first time a cyberwar was engaged parallel to a physical military operation.[25]

In fact, the cyberattacks against Georgia preceded the invasion of the southern part of the country by three weeks. By the time the ground invasion came, it was difficult for Georgian citizens to access websites, and those that could be accessed could often not be trusted because of the Russian information operations. As in Estonia, multiple sectors were affected by the cyberattacks. Financial, military, and government sites were inoperable or defaced. There were also information intrusions that may have allowed Russian forces to gather military intelligence.[26]

The cyberwar was unique in another way. Not only did it precede and occur alongside Russian military attacks, but there was a concerted effort to undermine Georgian hackers prior to the cyberattack.[27] Specifically, a well-known Georgian hacker website was attacked before the start of the cyber offensive. The attack, however, was not completely successful, as Georgian hackers launched a limited response during the course of the conflict.

As with the attacks against Estonia, there is no conclusive proof that the Russian government was involved. However, because of the coordination between physical and cyberattacks during the conflict with Georgia, it is very unlikely that the Russian government was not involved. Moreover, the strategy carried out by those engaging in the cyberattacks mirrored the Russian strategy overall. They hit websites that were problematic for Georgian citizens but none that directly affected the infrastructure of the country—though those attacking made it clear that they could target infrastructure if necessary. This same approach was taken by the Russian physical military operations, particularly in regards to Georgia's oil resources.

In many respects, the cyberwar between Russia and Georgia represents cyberwar as an adjunct to military operations, though it did target civilian websites and servers. The elements that this cyberwar demonstrated indicates the problems that can be faced when dealing with a combined physical and cyberattack. While those involved in the attacks refrained from targeting critical infrastructure, the capability of doing so was apparent,[28] and thus the conflict represents a paradigm shift for dealing with warfare, physical or otherwise, in the future.

Titan Rain

Though the United States has not been directly involved in a cyberwar in the same way as the two previous examples, that does not mean it has not been targeted by other nation-states in the context of the Internet. In particular, the United States has been regularly targeted by what is thought to be elements of the Chinese government—though to what extent they are directly involved is unclear. The most well-known cases of cyberattack against the United States is perhaps what has come to be known as Titan Rain.

Titan Rain was not a single attack but a set of attacks carried out between 2003 and 2005 (though some elements of the attack may have started before or continued after those dates). The attack is considered part of an advanced persistent threat or a targeted attack that takes place covertly over a long period of time. The goal of Titan Rain seems to have been to gather sensitive information on individuals and government programs. To date, the attacks have not been considered destructive but are more closely linked to espionage.

While the government is often the target of hackers, who are mostly trying to expose vulnerabilities for sport, Titan Rain was unique in the persistent nature and advanced level of those engaging in the hacking. Because of these elements, in addition to the fact that much of what was taken aligned with Chinese interests, the attacks are thought to have been directed, and perhaps even carried out, by the Chinese military. However, as in other cases of cyberwar, there is no conclusive proof that the attacks were government directed.

Though Titan Rain ostensibly ended in 2005 or 2006, there have been ongoing allegations of Chinese government–led hacking of U.S. systems, often causing friction between the Chinese and U.S. governments. Most recently, in June 2015, President Obama announced that there was a breach of security within the Office of Personnel Management, leading to the exposure of the personal information of at least 4 million current and former government workers. Among the data hacked was the SF-86 forms of those workers, which contains most of the information required to gain a security clearance.

While China seems to be leading the way in terms of potential adversaries with a significant cyber capability, other countries have also attempted to develop them. Russia clearly has some capabilities, but India and China both have seemingly greater ability to engage in cyberwar. Given the recent unstable relationships with countries around these nations, it is clear that cyberwar could present an ongoing challenge, not just for the United States but also for countries around the world.

Why No Cyberwar?

Given that cyberwar is generally inexpensive compared with more mechanized forms of warfare, and given that there seems to be a general utility in performing cyber operations, it is important to ask why we have not seen more cyberwar. Three reasons in particular, are important to understand.

The Reluctance to Use the Term

One reason we have not seen more cyberwarfare is the reluctance to use the term. There are several reasons for this reluctance. First, by calling it warfare, the action is placed squarely in the hands of the military. While the military is, in many ways, best equipped to deal with the threat of cyberwar, there are elements that should be handled by law enforcement or the Department of Homeland Security, both of which become secondary actors when the term cyberwar is invoked.

In addition to the change in actors, by using the term cyberwar a significant number of other issues arise. As mentioned earlier in this chapter, the idea of cyberwar can invoke treaty obligations and other elements with potentially unforeseen consequences. Because of this, other cyber terms have proliferated. In short, we may experience what could be considered cyberwar regularly, but we may not be terming it such.

Infrastructure Security

Behind much of the talk of cyberwar is the assumption that civilian and private infrastructure, and even in some cases governmental infrastructure, has the same level of connectivity and protection that critical infrastructure does. While it is understandable to make this assumption, upon evaluation it is generally false. James Lewis, a scholar with the Center for Strategic and International Studies, said:

> Computer network vulnerabilities are an increasingly serious business problem but their threat to national security is overstated. Modern industrial societies are more robust than they appear at first glance. Critical infrastructures, especially in large market economies, are more distributed, diverse, redundant and self-healing than a cursory assessment may suggest, rendering them less vulnerable to attack. In all cases, cyberattacks are less effective and less disruptive than physical attacks. Their only advantage is that they are cheaper and easier to carry out than a physical attack.[29] (p. 2)

Lewis wrote this in 2002, but it still holds true. Thus far cyberattacks, and in particular cyberwar, have been a more significant problem for private than public interests. This is even true with attacks that are thought to originate from other nation-states. The recent hack from North Korea in response to the movie *The Interview* is a case in point.[30]

Limited Strategic Effectiveness

A final reason why the United States may not have experienced cyberwar is because of the preparations the nation has made in regards to its cybersecurity. While certainly remaining vulnerable, as the recent exposure of private information shows, it is possible that the networks to which adversaries would need access are increasingly resilient. Though it is never possible to win the game against cyber adversaries in terms of completely securing a system from attack, the more secure a system, the more difficult it is to create widespread damage, even if the network is breached.

This means that successfully engaging in a cyberwar, specifically a limited cyberwar, may not serve much purpose for most governments. While it can certainly provide an annoyance, and in some cases my yield short-term benefits for the attacker, there is little chance that a cyberwar would cause enough damage to politically alter the landscape of the country being attacked. This has a dampening effect on cyberwar because the primary reason sates engage in warfare at all is to change the political elements in the losing nation.[31]

Fighting Cyberwar

One of the difficulties a country faces in fighting against cyberwar is that it is often difficult to know who is attacking. Compounding this difficulty is the fact that if an attack is being successfully carried out (depending on the extent and the systems affected), the attack itself can cripple the country's investigative ability for the time that the attack is underway. Because of this, many nations, including the United States, have tried to prepare for all three levels of cyberwar mentioned earlier.

Within the United States, the organization primarily responsible for cyberwarfare is USCYBERCOM. One of the sub-combatant commands under the United States Strategic Command, USCYBERCOM is tasked with defending the nation's military infrastructure and systems from attack. Following is USCYBERCOM's mission statement[32]:

> USCYBERCOM plans, coordinates, integrates, synchronizes and conducts activities to: direct the operations and defense of specified Department of Defense information networks and; prepare to, and when directed, conduct full spectrum military cyberspace operations in order to enable actions in all domains, ensure US/Allied freedom of action in cyberspace and deny the same to our adversaries.

What is perhaps most important about USCYBERCOM, as well as the increasing capability within intelligence agencies, is its ability to engage in offensive actions. In the year 2011, for instance, the United States engaged in at least 231 offensive cyber operations, most of which were aimed toward Iran, North Korea, and other countries the United States considers significant problems. The original release of this information came from Edward Snowden, but the National Security Agency (NSA) has acknowledged that the United States engages in offensive operations in cyberspace, though specifics are seldom released. It should be noted that the head of USCYBERCOM is also the director of the NSA, linking those organizations' operations closely together.

Perhaps the best known offensive attack that the United States has engaged in was the Stuxnet attack, which disabled centrifuges in an Iranian nuclear enrichment facility, setting back their nuclear weapons program significantly. Though the United States has never acknowledged that it developed the worm, it is widely attributed to a joint development effort between the United States and Israel.

Conclusion

While there are still many debates surrounding cyberwarfare, it is clear that it represents a significant challenge for the United States and other countries. With the increasing instances of cyberattacks, cyberespionage, and other network-based events, cyberwar has become a part of nations' military planning. The cyberwars in Estonia and Georgia were limited, but they could represent the leading edge of a significant change in the ways wars are fought. Including a fifth domain of war, the Internet, one that touches all of the others, making information and cybersecurity more important than ever.

To that effect, the United States has instituted a new sub-combatant command, USCYBERCOM. That organization, along with the intelligence agencies and the DHS, represent both the best defense the United States has against cyberwarfare as well as an offensive cyber capability that is being increasingly used. Through operations like Stuxnet, as well as others that remain classified, the United States is trying to move its military supremacy in the physical world to the online world. With this shift, it is hoped that there can be a deterrent effect, much like nuclear deterrence, keeping unrestricted cyberwar from happening.

Review Questions

1. What are the problems with defining cyberwar?
2. What are the implications if a nation gets involved in a cyberwar?
3. What was unique about the alleged 2008 cyberwar between Russia and Georgia?
4. Why have we not seen more extensive cyberwar against the United States?
5. What are the different kinds of cyberwar and what makes each kind unique?

Key Terms

Cyberwar
Cyberwar as an adjunct to military operations

Notes

1. John Arquilla and David Ronfeldt, "Cyberwar Is Coming!," *Comparative Strategy* 12 (1993): 141–165.

2. Ibid.

3. Bruce Schneier, "The Nature of Cyberwar," January 30, 2012, https://www.schneier.com/blog/archives/2012/01/the_nature_of_c.html.

4. Thomas Rid, *The Cyber War Will Not Take Place* (Oxford: Oxford University Press, 2013).

5. Gal Beckerman, "Is Cyberwar Really Real?," *Boston Globe Online*, September 15, 2013, https://www.bostonglobe.com/ideas/2013/09/15/cyberwar-really-war/4lffEBgkf50GjqvmV1HlsO/story.html.

6. Erik Gartzke, "The Myth of Cyberwar: Bringing War in Cyberspace Back Down to Earth," *International Security* 38 (2013): 41–73.

7. "War in the Fifth Domain," *The Economist*, June 2, 2010, http://www.economist.com/node/16478792.

8. RAND, "Cyber Warfare," 2015, http://www.rand.org/topics/cyber-warfare.html.

9. NATO, "Wales Summit Declaration," September 5, 2014, http://www.nato.int/cps/en/natohq/official_texts_112964.htm.

10. James A. Lewis, "A Note on the Laws of War in Cyberspace," Center for Strategic and International Studies, April 25, 2010, http://csis.org/files/publication/100425_Laws%20of%20War%20Applicable%20to%20Cyber%20Conflict.pdf.

11. Murray Brewster, "NATO Struggles to Define Collective Defense in the Age of Cyberwarfare," September 2, 2014, http://www.cbc.ca/news/politics/nato-struggles-to-define-collective-defence-in-the-age-of-cyberwarfare-1.2753382.

12. Timothy Shimeall, Phil Williams, and Casey Dunlevy, "Countering Cyber War," *NATO Review* 49 (2010): 16–18.

13. Ibid.

14. Ibid.

15. James A. Lewis, "Cybersecurity and Digital Infrastructure Protection," Center for Strategic and International Studies, 2006, http://csis.org/files/media/csis/pubs/0601_cscip_preliminary.pdf.

16. Office of Management and Budget, *Annual Report to Congress: Federal Information Security Act*, 2015, https://www.whitehouse.gov/sites/default/files/omb/assets/egov_docs/final_fy14_fisma_report_02_27_2015.pdf.

17. David Hollis, "Cyberwar Case Study: Georgia 2008," *Small Wars Journal*, January 6, 2011, http://smallwarsjournal.com/blog/journal/docs-temp/639-hollis .pdf.

18. J. Richards, "Denial-of-Service: The Estonian Cyberwar and Its Implications for US National Security," *International Affairs Review* 18 (2009), http://www .iar-gwu.org/node/65.

19. Ian Traynor, "Russia Accused of Unleashing Cyberwar to Disable Estonia," *The Guardian Online*, May 16, 2007, http://www.theguardian.com/world/2007 /may/17/topstories3.russia.

20. Hollis, "Cyberwar Case Study: Georgia 2008."

21. Richards, "Denial-of-Service."

22. NATO, "About Cyber Defense Center," 2015, https://ccdcoe.org/about-us .html.

23. Eneken Tikk and Kadri Kaska, "Legal Cooperation to Investigate Cyber Incidents: Estonian Case Study and Lessons," *Proceedings of the European Conference on Information Warfare*, 2010, 288.

24. David J. Smith, "Russian Cyber Strategy and the War against Georgia," *Infocus Quarterly*, January 17, 2014, http://www.atlanticcouncil.org/blogs/natosource /russian-cyber-policy-and-the-war-against-georgia.

25. John Markoff, "Before the Gunfire, Cyberattacks," *New York Times*, August 12, 2008, http://www.nytimes.com/2008/08/13/technology/13cyber.html.

26. Hollis, "Cyberwar Case Study: Georgia 2008."

27. Ibid.

28. Ibid.

29. Lewis, "Cybersecurity and Digital Infrastructure Protection."

30. FBI National Press Office, "Update on Sony Investigations," December 19, 2014, https://www.fbi.gov/news/pressrel/press-releases/update-on-sony-investi gation.

31. Martin Libicki, *Cyberdefense and Cyberwar* (Santa Monica, CA: RAND, 2009).

32. U.S. Department of Defense, "Cyber Command Fact Sheet," May 21, 2010.

CHAPTER NINE

Domestic Response

Introduction

IN RESPONSE TO THE GROWING PROBLEM OF CYBERCRIMES, the federal government (the president and Congress) and state officials have passed laws that define new crimes and punishments associated with those actions. The laws are also designed for other functions: to deter people from committing those crimes in the future and to mitigate the possible harmful effects of these offenses. This chapter will describe domestic actions being taken regarding cybercrime. It will describe what different presidents have said in their speeches about cybercrimes as well as the different laws proposed or passed by members of Congress. A description of state-level legislation is then provided.

Presidents and Cybercrime

Presidents sometimes discuss issues in their speeches as a way to bring attention to a particular problem or to tell the public how they will address that problem. This is true of cybercrime. Recent presidents have mentioned cybercrime in their public rhetoric to inform people about the dangers and to propose solutions. Because cybercrime was still an emerging phenomenon, it was not an issue mentioned by presidents until Democrat Bill Clinton came into office. He discussed options for controlling cybercrime and even signed legislation that defined acts of cybercrime as criminal. Presidents George W. Bush and Barack Obama have each considered cybercrime, too. The actions of each president are outlined in the following sections.

Bill Clinton

President Bill Clinton realized that the federal government had to work alongside private agencies and businesses to effectively control cybercrime.

Box 9.1   Cybercrime and the Politics of Fear

Presidents spend a good deal of their time speaking, through speeches, responses to questions from reporters, and other methods of addressing the public. While it often seems like this is wasted effort, research has shown that what the president says matters. This is as true for areas of crime policy as it is for other issues the government deals with.

In recent years, presidents have begun to speak about the problems presented by cybercrime. Beginning with President Clinton, they have addressed specific problems, including online child pornography, the availability of weapons designs, and cyberterrorism. Speeches have often focused on these issues in an attempt to help the public understand the complex issues but have sometimes been necessitated in response to breaches of government data.

However, there is another reason presidents talk about cybercrime, and it influences *how* they speak about it. Because cybercrime, along with issues like terrorism and national security, are complex and frightening, presidents have used the opportunity to further security agendas based on these speeches. Called the *politics of fear*, this approach allows executive agencies to gain support for programs that might otherwise be rejected by the public.

Thus, when you listen to the president speak about cybercrime, pay attention to what he says surrounding the issue. Is the speech really about cybercrime, or is there more to it, like issues of national security? If so, it might be that the president is trying to link those together to create a situation for more policy action.

In May 1998, he asked government agencies to cooperate with businesses in order to better secure the country's infrastructure, as most of that is privately owned and operated. That same year, he appointed a national coordinator for security, infrastructure protection and counterterrorism. This person would oversee the federal effort in fighting cybercrime, terrorism, and related issues.[1]

In 1999, Clinton established a working group that was given the task of providing an analysis of legal and policy issues surrounding those who use the Internet to commit crimes.[2] The working group's final report, *The Electronic Frontier: The Challenge of Unlawful Conduct Involving the Use of the*

Internet, was published in March 2000. The report recommended three approaches for addressing unlawful conduct on the Internet[3]:

1. Online conduct should be treated legally in a way that is consistent with the way off-line conduct is treated, and in a way that other concerns such as privacy and protection of civil liberties are handled.
2. The needs of law enforcement that are posed by the Internet should be recognized. Law enforcement agencies are in need of increased resources, training, and new investigative tools. There is also a need for coordination of efforts between federal, state and local law enforcement, as well as international agencies.
3. There should be continued support for private sector leadership. Efforts to provide programs to educate Internet users to prevent and minimize the risks of unlawful activity are also needed.

The following year, on May 4, 1999, Clinton again took action against cybercrime when he announced the Financial Privacy and Consumer Protection Initiative. Through this program, Clinton intended "to give all Americans both the tools and the confidence they need to fully participate in a thriving but highly complex 21st century economy." The initiative had five key principals[4]:

1. We have to do more to protect every American's financial privacy.
2. We must require greater public disclosure and enhance every consumer's right to know.
3. We have to do more to combat consumer fraud.
4. We must provide financial services for those who have been denied access to credit and basic banking services for too long.
5. We have to increase the financial literacy of the American people.

Later in that year, on November 6, 1999, Clinton announced a kNow Fraud project, a partnership between the U.S. Postal Service, the American Association of Retired Persons, the Council of Better Business Bureaus, the Department of Justice, the Federal Trade Commission (FTC), the National Association of Attorneys General, and the Securities and Exchange Commission that was designed to help consumers protect themselves from telemarketing fraud and other crimes.[5]

George W. Bush

By the time Republican George W. Bush was elected president, cybercrime was more common and thus received more attention from the administration. His attention to organized crime began in October 2001, when he signed an Executive Order in which he mandated efforts to protect the country's information systems from a cyberattack, including emergency preparedness communication and the physical assets that support these systems. As a way to protect against the possible disruption of these systems, Bush created the President's Critical Infrastructure Protection Board, which would be responsible for coordinating federal efforts related to protecting information systems. He asked the director of the Office of Management and Budget, the secretary of defense, and the director of the Central Intelligence Agency to develop policies that would protect information systems.[6]

On February 4, 2002, Bush announced Proclamation 7523, which established a National Consumer Protection Week with the theme "Consumer Confidential: The Privacy Story." The goal was to help Americans learn more about securing their personal information. He noted that while advances in computer technology have enabled the more efficient use of information and has benefited society as a whole, it has also made personal information more accessible. Therefore, corporations and government agencies must take precautions against the misuse of that information.

Bush specifically indicated that one of the most harmful abuses of personal information is identity theft. He sought to establish vigorous law enforcement efforts as a way to prevent this crime, but he also noted the importance of consumer education. He encouraged all Americans to learn more about ways to safeguard their personal information, recognize fraudulent telemarketers, and identify fraudulent email as a way to better protect their financial security.[7]

Bush announced National Consumer Protection weeks in 2003, 2005, 2007 and 2008. Each time, he noted that consumers, corporations, and government agencies must take precautions against the misuse of personal information, and he sought to help all Americans learn how to keep their personal information secure by using effective passwords, firewalls, and antivirus software.[8]

After meeting with victims of identity theft in May 2006, Bush acknowledged that identity theft is a serious problem in America and noted that the federal government can help by not only dealing with those who commit the crime but helping those who have been victimized.[9] He then signed Executive Order 13402, entitled Strengthening Federal Efforts to Protect Against Identity Theft. In this, Bush promised to use federal resources to deter, prevent, detect, investigate, proceed against, and prosecute the unlawful use of identifying information. He explained that this would be accomplished through increased aggressive law enforcement, outreach by the federal government to educate the public about identity theft, and more safeguards imposed by the federal government to better secure personal data.

As a way to provide more assistance, Bush then established an Identity Theft Task Force that would consist of the top administration officials (including the attorney general, the chairman of the Federal Trade Commission, the secretary of the Treasury, the secretary of commerce; the secretary of health and human services, the secretary of veterans affairs, the secretary of homeland security, the chairman of the Board of Governors of the Federal Reserve System; and many others). The role of the task force was to review the activities of Executive Branch departments and propose a new plan to improve the federal government's activities related to identity theft awareness, prevention, detection, and prosecution.[10]

In 2008, Bush created the Comprehensive National Cybersecurity Initiative within the Department of Homeland Security as a way to improve the security of government computer networks. This initiative remained largely out of the public eye for many months until some of its work was revealed because of national security concerns. The intent of the initiative, however, was to protect the computers used by government employees from cyberattacks.[11]

Barack Obama

Like President Bush, President Barack Obama continued to proclaim one week out of the year as National Consumer Protection Week to focus on cyber offenses. In doing so, Obama said that consumer education helps all Americans know their rights, which allows them to make sound decisions and protects them from fraud and abuse. Consumer vigilance also prevents problems before they arise. During National Consumer Protection Week, he sought to highlight consumer education efforts that help Americans make wise decisions, and then teach them about the importance of seeking a credit report. He had the FTC provide tips on how to prevent identity theft.[12]

Obama also designated a National Crime Victims' Rights Week. By doing so, he sought to bring attention to the millions of Americans who must rebuild after financial fraud or identity theft. He promised to ensure that victims get the services they need—from care and counseling to justice under the law.[13]

One month of the year was designated National Cybersecurity Awareness Month, a time devoted to expanding the public's awareness about cybersecurity. Obama reinforced his commitment to enhancing the security of our nation's infrastructure during this time.[14] For example, in 2011, Obama chose this month to release the National Strategy for Trusted Identities in Cyberspace, a plan to improve security for consumers conducting e-commerce by helping prevent fraud and identity theft and making it easier for businesses to operate online. He called on the people of the United States to recognize the importance of cybersecurity and to observe this month with activities, events, and training that would enhance our national security and resilience.[15]

Obama frequently discussed the dangers of cybercrime. In April 2009, he told employees at the Federal Bureau of Investigation (FBI) that they had to face new types of crimes, such as cybercrimes.[16] He reminded citizens of the same in a speech on May 29, 2009, when he remarked that spyware, malware, phishing, and botnets have caused millions of Americans to become victims and to have their privacy violated, identities stolen, lives upended, and wallets emptied. He said the dangers can come from cyber thieves who troll for sensitive information, a disgruntled employee, a hacker, organized crime, the industrial spy, or foreign intelligence services. Thus, there is a need to protect America's digital infrastructure.[17]

In this speech, Obama also noted that the danger is that the United States is not as prepared as it should be when it comes to cybercrime. He noted that the United States has failed to invest in the security of our digital infrastructure, and that agencies do not coordinate and communicate as well as they should. To resolve this problem, Obama announced a new comprehensive approach to securing America's digital infrastructure. The approach Obama has taken seeks to make networks secure as a way to deter, prevent, detect, and defend against attacks and recover quickly from any disruptions or damage.

The administration's comprehensive approach to fighting cybercrime included a new position that would be responsible for addressing the problem of computer attacks against the government, businesses and the government. The person would be called the "cyber czar." Obama also used the speech to announce a new office at the White House, led by a cybersecurity coordinator, who would oversee all matters related to cybersecurity. This new coordinator would be dedicated to safeguarding the privacy and civil liberties of the American people. In addition, Obama announced actions in five key areas.[18]

First, he planned to develop a new comprehensive strategy to secure America's information and communications networks. To ensure a coordinated approach, the newly developed cybersecurity coordinator would work closely with others agencies. Another approach to ensure coordinated action was to designate cybersecurity as a key management priority.

Second, Obama planned to work with other key players, including state and local governments and the private sector, to ensure a unified response to prevent future cyber incidents. He said that a plan and resources need to be in place before a crisis hits.

Third, Obama sought to strengthen the public/private partnerships needed to combat cybercrime, especially because the vast majority of our critical information infrastructure in the United States is owned and operated by the private sector. He sought to collaborate with industry to find technology solutions that ensure our security.

Fourth, he announced an investment in cutting-edge research and the development that is needed to discover how to meet the digital challenges of our time. Last, Obama announced a national campaign to promote cybersecurity awareness and digital literacy for consumers.

Through Executive Order 13636, issued on February 12, 2013, Obama announced improvements to critical infrastructure cybersecurity. Alongside that he announced Presidential Policy Directive 21, Critical Infrastructure Security and Resilience. In these documents, the president noted that there had been repeated intrusions into the nation's critical infrastructure that posed potential harm to national security. While the country had response plans for potential threats, some of these were outdated. He ordered that the National Infrastructure Protection Plan be updated to reflect the new threats and advances in technology.[19]

Obama took further action on cybercrime in February 2015, issuing Executive Order 13691, Promoting Private Sector Cybersecurity Information Sharing. In it, he asked that executive departments and agencies share information more readily and collaborate with those in the private sector as a way to coordinate the nation's response to a potential cyberattack.[20] Obama also sponsored a Summit on Cybersecurity and Consumer Protection in February 2015, and announced financial grants to historically black colleges to be used for training students on cybersecurity.

A few days later, Obama announced the establishment of the Cyber Threat Intelligence Integration Center, which was to analyze intelligence on foreign cyber threats or incidents that may affect the United States as well as implement intelligence-sharing policies that may enhance awareness of threats.[21] In that same speech, Obama called cyberspace the "new Wild West," with everyone expecting the government to be the sheriff. He also said that the private sector must do more to stop cyberattacks aimed at the United States,[22] Noting that cyber threats are a challenge to U.S. national security, public safety, and the economy, Obama asked administration officials, tech CEOs, law enforcement officers, and consumer and privacy advocates to work together to do what none can achieve alone.[23]

Congressional Legislation

The U.S. Congress has proposed and passed different pieces of legislation about crimes committed on the Internet. However, the laws quickly become outdated and unenforceable as cybercrime evolves and new crimes develop. Because of this constant evolution, it is difficult for lawmakers to fully understand these issues. Moreover, most constituents do not know enough to demand action. Thus, Congress has not passed an abundance of anti-cybercrime laws. Even fewer laws have been passed at the state government level. In fact, when it comes to policy regarding computer crimes, there is a lack of effective legislation against cybercrime.

One reason why few laws exist is that some members of Congress are reluctant to pass legislation that requires businesses to act in a particular way or to implement a particular level of cybersecurity, even a minimal one. They would prefer that Congress make no laws (or as few as possible) that regulate business. Another reason for the low amount of legislation is that it is difficult to make laws that define appropriate and inappropriate behavior because the definition of appropriate behavior varies from one person to the next. For example, some believe limits should be placed on speech, whereas others disagree.

At this point, the U.S. cybercrime law consists of federal law and 51 other sets of laws (in the 50 states and the District of Columbia). There is a great deal of consistency in state and federal cybercrime law,[24] but at the same time not all of the laws are standard. In the long run, many of the laws are ineffective simply because they address crimes on the national level, whereas cybercrimes are often transnational and not contained in one country.

Federal Cybercrime Legislation

Federal provisions on cybercrime are outlined in the Federal Criminal Code (U.S.C. Title 18). These are described in Box 9.2.

Congressional Legislation

The Digital Millennium Copyright Act of 1976

One of the earliest pieces of legislation passed by Congress to limit cybercrimes was the Digital Millennium Copyright Act of 1976. This law created new criminal offenses related to copyrights and intellectual property. Some of the new crimes defined were copyright infringement, removal of copyright notice, and false representation of copyrighted goods.

Box 9.2   Federal Code Pertaining to Cybercrime

1. Section 1029, Fraud and Related Activity in Connection with Access Devices, makes it illegal for a person to knowingly and without authority produce an identification document.
2. Section 1030, Fraud and Related Activity in Connection with Computers, makes it illegal to intentionally access a computer without authorization and obtain information from any department of the United States.
3. Section 1362, Communication Lines, Stations, or Systems, makes it illegal to injure or destroy any material related to radio, telegraph, telephone, or cable lines operated or controlled by the U.S. government.
4. Section 2510, Wire and Electronic Communications Interception and Interception of Oral Communications, provides definitions of wire communications, oral communications, intercept, and other key concepts.
5. Section 2512, Manufacture, Distribution, Possession, and Advertising of Wire, Oral, or Electronic Communication Intercepting Devices Prohibited, makes it illegal to send through the mail any device that is intended to be used for the interception of communication.
6. Section 2517, Authorization for Disclosure and Use of Intercepted Wire, Oral, or Electronic Communications, permits law enforcement agencies to share intercepted communications with another law enforcement agency.
7. Section 2520, Recovery of Civil Damages Authorized, specifies that any person whose communication is intercepted illegally may recover relief through a civil action.
8. Section 2701, Unlawful Access to Store Communications, makes it illegal to intentionally access a facility through which an electronic communication service is provided.
9. Section 2702, Voluntary Disclosure of Customer Communications or Records, makes it illegal for a person who provides an electronic communication service to divulge contents of a communication while in storage.
10. Section 2703, Required Disclosure of Customer Communications or Records, provides that the government may require the provider of electronic communication service to disclose information in electronic storage if a warrant is obtained.
11. Section 3121, Recording of Dialing, Routing, Addressing, and Signaling Information, makes it illegal for a person to install a pen register or a trap-and-trace device without first obtaining a court order.
12. Section 3125, Emergency Pen Register and Trap-and-Trace Device Installation, says that law enforcement may install a pen register or trap-and-trace device under certain emergency situations.

The law also made it illegal to evade software access controls and to produce technology that was intended to circumvent access controls.[25] What is significant about this early law was that it demonstrated that Congress was aware of the harm done by Internet theft of intellectual property and its willingness to act on it.

The Ribicoff Bill

Another early attempt to prohibit the misuse of computers was as the proposed Federal Computer Systems Protection Act of 1977, or the Ribicoff Bill, named after the bill's sponsor, Senator Abe Ribicoff. The bill was the result of a 1977 study carried out by the Senate Government Operations Committee, chaired by Ribicoff. After researching the potential problems associated with computers, the committee recommended that Congress pass new laws prohibiting unauthorized use of computers. This ensuing proposal (S 1766, proposed in the 95th Congress) became the first federal proposal to address computer crime. Even though the bill did not pass Congress and become law, it was notable because it was another attempt to address the possible harm that could be accomplished through computers. The debate that took place while the bill was being considered helped to educate members of Congress and the public about the potential for harm that could be caused by the new technology.

Amendments to the Comprehensive Crime Control Act of 1984

In 1983, deputy assistant FBI director Floyd Clarke testified in front of a House subcommittee that a computer could be used much like "a gun, a knife or a forger's pen." He urged Congress to pass new laws on computer hacking.[26] By this time, cybercrime was a growing problem, and members of Congress realized that there was a need for new laws to address it. A less complicated way to get this done was to make amendments to the Comprehensive Crime Control Act of 1984, which included provisions designed to deter the unauthorized use of computers and networks. The amendments made it a felony to access classified information in a computer without authorization. Moreover, Congress made accessing financial records in a computer system a misdemeanor.

The Computer Fraud and Abuse Act of 1984

In 1984, members of Congress passed the Computer Fraud and Abuse Act in response to the growing number of computer crimes being reported. It was also partly based on the fear generated from the movie *WarGames*.[27] The new law made it a misdemeanor to fraudulently obtain a person's financial or credit information through a computer. It also made it illegal to access the computer systems of a bank or federal government without permission. It also gave federal prosecutors more power to prosecute criminal computer activity. This law was the cornerstone of the federal government's war on computer crime for many years.

At the time it was passed, the act was criticized for being overly vague and narrow in scope. Because of that, Congress amended the original act in 1986. It also underwent minor changes in 1988, 1989, and 1990, largely to clarify terms. It was then amended by the 2001 USA PATRIOT Act and the 2008 Identity Theft Enforcement and Restitution Act.[28]

The changes in 1986 created three new felony offenses: computer fraud, trafficking in network passwords, and hacking. Amendments made in 1996 made it a felony to intentionally damage a computer by knowingly transmitting a harmful program or to intentionally access a computer without permission to cause damage. The law also defined a new misdemeanor offense: intentionally accessing a computer without authorization and negligently causing damage to that system.

When Congress passed the PATRIOT Act after the terrorist attacks of September 11, 2001, the law was again amended to combat the threat of cyberterrorism. The new provisions gave more power to prosecutors to charge computer criminals with a felony offense. Now, prosecutors did not have to show that $5,000 in damage occurred if the computers attacked were used for national security or criminal justice. The amendments also raised the penalties for cybercrimes. The maximum punishment for first-time offenders was set at 10 years (instead of five). For repeat offenders, the maximum punishment was raised from 10 to 20 years. New provisions now allowed state convictions for related crimes to be counted as prior offenses.

The PATRIOT Act made it a federal crime to, without prior permission, access a computer in order to obtain national security information, financial records, information from a consumer reporting agency, or information from any department or agency of the United States, without permission. Moreover, the law made it a federal crime to simply access a federal government computer without permission, even if there was no damage to or theft of any confidential data. The law also made it a federal crime to traffic in or sell personal information, such as passwords, that could be used to access computer systems without authorization.

Finally, the law made it a crime to knowingly cause the transmission of a program, code, or command that causes damage or intentionally accessing a computer without authorization and, as a result of such conduct, causing damage that results in the following:

- Loss to one or more persons during any one-year period aggregating at least $5,000 in value
- The modification or impairment, or potential modification or impairment, of the medical examination, diagnosis, treatment, or care of one or more individuals
- Physical injury to any person
- A threat to public health or safety
- Damage affecting a government computer system

This provision made almost all forms of hacking, viruses, denial-of-service attacks, and session hijacking federal crimes.[29]

The law was again amended by the Identity Theft Enforcement and Restitution Act of 2008. The amendment made it a felony to merely threaten to damage a computer, computer system, or steal data, but not actually perform the act. The amendment also expanded the scope of the original law, making any hacking of a system or even conspiring to hack a system a felony offense.

New laws were created as well. Computer fraud offenses taking place in one state were now considered federal offenses. Additionally, an organization could now be considered to be a victim of identity theft. Prior to this, only an individual could be a victim. It also made it a criminal offense to conspire to commit computer fraud, and expanded the definition of cyber extortion to include threats made to damage computer systems or steal data.[30]

Computer Security Act of 1987

This new law, passed in 1987, directed the National Bureau of Standards to establish a computer standards program for federal computer systems. Part of the mandate was to set guidelines for the security of federal computer systems. Signed by President Reagan, this was an early attempt to protect the computer databases held by federal agencies.

Child Pornography Protection Act of 1996

In 1996, Congress was concerned about an increase in the availability of child pornography on the Internet. Congress had first outlawed child pornography in the Protection of Children Against Sexual Exploitation Act of 1977. The 1996 law banned the use of real children in the production of child pornography. By the end of the 20th century, computers and software programs allowed offenders to create "virtual" child pornography, or pornography that does not involve the use of actual children. The Internet also made pornography much easier to create and distribute. In response to these concerns, Congress passed the Child Pornography Protection Act to make the federal laws more current by dealing with computer-generated child pornography and making simulated child pornography illegal. However, the Supreme Court struck down the relevant portions of the act on First Amendment grounds.

Economic Espionage Act of 1996

The Economic Espionage Act of 1996 (PL 104-294) was passed by Congress to deter the theft of trade secrets. One provision specifies that to meet the statute the theft of the trade secret must be done with the intent to benefit a foreign government. The second provision revolves around the more commonly recognized crime of theft of trade secrets, regardless of who benefits. If convicted under this law, the government can seize the property or proceeds of offenders.

The National Information Infrastructure Protection Act of 1996

The National Information Infrastructure Protection Act of 1996 made changes to the federal criminal code regarding fraud and related activities if it is committed with the use of a computer. The law established penalties for those who knowingly and without permission access a computer to obtain restricted information or data and gives that information to another person, knowing that the information could be used to harm the United States.

The Communications Decency Act of 1996

The Communications Decency Act of 1996, which was Title V of the Telecommunications Act, was not only intended to curtail Internet pornography but also to limit children's access to pornography. Under the law, any person who knowingly uses a computer to send pornographic material (material that is obscene, lewd, indecent or immoral, or "patently offensive") to a person who is under 18 years old, or uses a computer to communicate with a person who is under 18 years of age, may be guilty of a crime.[31]

In July 1996, a U.S. federal court in New York struck down a portion of the Communications Decency Act, ruling that the part of the law that was meant to protect children from indecent speech was too broadly written. The decision was appealed to the U.S. Supreme Court in June 1997, and the justices upheld the lower court's ruling (*Reno v. American Civil Liberties Union*). The effect of this ruling was to strike down significant portions of the Communications Decency Act. The court ruled that the indecency provisions violated the First Amendment and the right to free speech because it did not allow parents to decide what material was acceptable for their children to view. The court also explained that the law did not define what was meant by the term "patently offensive."

Wire Fraud Act of 1997

Part of the Wire Fraud Act of 1997 made it a crime for hacker to allow others to download software for free. Thus, even if a hacker did not financially profit from the hacking, he or she would still be committing a crime. Before this, it had to be shown that the offender profited from the hacking.

No Electronic Theft Act of 1997

The No Electronic Theft Act of 1997 was signed into law by President Clinton. The goal of the law was to provide new tools for law enforcement and prosecutors to more effectively investigate violations of copyright laws and intellectual property. This new law made it a federal crime to reproduce, distribute, or share copies of electronic copyrighted works. This applied to software, music, videos, and electronic versions of printed material. As defined by Congress, the act made it illegal to distribute those types of material, even if the person does not gain financially. However, the value of the material must be over $1,000. If found guilty of these acts, a person could face a maximum of three years in prison and a $250,000 fine.

The law also made it a criminal act to remove a copyright notice from an electronic product and replace it with a false copyright notice. Further, a person could no longer record a live performance without the permission of the artist for distribution. A victim of this type of act was now permitted to submit a victim impact statement to describe the extent of the harm caused by the crime, as well as the estimated economic impacts of the offense.[32]

Identity Theft and Assumption Deterrence Act of 1998

On October 30, 1998, President Clinton signed the Identity Theft and Assumption Deterrence Act of 1998, which made identity theft a federal crime, punishable by up to three years in prison and a fine of $250,000. It was now a federal crime for a person to steal personal information of another individual as a way to obtain fraudulent loans or credit cards. Clinton also put some attention on the victims of cybercrime in this new law. Now, the FTC would institute programs intended to help victims deal with the consequences of this crime.[33]

Digital Millennium Copyright Act 1998

The Digital Millennium Copyright Act was signed into law on October 28, 1998. The law made it illegal to attempt to circumvent copy-protection technologies. Clearly, the bill was supported during the debate before its enactment by those who manufacture CDs, DVDs, and other types of media. However, the law mandates that an Internet service provider is not liable if one of its customers uses its service to violate the law.

Child Online Protection Act of 1998

The Child Online Protection Act made it a crime for a minor to access material that would be considered harmful to them online. A communication was considered harmful if it was obscene, designed to appeal to the "prurient interest" of the child, or depicted a sexual act or lewd representation of genitals. In general, to be considered obscene, it had to lack any serious value.[34] The law has been litigated in the federal courts, with two different courts holding that the law is unconstitutional. The case was later reviewed by the Supreme Court after challenged as violating the First Amendment's freedom of speech, but the court refused to grant a hearing, letting the lower courts' rulings on the law as unconstitutional stand.[35]

Children's Internet Protection Act 2000

The Children's Internet Protection Act was signed into law on December 21, 2000. The intent of the new law was protect children from accessing pornographic or indecent material on the Internet. To do that, libraries and schools were now required to filter the content to which children had access. However, if an adult patron asked for the filter to be removed, the library could do so. Unless a library had a system in place to ensure that children could not access inappropriate material on the Internet, the library would receive no federal funds to purchase computers.[36] Schools and libraries were also asked to educate children about appropriate online behavior, including cyberbullying and how to interact safely with other people on social-networking sites and in chat rooms. The law was criticized because it was too broad and unconstitutionally restricted a person's access to a public forum. However, upon review, the Supreme Court upheld the act.

The Cybersecurity Research and Development Act of 2002

The Cybersecurity Research and Development Act was signed by President Bush in November 2002. The legislation provided $900 million over the following five years to pay for research into computer security issues and education. The bill provided grants for, among other things, establishing graduate programs at universities and research centers so that students could pursue academic careers in cybersecurity.

Cyber Security Enhancement Act of 2002

The Cyber Security Enhancement Act of 2002 was a provision in the Homeland Security Act that directed the Sentencing Commission to upgrade the penalties assessed under the CVAA. The commission then changed the guidelines in April 2003, so that those convicted of computer crimes from that point on would face substantially higher penalties for their crimes. The law changed the reporting process for Internet security providers. Now, companies would be able to give records of customers' emails, phone calls, and purchases to the government without a warrant. So if the company believes there is an "immediate threat to a national security interest," they can report the information if they can show they had "good faith" in doing so. Moreover, customers cannot sue the company for reporting them.

Dot Kids Act of 2002

This law was an attempt to protect children from viewing inappropriate material online. According to this law, the registry that is in charge of all websites should ensure that all sites that use the U.S. country domain, that is, websites that end in ".us" should establish a second-level country domain that is ".kids." This domain would only be available to websites whose content is suitable for children. This means that the material serves educational, intellectual, cognitive, emotional, social, or entertainment needs of children and is not psychologically or intellectually inappropriate for them.[37]

CAN-SPAM Act of 2003

In 2003, the U.S. Congress passed the Controlling the Assault of Non-Solicited Pornography and Marketing Act of 2003, otherwise known as the CAN-SPAM Act. Effective on January 1, 2004, this law requires anyone who sends spam emails to provide an opt-out choice for all recipients. This means someone who is receiving the spam can choose to stop any further emails from that company. This law was pivotal because it was the first law concerning the transmission of commercial email.

Critics of the bill claim that the law has too many loopholes. For example, a person does not need to seek permission before sending email, which means they would be sending out unsolicited email, which is the definition of spam. Because the law defines commercial email as "any electronic mail message the primary purpose of which is the commercial advertisement or promotion of a commercial product or service (including content on an Internet website operated for a commercial purpose)," it means mass mailings that have no commercial purpose are not covered by this law. It also means mass emailings for political or religious purposes that do not represent a commercial interest are exempt from this law. The only requirement is that the sender must provide a method whereby the receiver can opt out, and that method cannot require the receiver to pay a fee to opt out.

The opt-out methods must follow particular guidelines, as outlined in the law. First, there must be a visible and operable way to unsubscribe in all emails. Additionally, all consumer opt-out requests must be are honored within 10 days, and any opt-out lists may not be sold to other vendors/senders. Perhaps the most controversial portion of this law is the fact that it supersedes all other state and local ordinances.

Prosecutorial Remedies and Other Tools to End the Exploitation of Children Today Act of 2003

A law to protect children was the Prosecutorial Remedies and Other Tools to End the Exploitation of Children Today Act, otherwise known as the PROTECT Act. The law, passed in 2003, was intended to criminalize virtual child pornography by making illegal any material that has "a visual depiction of any kind, including a drawing, cartoon, sculpture or painting or that depicts a minor engaging in sexually explicit conduct and is obscene." The material is also illegal if it "depicts an image that is, or appears to be, of a minor engaging in . . . sexual intercourse . . . and lacks serious literary, artistic, political, or scientific value."[38]

Another provision in the PROTECT Act made service providers responsible for reporting any suspected cases of child pornography to the Cyber-Tipline at the National Center for Missing and Exploited Children. Personnel at the center then forward the information to local law enforcement for investigation. If the service provider fails to report suspected pornography, it may be fined up to $150,000 for a first violation and $300,000 for subsequent violations.[39]

Fair and Accurate Credit Transactions Act of 2003

On December 4, 2003, President Bush signed the Fair and Accurate Credit Transactions Act to protect victims of identity theft. The law would permit users to get a free copy of their credit report each year so they can keep it accurate and challenge any errors. The new law also required merchants to delete all but the last five digits of a credit card number on store receipts. A national system of fraud detection was created so that cases of identity theft could be traced and handled as early as possible. The law also encouraged lenders and credit agencies to take action before a victim even knows an identity crime has occurred. In many cases, identity thieves follow predictable patterns. Bank regulators working with credit agencies were tasked with drawing up guidelines to identify these patterns.[40]

Identity Theft Penalty Enhancement Act of 2004

On July 15, 2004, Bush signed the Identity Theft Penalty Enhancement Act. According to Bush, the intent of the law was to punish those who committed identity theft by creating prison sentences for those found guilty. The new law also established the offense of "aggravated identity theft." A person who is convicted of that crime will be punished more harshly, receiving the punishment for the crime committed (i.e., using a fake passport) plus an extra 2- to 5-year mandatory sentence for the identity theft. Further, sentencing judges would not be permitted to let those convicted of aggravated identity theft serve their sentence on probation.[41]

Cybersecurity Enhancement Act of 2014

When this law was passed, the secretary of commerce, acting through the director of the National Institute of Standards and Technology, was required to develop new standards and procedures, with the help of the computer industry, to reduce the risk of a cybercrime attack on the country's critical infrastructure. The law required the director to work with private-sector personnel, owners of critical infrastructure, and other groups to come up with this plan.

National Cybersecurity Protection Act of 2014

The National Cybersecurity Protection Act, passed in 2014, made changes to the Homeland Security Act of 2002 and created a National Cybersecurity and Communications Integration Center housed within the Department of Homeland Security. The center was created to be a federal agency that would facilitate sharing of information pertaining to cybersecurity risks, incidents, analyses, and warnings for federal and nonfederal entities. Center personnel facilitate cross-sector coordination to address risks and incidents that may be related or could have consequential impacts across multiple sectors. They also conduct and share information pertaining to the analysis of information and provide technical assistance, risk management, and security measure recommendations.

State Cybercrime Laws

In additional to federal legislation to deter cybercrime, individual states have also passed laws on cybercrime. For example, in California, according to a law signed on September 25, 2002, that amended the California

Civil Code, notice must be given to the Department of Defense regarding security breaches involving unencrypted personal information. The California Security Breach Information Act requires a state agency, person, or business that conducts business in California, and owns or licenses computerized data that includes personal information, to disclose any breach of the security of that data to any resident of California whose unencrypted personal information was, or is reasonably thought to have been, acquired by any unauthorized person. A law passed in Texas gave the Texas attorney general the power to prosecute identity thieves in that state.

Each state is responsible for its own laws. Most states, if not all, have passed statutes specifically addressing cyber harassment or cyberstalking, identity theft, hacking, child pornography, or all of these offenses.[42] Some states have added extra punishments for aggravated offenses. For example, there may be a law that bans hacking and another law that bans aggravated hacking as distinct crimes. In this case simple hacking might be unauthorized access, unauthorized use, or "computer tampering," whereas aggravated hacking would be unauthorized access of computers that results in the copying, alteration, and/or deletion of data, or damage to a computer system. Some states also include provisions that criminalize the use of a computer to engage in other criminal acts.[43] In most states, simple hacking is a misdemeanor offense and aggravated hacking is a felony. Some states use a single statute to criminalize both.

Malware

Many states have made the dissemination of viruses, worms, and other types of malware illegal. For example, in California, it is illegal to knowingly "introduce any computer contaminant into any computer, computer system, or computer network" (California Penal Code § 502(c)(7)). Some states have also outlawed attempts to disseminate malware.

Denial of Service

A few states have made denial-of-service attacks illegal. For example, Arkansas has made it a crime to use a computer to launch a denial-of-service attack.

Computer Fraud and Theft

Many states have banned the use of computers to commit fraud. Some states have made computer fraud a distinct crime, whereas others have increased the penalties for aggravated hacking if the crime is carried out with the purpose of defrauding another person.[44]

Other states have made specific laws regarding "computer theft." These laws encompass many different crimes, such as the theft of information, software or hardware, or computer services. It can also include using a computer to steal other types of property (e.g., Michigan Compiled Laws § 752.795).

Crimes against Children

Most states have made it a crime to use a computer to solicit a minor for sex. In Texas, offenders are guilty of the offense if they believe the person whom they were soliciting for sex is a minor, even if that is not true (Texas Penal Code § 15.031). Most states also have laws outlawing the use of computers to create, possess, and/or distribute child pornography.

Cyberstalking Laws

Cyberstalking often leads to other crimes, such as assault, rape, or murder. Since most offenders are local (i.e., in the same city or town), and are investigated by local law enforcement, the offenses are often banned by state legislatures. The first cyberstalking laws were passed in California in 1991. Some states do not have specific statutes for cyberstalking but instead apply existing stalking and harassment laws to cyberstalking behavior. A description of an early cyberstalking law is presented in Box 9.3.

Box 9.3   Anti-Stalking Laws

The first and perhaps most famous conviction under California anti-stalking laws occurred in 1999. Gary S. Dellapenta, a 50-year-old security guard, had been making advances toward a woman at his church, which she rejected. He reacted aggressively, and his behavior became such a concern that church elders asked him to leave the church. To retaliate against the woman, Dellapenta took out fake ads on the Internet, purporting to be from the woman in question, claiming she enjoyed rape fantasies. When men contacted the email address in the ad, it went to Dellapenta, who responded with the address and phone number of the victim. On at least six separate occasions, men actually showed up at the victim's home. Dellapenta was arrested, convicted, and received a six-year prison sentence.

The Louisiana legislature included a very explicit definition of cyber-stalking. They define it as the use of email or electronic communication in which there are threats to inflict bodily harm to a person and/or the person's sibling, spouse, or dependent. It is also illegal for a cyberstalker to send damaging or threatening electronic communications about the victim to another person. The penalties for stalking vary. For second-time offenders, the penalties typically include time in prison and a fine.

Some states have simply added a clause to the existing statute on stalking to make it apply to cyberstalking as well. For example, the Arizona legislature added one sentence to the law banning traditional stalking: "Anonymously or otherwise contacts, communicates or causes a communication with another person by verbal, electronic, mechanical, telegraphic, telephonic or written means in a manner that harasses." Other examples of state cyberstalking laws are presented in Table 9.1.

Identity-Theft Laws

Since the crime of identity theft often crosses state lines or involves financial institutions, it is often considered to be a federal crime. Thus, laws on identity theft vary tremendously from state to state. Where some states have created new legislation that specifically deals with this new crime, others have opted to modify existing laws. However, some cases of identity theft occur solely within a state, so there is a need for state laws that outlaw these behaviors. Examples of state-level identity theft laws are presented in Table 9.2.

Most states have statutes outlawing a person from stealing another person's identity and using that to commit crimes. In general, these laws make

Table 9.1 Examples of State Cyberstalking Laws

State	Statute
Arizona	Ariz. Rev. Stat. 13-2921
Florida	Fla. Stat. 817.568, 784.048
Hawaii	Hawaii Rev. Stat. 711-1106
Kansas	Kan. Stat. 21-3438
Maine	Me. Rev. Stat. title 17A 210-A
New York	New York Penal Law 240.30
Utah	Utah Code 76-5-106.5
Wisconsin	Wis. Stat. 947.0125

Table 9.2   Examples of State Identity-Theft Statutes

State	Statute
Alabama	13A-8-190 to 13A-8-201: The Consumer Identity Protection Act
Florida	817.568: Criminal Use of Personal Identification Information
Indiana	34-43-5-3.5: Identity Deception
Louisiana	RS 14:67.16: Identity Theft
Maine	17-A905-A: Misuse of Identification
Michigan	445.61 et seq.: Identity Theft Protection Act
New Hampshire	638:25 to 638:27: Identity Fraud
Nebraska	28-608: Criminal Impersonation

it a crime to "knowingly and with intent to defraud for economic benefit" obtain, possess, transfer, use, or attempt "to obtain, possess, transfer or use, one or more identification documents or personal identification number" of someone else (Alabama Code § 13A-8-193). Some states also make it a crime to traffic in stolen identities (Alabama Code § 13A-8-193).

In Alabama, the crime of identity theft is defined in the Consumer Identity Protection Act. The legislature realized how serious this crime could be and made it a felony offense. Florida also made identity theft a felony. In Florida, identity theft occurs when a person uses another person's identification without his or her permission. Under this law, even if a person does not use the stolen personal information for financial purposes, it is still a felony. So if a criminal in Florida steals someone's personal information and uses it to embarrass another person, it is a felony crime.

If a crime is committed for financial gain, the punishments are based on the damages caused by the act. If a crime results in damages between $5,000 and $50,000 and/or affects between 10 and 20 people, the penalty is a minimum of three years in prison. If a crime causes damages between $50,000 and $100,000 and/or affects between 20 and 30 people, the penalty is a minimum of five years in prison. If, however, the damages exceed $100,000 and/or affects more than 30 people, the penalty is a minimum of 10 years in prison.

In Idaho, the law against identity theft states, "It is unlawful for any person to obtain or record personal identifying information of another person without the authorization of that person, with the intent that the information be used to obtain, or attempt to obtain, credit, money, goods or services without the consent of that person" (Idaho Statutes § 18-3126). Another part of the law makes receiving goods purchased through fraud to be a crime.

Child Pornography Laws

Every state has some laws that address child pornography. Some of these are listed in Table 9.3. Many state laws require information technology workers (or anyone else) to report any evidence of child pornography to law enforcement if they find it. In Arkansas, the laws against child pornography make it illegal to knowingly receive, sell, manufacture, lend, trade, mail, deliver, transfer, publish, distribute, circulate, disseminate, present, exhibit, advertise, offer, or agree to offer child pornography, through any means, including the Internet. This can be any photograph, film, videotape, computer program or file, computer-generated image, video game, or any other reproduction or reconstruction that depicts a child engaging in sexually explicit conduct. In Connecticut, the law defines child pornography as any material that depicts a minor in a prohibited sexual act. In Oregon, the law has made online sexual discussions with a minor a criminal offense.

Sexting

Sexting involves the use of cell phones to send sexually explicit material to others. Many states have not passed any laws related specifically to sexting. The Ohio General Assembly, however, has done so, and it makes sexting a criminal act. The law says that no minor shall recklessly create,

Table 9.3   Examples of State Child Pornography Laws

State	Statute
Arizona	Statute 13-3551–3553
California	Penal Code 311
Colorado	Statute 8-16-403 and 404
Idaho	Code 1801707
Kansas	Statute 21-3516
Massachusetts	General Law 272 29-30
Vermont	Title 13 2821, 2825, 2826, and 2827
Virginia	Code 18.2-374

receive, exchange, send, or possess a photograph, video, or other material that shows a minor in a state of nudity. If so, the person is guilty of a misdemeanor offense.

Hacking Laws

Many hackers are convicted under federal laws, but many states have also passed laws on hacking. These are needed because some hackers, for example, a student who hacks into a school computer system, do not affect computers outside of a small area.

One state that has passed anti-hacking laws is Maine. In that state, a person is guilty of "criminal invasion of computer privacy" if the person intentionally accesses a computer when not authorized to do so. In Montana, the law states that any person who obtains the use of a computer or network without the consent of the owner and destroys or alters software or data is guilty of unlawful use of a computer. The crime is punishable by a fine of up to $1,500, or a term in jail of up to 6 months, or both. If the value of the property that was lost or stolen is higher, then the punishment is higher. Table 9.4 gives some examples of state laws related to unauthorized computer access.

Spyware

Spyware and adware have become major problems for computer users. As a result, many state legislatures have passed laws against them. In Arizona, the law emphasizes the use of spyware to carry out identity theft and addresses phishing. The law makes it a class 5 felony to use a web page or

Table 9.4   Examples of State Laws on Unauthorized Computer Access

State	Statute
Alabama	Code 13A-8-102, 13A-8-103
Connecticut	Gen. Statute 53a-251
Idaho	Code 18-2202
Kansas	Statute Ann. 21-3755
Mississippi	Code Ann. 97-45-1 to 97-45-13
New Jersey	Statute 2A:38A-3
North Carolina	General Statute 14-453 to 14-458
Vermont	Statute 13, 4101 to 4107

an email message to solicit or induce another person to provide identifying information by representing or implying that the person is an online business without the authority or approval of the online business. In other words, sending an email claiming to be from Bank of America and asking people to go to a web page and enter their username and password is a class 5 felony.

Furthermore, this law explicitly addresses spyware. It bans any person from transmitting computer software if that software will change Internet control settings, collect personally identifiable information, prevent the user's efforts to block the installation or execution of the software, falsely claim that software will be disabled by the operator's actions, remove or disable security software installed on the computer; or take control of the computer. In Texas, the law makes the creation of zombies or botnets illegal. If one is used against a victim, that person can recover actual damages of up to $100,000 for each zombie used. Table 9.5 provides some examples of state-level anti-spyware laws.

Conclusion

Often, laws and policies to regulate cybercrime lag behind advances in technology. Legislators at the federal and state level may attempt to address all avenues of cybercrime, but it is almost impossible as technology is constantly changing and adapting. Thus, new laws that are passed may be effective for a short time but become ineffective or irrelevant quickly. They may also have unintended consequences for companies or users.[45]

As cybercrime increases, there will be more demands for more regulation of the Internet. Additional legislation will be needed, and legislators

Table 9.5 Examples of State Spyware Laws

State	Statute
Alaska	Alaska Stat. 45.45.792, .794, .798;45.50.471(51)
Georgia	Ga. Code 16-9-152 to -157
Illinois	720 ILCS 5/16D-5.5
Iowa	Iowa Code 715.1 to 715.8
Louisiana	La. Rev. Stat. Ann. 51:2006 to 51:2014
Nevada	Nev. Rev. Stat. 205.4737
Utah	Utah Code Ann. 13-40-101 to 13-40-401
Washington	Wash. Rev. Code 19.270.101 to 19.270.900

must continue to recommend and pass new laws or add provisions to existing laws to stop these ever-changing crimes.

Review Questions

1. Describe the presidential response to cybercrime over the years. Has one approach been more effective than another? If so, how?
2. What are some of the laws Congress has passed to attack cybercrime?
3. What legislation should Congress pass in the next five years to deter cybercrime?
4. Describe the actions taken by states as a result of crimes on the Internet.
5. What are the laws pertaining to cybercrime in your state?

Key Terms

Amendments to the Comprehensive Crime Control Act of 1984
CAN-SPAM Act of 2003
Child Pornography Protection Act of 1996
Children's Internet Protection Act of 2000
Children's Online Protection Act of 1998
Communications Decency Act of 1996
Computer Fraud and Abuse Act of 1984
Computer Security Act of 1987
Cybersecurity Enhancement Act of 2002
Cybersecurity Enhancement Act of 2004
Cybersecurity Research and Development Act of 2002
Digital Millennium Copyright Act of 1998
Dot Kids Act of 2002
Economic Espionage Act of 1996
Fair and Accurate Credit Transactions Act of 2003
Identity Theft and Assumption Deterrence Act of 1998
Identity Theft Penalty Enhancement Act of 2004
National Information Infrastructure Protection Act of 1996
No Electronic Theft Act of 1997
Prosecutorial Remedies and Other Tools to End the Exploitation of Children Today 2003
Ribicoff Bill
Wire Fraud Act of 1997

Notes

1. William J. Clinton, "Commencement Address at the United States Naval Academy in Annapolis, Maryland," May 22, 1998, The American Presidency Proj-

ect, Gerhard Peters and John T. Woolley, http://www.presidency.ucsb.edu /ws/?pid=56012.

2. "Timeline: The US Government and Cybersecurity," TechNews.com, *Washington Post*, May 16, 2003, http://www.washingtonpost.com/wp-dyn/articles /A50606-2002Jun26_2.html; William J. Clinton, "Executive Order 13133— Working Group on Unlawful Conduct on the Internet," August 5, 1999, The American Presidency Project, Gerhard Peters and John T. Woolley, http://www.presidency .ucsb.edu/ws/?pid=58014.

3. U.S. Working Group on Unlawful Conduct on the Internet, "The Electronic Frontier: The Challenge of Unlawful Conduct Involving the Use of the Internet: A Report of the President's Working Group on Unlawful Conduct on the Internet" (Washington, DC: U.S. Government Printing Office, 2000), http://purl.access .gpo.gov/GPO/LPS5093.

4. William J. Clinton, "Remarks Announcing the Financial Privacy and Consumer Protection Initiative," May 4, 1999, The American Presidency Project, Gerhard Peters and John T. Woolley, http://www.presidency.ucsb.edu/ws/?pid=57513.

5. William J. Clinton, "Memorandum on Protecting Consumers from Fraud," November 6, 1999, The American Presidency Project, Gerhard Peters and John T. Woolley, http://www.presidency.ucsb.edu/ws/?pid=56885.

6. George W. Bush, "Executive Order 13231—Critical Infrastructure Protection in the Information Age," October 16, 2001, The American Presidency Project, Gerhard Peters and John T. Woolley, http://www.presidency.ucsb.edu/ws /?pid=61512.

7. George W. Bush, "Proclamation 7523—National Consumer Protection Week, 2002," February 4, 2002, The American Presidency Project, Gerhard Peters and John T. Woolley, http://www.presidency.ucsb.edu/ws/?pid=61820.

8. George W. Bush, "Proclamation 7643—National Consumer Protection Week, 2003," January 27, 2003, The American Presidency Project, Gerhard Peters and John T. Woolley, http://www.presidency.ucsb.edu/ws/?pid=61934; George W. Bush, "Proclamation 7869—National Consumer Protection Week, 2005," February 7, 2005, The American Presidency Project, Gerhard Peters and John T. Woolley, http://www.presidency.ucsb.edu/ws/?pid=62153; George W. Bush, "Proclamation 7979—National Consumer Protection Week, 2006," February 3, 2006, The American Presidency Project, Gerhard Peters and John T. Woolley, http://www.presidency.ucsb.edu/ws/?pid=65092; George W. Bush, "Proclamation 8105—National Consumer Protection Week, 2007," February 2, 2007, The American Presidency Project, Gerhard Peters and John T. Woolley, http://www .presidency.ucsb.edu/ws/?pid=24497; George W. Bush, "Proclamation 8224— National Consumer Protection Week, 2008," February 29, 2008, The American Presidency Project, Gerhard Peters and John T. Woolley, http://www.presidency .ucsb.edu/ws/?pid=76591.

9. George W. Bush, "Remarks Following a Meeting with Victims of Identity Theft," May 10, 2006, The American Presidency Project, Gerhard Peters and John T. Woolley, http://www.presidency.ucsb.edu/ws/?pid=72908.

10. George W. Bush, "Executive Order 13402—Strengthening Federal Efforts to Protect Against Identity Theft," May 10, 2006, The American Presidency Project, Gerhard Peters and John T. Woolley, http://www.presidency.ucsb.edu/ws/?pid=72902; George W. Bush, "Executive Order 13414—Amendment to Executive Order 13402, Strengthening Federal Efforts to Protect against Identity Theft," November 3, 2006, The American Presidency Project, Gerhard Peters and John T. Woolley, http://www.presidency.ucsb.edu/ws/?pid=24265.

11. The White House, "The Comprehensive National Cybersecurity Initiative," https://www.whitehouse.gov/issues/foreign-policy/cybersecurity/national-initiative.

12. Barack Obama, "Proclamation 8347—National Consumer Protection Week, 2009," February 27, 2009, The American Presidency Project, Gerhard Peters and John T. Woolley, http://www.presidency.ucsb.edu/ws/?pid=85817; Barack Obama, "Proclamation 8782—National Consumer Protection Week, 2012," March 5, 2012, The American Presidency Project, Gerhard Peters and John T. Woolley, http://www.presidency.ucsb.edu/ws/?pid=99971; Barack Obama, "Proclamation 8937—National Consumer Protection Week, 2013," March 1, 2013, The American Presidency Project, Gerhard Peters and John T. Woolley, http://www.presidency.ucsb.edu/ws/?pid=103302.

13. Barack Obama, "Proclamation 8959—National Crime Victims' Rights Week, 2013," April 19, 2013, The American Presidency Project, Gerhard Peters and John T. Woolley, http://www.presidency.ucsb.edu/ws/?pid=103520.

14. Barack Obama, "Proclamation 9029—National Cybersecurity Awareness Month, 2013," September 30, 2013, The American Presidency Project, Gerhard Peters and John T. Woolley, http://www.presidency.ucsb.edu/ws/?pid=104297.

15. Barack Obama, "Proclamation 8725—National Cybersecurity Awareness Month, 2011," October 3, 2011, The American Presidency Project, Gerhard Peters and John T. Woolley, http://www.presidency.ucsb.edu/ws/?pid=96842.

16. Barack Obama, "Remarks to Federal Bureau of Investigation Employees," April 28, 2009, The American Presidency Project, Gerhard Peters and John T. Woolley, http://www.presidency.ucsb.edu/ws/?pid=86063.

17. Barack Obama, "Remarks on Securing the Nation's Information and Communications Infrastructure," May 29, 2009, The American Presidency Project, Gerhard Peters and John T. Woolley, http://www.presidency.ucsb.edu/ws/?pid=86215.

18. Barack Obama, "Remarks on Securing the Nation's Information and Communications Infrastructure," May 29, 2009, The American Presidency Project, Gerhard Peters and John T. Woolley, http://www.presidency.ucsb.edu/ws/?pid=86215.

19. Barack Obama, "Executive Order 13636—Improving Critical Infrastructure Cybersecurity," February 12, 2013, The American Presidency Project, Gerhard Peters and John T. Woolley, http://www.presidency.ucsb.edu/ws/?pid=103245.

20. Barack Obama, "Executive Order 13691—Promoting Private Sector Cybersecurity Information Sharing," February 13, 2015, The American Presidency Project, Gerhard Peters and John T. Woolley, http://www.presidency.ucsb.edu/ws/?pid=109407.

21. Barack Obama, "Memorandum on Establishment of the Cyber Threat Intelligence Integration Center," February 25, 2015, The American Presidency Project, Gerhard Peters and John T. Woolley, http://www.presidency.ucsb.edu/ws/?pid=109683.

22. The White House, Office of the Press Secretary, "Securing Cyberspace—President Obama Announces New Cybersecurity Legislative Proposal and Other Cybersecurity Efforts," January 13, 2015, https://www.whitehouse.gov/the-press-office/2015/01/13/securing-cyberspace-president-obama-announces-new-cybersecurity-legislat.

23. Darlene Superville and Martha Mendoza, "Obama Calls Cyberspace the New 'Wild West'," *The Repository (Ohio)*, February 14, 2015, A-15.

24. Susan W. Brenner, "Cybercrime Law: A United States Perspective," in *Digital Evidence and Computer Crime*, ed. Eoghan Casey, 3rd ed. (Boston: Academic Press, 2011), 85–121.

25. Salil K. Mehra, "Law and Cybercrime in the United States Today," *American Journal of Comparative Law* 58 (2010): 659–685.

26. "Timeline: The US Government and Cybersecurity," *Washington Post*.

27. Reid Skibell, "Cybercrimes and Misdemeanors: A Reevaluation of the Computer Fraud and Abuse Act," *Berkeley Technology Law Journal* 18 (2003): 909–944.

28. Salil K. Mehra, "Law and Cybercrime in the United States Today."

29. Brenner, "Cybercrime Law."

30. Ibid.

31. Salil K. Mehra, "Law and Cybercrime in the United States Today."

32. Ibid.

33. William J. Clinton, "Statement on Signing the Identity Theft and Assumption Deterrence Act of 1998," October 30, 1998, The American Presidency Project, Gerhard Peters and John T. Woolley, http://www.presidency.ucsb.edu/ws/?pid=55196.

34. Salil K. Mehra, "Law and Cybercrime in the United States Today."

35. Grainne Kirwan and Andrew Power, *The Psychology of Cyber Crime: Concepts and Principles* (Hershey, PA: Information Science Reference, 2012).

36. Salil K. Mehra, "Law and Cybercrime in the United States Today."

37. Ibid.

38. Ibid.

39. Ibid

40. George W. Bush, "Remarks on Signing the Fair and Accurate Credit Transactions Act of 2003," December 4, 2003, The American Presidency Project, Gerhard Peters and John T. Woolley, http://www.presidency.ucsb.edu/ws/?pid=62888.

41. Ibid.

42. Steven D. Hazelwood and Sarah Koon-Magnin, "Cyber Stalking and Cyber Harassment Legislation in the United States: A Qualitative Analysis," *International Journal of Cyber Criminology* 7, no. 2 (2013): 155–168.

43. Brenner, "Cybercrime Law." 50.

44. Brenner, "Cybercrime Law."

45. Nigel Pearson, "A Larger Problem: Financial and Reputational Risks," *Computer Fraud and Security,* April 2014, 11–13, www.computerfraudandsecurity.com.

CHAPTER TEN

International Response

Introduction

CYBERCRIME DOES NOT OCCUR IN A SINGLE PLACE. INSTEAD, cyberattacks affect victims across boundaries and geographic borders. A cybercrime can easily originate in one country, and then rapidly impact thousands around the globe. Criminals can easily move from one point to another, making it difficult to track them. Since cybercrime is a worldwide phenomenon, there have been calls for international regulation and governance of Internet activity. While most national leaders agree that cybercrimes pose a significant problem, there is little consensus in different countries about how to solve that problem. Thus, each country has developed its own laws regarding cybercrimes, and there is sometimes very little consistency among them.

Yet most nations agree that there must some level of international cooperation to have a concerted effort to attack cybercriminals, and many officials have debated and passed consistent policies to regulate cybercrime and give investigators the powers they need to investigate these offenses. This chapter will discuss the international responses to cybercrime to show how these laws and policies have evolved and what their status is today.

International Actions

Officials in most countries around the world have been quick to realize the dangers posed by cybercrimes. Many have passed laws and policies aimed at reducing the likelihood of a cyberattack. But most of the laws pertain to cybercrime in a particular country rather than internationally. The laws each country has passed to reduce cybercrime vary greatly.

For example, in Israel, Section 4 of the Computer Law of 1995 states that any person who unlawfully obtains access to data in a computer shall be sentenced to imprisonment not exceeding three years. In Italy, according to the Penal Code Article 615, those who have unauthorized access into a computer or telecommunication system that is protected by security measures, or who remains in that site against the expressed or implied will of the one who has the right to exclude him, shall be sentenced to imprisonment not exceeding three years. If that person uses violence to commit the crime, of if the act causes the destruction or the damage to the system, then the punishment is either a sentence of one to five years or three to eight years' imprisonment, respectively.

The Malaysian law concerning cybercrimes is the Computer Crimes Act of 1997. Part II of the law states that a person is guilty of an offense if he or she causes a computer to perform any function with the intent to secure access to any program or data held in any computer that is unauthorized if the person knows at the time that the program is unauthorized. In Norway, the relevant law is Penal Code 145, which states that any person who unlawfully opens a closed document or in some manner gains access to its contents, shall be liable to fines or to imprisonment for a term not exceeding six months. In 2003, the United Kingdom introduced legislation requiring people to "opt in" to unsolicited emails. Called the Privacy and Electronic Communications Regulations, the law outlawed spam email without the prior consent of the recipient.

In South Africa, The Electronic Communications and Transactions Act of 2002 outlaws the unauthorized access to, interception of, or interference with data. Anyone who breaks this law faces a fine or imprisonment not exceeding 12 months. The Philippine government passed an act providing for the recognition and use of electronic commercial and noncommercial transactions. Those who violate the law are subject to a fine and a mandatory term of imprisonment from six months to three years. The German Penal Code has many provisions related to cybercrime, including Section 202a on data espionage, Section 303 on alteration of data, and Section 303b on computer sabotage.

England was the first European country to enact a law specifically on computer crime. In the Computer Misuse Act of 1990, three new offenses were defined: unauthorized access to a computer, unauthorized access with intent to commit or facilitate the commission of further offenses, and unauthorized modification of computer material. The Police and Justice Act of 2006 amended that law. The courts have also relied on the U.K. Criminal Damage Act of 1971 to prosecute computer crimes. The Protection of Children Act of 1978 protects children in child pornography.

The offenses of fraud and forgery are found in the Fraud Act of 2006 as well as the Forgery and Counterfeiting Act of 1981. Copyright statutes are found in the Copyright and Rights Related Acts.[1] More examples of anti-cybercrime laws from various countries are provided in Box 10.1.

Box 10.1   Examples of Anti-Cybercrime Legislation

Australia
The federal Cybercrime Act of 2001 amended the Criminal Code Act of 1995 to replace existing outdated computer offenses. In it, a person is guilty of an offense if he or she causes any unauthorized access to, or modification of, restricted data; intends to cause the access or modification; and knows that the access or modification is unauthorized. One or more of the following must also apply: the restricted data is held in a Commonwealth computer or held on behalf of the Commonwealth and the access to, or modification of, the restricted data is caused by means of a telecommunications service. The penalty is two years in prison.

Austria
The Privacy Act of 2000: Section 10 states:

> Provided that the offenses does not meet the statutory definition of a punishable action within the relevant jurisdiction of the court nor is threatened by a more severe punishment under a different administrative penalty clause, a minor administrative offense shall be pronounced with a fine of up to S260.00. Parties who: 1. willfully obtain unlawful access to a data application or willfully maintain discernible, unlawful and deliberate access, or 2. intentionally transmit data in violation of the Data Secrecy Clause (Section 15), especially data that were entrusted to him/her according to Section 46 and Section 47, for intentional use for other purposes or, 3. use data contrary to a legal judgment or decision, withhold data, fail to correct false data, fail to delete data, or 4. intentionally delete data contrary to (S) 26, Section 7

Brazil
Law no. 9,983 of July 14, 2000: has been adopted covering provisions

A. Entry of False Data into the Information System: Entry, or facilitation on the part of an unauthorized employee of the entry, of false data, improper alteration or exclusion of correct data with respect to the information system or the data bank of the Public Management for purposes of achieving an improper advantage for himself or for some other person, or of causing damages. Penalty is imprisonment for 2 to 12 years, and fines

B. Unauthorized Modification or Alteration of The Information System: article 313-B: Modification or alteration of the information system or computer program by an employee, without authorization by or at the request of a competent authority; penalty: detention for three months to two years and fines.

   a. The penalties are increased by one-third until one-half if the modification or alteration results in damage to the Public Management or to the individual.

Canada

The Canadian Criminal Code Section 342.1 states:

1. Everyone who fraudulently and without color of right,

   a. obtains directly or indirectly, any computer service,
   b. by means of an electro-magnetic, acoustic, mechanical or other device, intercepts or causes to be intercepted, directly or indirectly, any function of a computer system
   c. uses or causes to be used, directly or indirectly, a computer system with intent to commit an offense under paragraph (a) or (b) or an offense under section 430 in relation to data or a computer system, or
   d. uses, possesses, traffics in or permits another person to have access to a computer password that would enable a person to commit an offenses under paragraph (a), (b), or (c) is guilty of an indictable offense is liable to imprisonment for a term not exceeding ten years or is guilty of an offense punishable on summary conviction

Hong Kong

Telecommunication Ordinance: Section 27A: Unauthorized access to computer by telecommunication states the following:

(1) Any person who, by telecommunication, knowingly causes a computer to perform any function to obtain unauthorized access to any program or data held in a computer commits an offense and is liable on conviction to a fine of $20000

(2) For the purpose of subsection (1)

(a) the intent of the person need not be directed at

    (i)   any particular program or data
    (ii) a program or data of a particular kind; or
    (iii) a program or data held in a particular computer;

(b) access of any kind by a person to any program or data held in a computer is unauthorized if he is not entitled to control access of the kind in question to the program or data held in the computer and

    (i)   he had not been authorized to obtain access of the kind in question to the program or data held in the computer by any person who is entitled
    (ii) he does not believe that he has been so authorized; and
    (iii) he does not believe that he would have been so authorized if he had applied for the appropriate authority

Section 161: Access to computer with criminal or dishonest intent

(1) any person who obtains access to a computer

    (a) with intent to commit an offense
    (b) with a dishonest intent to deceive
    (c) with a view to dishonest gain for himself or another or
    (d) with a dishonest intent to cause loss to another, whether on the same occasion as he obtains such access or on any future occasion, commits an offense and is liable on conviction upon indictment to imprisonment for five years

Source: "The Council of Europe's Convention on Cybercrime: An Exercise in Symbolic Legislation," *International Journal of Cyber Criminology,* January–July 2010, July–December 2010 (Combined Issue) Vol 4 (1&2): 699–712; available at http://www.cybercrimejournal.com.

International Organizations

The laws pertaining to cybercrime in each country are different, and there are a wide variety of approaches to containing cybercrime. This has led to a great deal of conflict when a cybercrime was committed. What country is responsible for investigating the crime, under what legal code, and what punishment would the offender receive? Because of the inconsistencies in the laws of different countries, it was possible for some computer offenders to go free after committing offenses, without facing any criminal sanctions for their actions. With that in mind, it was quickly recognized that there was a need for a comprehensive, international law on cybercrime. In order to have a serious attack on an international problem, there was a need for a consistent international solution that could be applied when a cyberattack occurred.

This became particularly relevant in 2000, when the ILoveYou or Love Bug computer virus was disseminated to computers worldwide through an email attachment. When the attachment was opened, the virus was loaded onto a user's hard drive. Once attached to the recipient's computer, the virus was able to erase music, photos, and other files, and then send copies of itself to other addresses in the victim's address book. In the end, the virus affected 45 million computers around the world and caused an estimated $10 billion in damages. After investigating the crime, law enforcement determined that a man in the Philippines was responsible for the virus. At the time the bug was disseminated, the Philippines had no law specifically outlawing computer crimes, so the offender was not punished for his acts. About a month after that, the Philippine Congress passed the Electronic Commerce Law, which could be used to prosecute a similar act in the future.

After the release of the Love Bug virus, other countries that had been affected by the virus, including the United States, sought to extradite and apply their laws to punish the offender. This did not happen, but political leaders from around the world realized the need for international cooperation to regulate the cyberworld. Leaders agreed to meet to discuss the problems associated with cybercrimes and how they could cooperate in the future. Leaders from Group of Eight countries met for three days in Paris, France, to discuss crimes committed via the Internet. At the same time, members from the 41-nation Council of Europe, with the help of nonmember nations of United States, Canada, Japan, and South Africa, were working to develop a treaty that would standardize cybercrime laws across nations.[2]

It became clear that many countries did not have laws that outlawed cybercrimes or specified punishments for those who commit Internet crimes. Moreover, the laws that did exist were sometimes outdated, inconsistent, or in conflict with other laws in that same country or international laws. This is because legislators often do not understand the extent or the technicalities of cybercrime. This sometimes makes it difficult to pass effective laws. A common international law that would make investigating and prosecuting cybercrimes easier was needed.

European Commission

The European Commission, the executive board that oversees the European Union, is a group of 28 representatives from nations located primarily in Europe. It makes policies and recommends legislation to member states on different issues of concern to European nations. Cybercrime is one of those policy areas. In 1995, the European Commission announced a Data Protection Directive. This document focused on protecting personal data on the Internet. A revised document was published in November 2011. Under the new document, mandatory data breach disclosure laws were extended to include telecommunication companies and Internet service providers.

In 2013, the European Commission considered new laws on cybercrime. One of those would require all European organizations, such as banks, power companies, airports, hospitals, and industries, to report all serious cyberattacks on their systems. Only very small organizations (those with under 10 employees) would not be required to do this.

The European Commission also issued a strategy for incident reporting titled "An Open, Safe and Secure Cyberspace." It announced proposals that became the Directive on Network and Information Security and was intended to ensure a common level of network and information security across Europe. Once the directive was announced, it would be up to individual member states to determine how to enact this directive in their own countries.[3]

Under the directive, member states were asked to launch a minimum level of network security by setting up Computer Emergency Response Teams and by adopting national strategies and modes of cooperation. Additionally, those who operate critical infrastructure organizations will be required to assess potential risks in their organizations and approve appropriate policies to ensure the safety of computer systems.[4] The aim of the strategy is to harden smart grids and industrial control systems, fight botnets, raise security awareness, develop security standards, encourage research, and develop industrial and technical resources.[5]

World Intellectual Property Organization

The World Intellectual Property Organization is an agency within the United Nations that is focused on protecting intellectual property. One matter under its jurisdiction is the dispute resolution process for domain names and dealing with cybersquatting. When there is a dispute, the case goes to arbitration. If the arbitrator decides cybersquatting is occurring, he or she may issue an order to the domain name registrar who will then simply reassign the domain name.[6]

NATO

NATO (the North American Treaty Organization) is made up of 28 member states that cooperate on issues of defense and security. The long-term aim is to prevent conflict between nations. NATO has established a Computer Incident Response Capability (NCIRC) that is responsible for the cyber defense of all NATO sites around the world. If an attack were to occur, experts would meet and devise a response plan to restore the computer systems and return the situation to normal as quickly as possible with minimum loss of data and damage to computers. In October 2013, NCIRC upgraded its computer systems so it would be better protected.

In 2012, NATO established rapid reaction teams that would assist member states in the case of an attack. The teams offer technical assistance to members, especially to countries that have not developed resources for their own cyber defense. Each team has a permanent core of six trained experts. Other professionals may join a team as needed. Each team has the necessary equipment to conduct an investigation, such as satellite telephones, equipment for digital evidence collection, cryptography, digital forensic analysis, vulnerability management, and network security. Once a rapid reaction team is activated, it responds within 24 hours.[7]

Asia-Pacific Economic Cooperation

The Asia-Pacific Economic Cooperation is a group of 21 nations; its goal is to support trade and economic issues in the Asia-Pacific region. The membership is divided into steering groups that recommend policies to the entire group. The Security and Prosperity Steering Group works with cybercrime issues. When it comes to crimes on the Internet, the steering group works to, among other things, promote security, trust, and confidence in computer networks and e-commerce. They encourage Computer Emergency Response Teams and Computer Security Incident Response Teams. A major topic is the prevention of spam, spyware, and other cybercrimes. The group sponsors training sessions and workshops to educate businesses about preventing and responding to cybercrime.[8]

Association of Southeast Asian Nations

The Association of Southeast Asian Nations (ASEAN) is a group of 10 nations that cooperate to support economic growth, peace, and stability in the region. One way the group does this is to make policies regarding cybercrime. ASEAN has been committed to addressing cybercrime as a security threat. In 2014, its Senior Officials Meeting on Transnational Crime (SOMTC) finalized a road map or plan for combating cybercrime that included increased regional cooperation for training, law enforcement, and legal matters.[9]

Organization for Economic Cooperation and Development

The Organization for Economic Cooperation and Development (OECD) was created in 1961 as a way for member countries to work together to promote policies that improve the economic and social well-being of people around the world. Through the OECD, governments can share information on many problems that affect people's lives, predict future trends, and set standards on a wide range of topics.

In 2012, OECD studied cybercrime, noting that cybercrime is now a national priority in many countries. However, a major concern is how to leave the Internet free, open, and a platform for innovation and growth, while at the same time making it a secure place that businesses, individuals and governments can use for their needed functions. The final report highlighted suggestions made by business, individuals, and the Internet community as to how to protect users from harm while at the same time supporting the Internet.[10] OECD has also written reports on malware and ways to reduce the risks of cybercrime.

Council of Europe Cybercrime Treaty

The Council of Europe (CoE) is an international organization of 47 European countries. In 1995, the council adopted recommendations regarding criminal procedural law on cybercrime. The members recommended that its member states adopt particular guiding principles to follow in regards to criminal procedures in cases regarding cybercrimes. In general, the proposed recommendations were related to searches of computer systems, seizure of data, technical surveillance, and required cooperation with law enforcement, among other things.

The early recommendations were not enough to fully attack cybercrime, so in 1997 the CoE appointed a Committee of Experts on Crime in

Cyberspace to identify and define new cybercrimes as well as establish jurisdictional rights and criminal liabilities for crimes that occur via the Internet. Four nonmember nations, Canada, Japan, South Africa, and the United States were invited to participate in the process as observer nations.

From the start, the committee members recognized the need for a consistent international approach to fighting cybercrime. Committee members sought to establish standard laws concerning cybercrimes for the global community and thereby create a common policy that would effectively deter cybercrimes but also allow for easier investigation and prosecution of offenders. Committee members also sought to increase cooperation within law enforcement agencies in different locations, leading to a more effective evidence collection process. The committee came up with definitions of crimes committed on the Internet and then proposed actions or punishments for those who committed the offenses.

The committee's recommendations formed the basis of the Convention on Cybercrime. Completed in 2001, the proposed treaty is an international policy that makes it easier for countries to gather evidence about, prosecute, and punish those who commit cybercrimes. This is the only international agreement to attack the harms resulting from cybercrime and currently the only global document geared toward stopping international cybercrimes.[11] It is also the only international document that provides a framework for international cooperation in cybersecurity.

If a country agrees to participate in the CoE Cybercrime Treaty, it must also agree to create a minimum set of laws that address particular computer crimes (i.e., unauthorized access to computer networks, computer fraud).[12] The countries must also agree to participate with other countries in investigating cyberattacks. To do this, the officials must provide the name of a contact in their country who will assist any other country that is investigating a computer crime.

The treaty was signed by 26 member states. The countries with observer status in the European Council (the United States, Mexico, Japan, and Canada) were then given the option to sign it. The treaty was then considered for ratification by each member state and observer state. After five states, including at least three CoE member states, ratified it, the treaty would go into effect. This happened on July 1, 2004. To date, the convention has been ratified by 44 countries; nine others have signed but not ratified it. In August 2006, the United States became the 16th nation to ratify the treaty. Immediately after, Congress passed new laws to implement the treaty's provisions. The convention went into force in the United States on January 1, 2007.

Convention on Cybercrime Treaty

In general, the treaty includes provisions geared toward fighting terrorism, child sexual exploitation and child pornography, organized crime, copyright infringement, hacking, and Internet fraud. It acts as a framework for international cooperation between countries in investigating and prosecuting possible cybercrimes. The treaty gives police agencies increased powers to investigate and prosecute offenders if the crime committed crosses national boundaries.[13] An additional provision was added to the original treaty, which focused solely on racist and xenophobic materials sent through computer networks.

The treaty is organized into four chapters, which are broken down into sections and then articles. Each chapter discusses a different aspect of the treaty, with specifics given in the articles. In all, there are 48 articles in the treaty. A general outline of the treaty is provided in Box 10.2.

Chapter 1: Use of Terms

Chapter 1 of the treaty begins with a simple description and definition of relevant terms used throughout the document, such as "computer system," "computer data," "service provider," and "traffic data." The term "traffic data," for example, is any computer data relating to the data's chain of communication, including its origin, destination, route, time, date, size, duration, or type of underlying service.

Chapter 2: Measures to Be Taken at the National Level

Section 1: Substantive Criminal Law

Chapter 2 of the Cybercrime Treaty provides details about the criminal laws that participating countries should adopt if they agree to abide by the convention. There are five titles in this chapter. Title 1 addresses offenses against the confidentiality, integrity, and availability of computer data and systems and comprises six articles that attempt to provide protection for computer systems while at the same time not criminalizing legitimate computer usage. The articles describe the laws each country should adopt if it ratifies the treaty. For example, if a state ratifies the treaty it promises to pass laws against illegal access to a computer system without permission or with the intent of obtaining computer data or with other dishonest purpose. Other laws should address the application of cookies to locate and retrieve information; illegal interception (interception of nonpublic transmissions of computer data); the illegal use of software, passwords, or codes to collect data; data interference (the damaging, deletion, deterioration, alteration, or suppression of computer data); inputting malicious codes, such as viruses;

system interference (hindering a computer system); deleting or altering computer data; or misuse of devices. The last article, Article 6, defines the term "illegal devices." It prohibits the unauthorized creation, distribution, and use of programs that may assist others to have illegal access to computers or to systems.

Title 2 of Chapter 2 is called "Computer Related Offenses." This includes a requirement that participating countries create new laws that will make computer-related forgery (Article 7) and computer-related fraud (Article 8) illegal. The treaty provides states with a general description of what those crimes entail as a way to help ensure at least a minimum consistency between the laws passed in different countries. For example, the treaty describes computer-related forgery as "the input, alteration, deletion, or suppression of computer data with the result that inauthentic data is considered or acted upon as if it were authentic." The treaty defines the term "computer-related fraud" as causing a person to lose property by alteration, deletion, or suppression of data, or interference with a computer system. Countries are not required to adopt these definitions, but they serve as a guide.

Title 3 of Chapter 2 of the Cybercrime Treaty consists of Article 9, which describes what the legislation on child pornography should include for those nations who adopt the treaty. The law must include provisions outlawing the production, distribution, manufacturing, or possession of electronic child pornography. According to the treaty, child pornography is the depiction of a minor (or a person who appears to be a minor) engaged in sexual activity. It can also be realistic images that represent a minor engaged in sexual conduct. This includes sending child pornography through a computer system. A minor is defined as a person under the age of 18 but can be a person under 16 if a country decides on a lower age-limit.

Title 4 of the first section of Chapter 2 provides cooperating countries with guidelines for creating laws meant to curtail the theft of copyrighted and intellectual property on the Internet. Countries should pass legislation that protects literary and artistic works from being intentionally stolen by others. This includes written and musical property.

The final title of Section 1, Ancillary Liability and Sanctions, provides participating countries with guidelines about the liability of those who aid and abet others in committing cybercrimes as well as suggestions for punishments for people and corporations that commit criminal acts.

Section 2: Procedural Criminal Law
Section 2 of Chapter 2 describes procedures that must be followed when cooperating countries investigate and punish cybercrimes. There are

five titles in Section 2. Title 1 states that each country that adopts the treaty should create laws to give law enforcement officials increased powers when investigating cybercrimes. However, Article 15 provides that the powers should be limited under the law. In other words, there should be safeguards to protect the human rights and liberties of citizens of a country.

Title 2 of this section describes methods for protecting data when crimes are being investigated. Each country should, according to the treaty, adopt legislation to enable authorities to preserve computer data after allegations that a computer-related crime has occurred. Any stored data or information must be kept confidential for the entirety of the investigation. The only article in Section 2 provides that each country should pass laws that will permit law enforcement to collect data that may be located in another country. Article 3 has to do with the jurisdiction of these cases. In other words, this section answers the question about what court will hear any cases arising from this treaty and these new laws.

Title 4 relates to the search and seizure of stored computer data that could be used as evidence against a defendant who is accused of a computer crime. The treaty indicates that each country should allow law enforcement to have access to records as needed if it is part of a criminal investigation. Law enforcement should also be permitted to seize a computer system if data related to a crime is stored on it. If this is not possible, agents should be provided with a copy the relevant data.

Title 5 includes two articles having to do with collection of computer data by law enforcement during criminal investigations. Under Articles 20 and 21, each participating country should pass laws that would allow authorities to compel a service provider to record communications sent through a computer and then collect that data and provide it to law enforcement.

Section 3: Jurisdiction

Section 3 of Chapter 2 of the cybercrime treaty includes a statement that each participating country should create new laws that establish jurisdiction over computer offenses. This should happen if the offense is committed within a country's territory, or on a ship flying the flag of a country, on board an aircraft registered under the laws of that country, or by a country's officials.

Chapter 3: International Cooperation

In Chapter 3, International Cooperation, had two sections: General Principles and Specific provisions.

Section 1: General Principles Relating to International Cooperation

Section 1 consists of four titles. The first describes the general principles of the treaty as they relate to international cooperation. As underscored in the treaty, cooperation is essential for the treated to be fully implemented. Article 23 states that each country shall cooperate with other countries by passing reciprocal legislation and by investigating criminal offenses related to computer systems that occur within their boundaries.

Title 2 concerns the extradition of a person accused of committing a cybercrime. This titles states that the offenses in the earlier sections of the treaty shall be considered extraditable offenses, if they are punishable under the laws of both nations.

Title 3 describes the general principles concerning mutual assistance between countries that have adopted the treaty. Article 25 specifies that the countries shall provide mutual assistance to the fullest extent possible during investigations. The second Article in Title 3, Article 26, states that each country shall provide other countries with any information they may have if it could assist in an investigation of a crime. Upon providing the requested information, the country providing the data may request that the information be kept confidential by the receiving country.

Title 4 relates to procedures for mutual assistance requests in situations where there are no formal international agreements. The two articles, Articles 27 and 28, in this title oblige countries to provide mutual assistance even if there is no mutual assistance treaty, and that if sensitive data is shared with another country it cannot be disseminated to others.

Section 2: Specific Provisions

Section 2 has three titles. The first concerns the preservation of stored data. Article 29 states that law enforcement agencies in one country can request that stored data in another country be preserved if an offense is under investigation. If the requesting nation wants the data to be preserved, it must provide reasons. A request for preservation of data can only be refused if the request concerns an offense that the requesting nation considers to be a political crime, or if the request is likely to prejudice the security or public order in that country. The second article in Section 2 deals with the expedited disclosure of preserved traffic data.

The second title under this section is the mutual assistance regarding access to stored computer data. A nation can ask another nation to search or seize data within its territory if it has been preserved. The request should be carried out quickly if there is a belief that the data in question is vulnerable to being lost or modified. Further, the treaty states that a country can access data if it is available to the public (open source), regardless of where it is located geographically (Article 32). Finally, countries should provide mutual assistance to collect real-time data (Article 33).

The last title in this section states that each country should have a point of contact who is available at all times and can give immediate assistance to any other country for collecting evidence of a possible crime.

Chapter 4: Final Provisions

The last chapter of the treaty includes some miscellaneous provisions relating to the passage and implementation of the treaty. The first article describes how the treaty will be ratified. This is important because the document can only be carried out if a certain number of countries have agreed to be bound by it. Article 37 of the treaty states that the CoE may invite nonmember states or territories to join the member states in the convention. According to Article 38, any state may extend the treaty to territories. The provisions of this treaty will supplement any preexisting treaties, according the Article 39. Other articles allow for a country to declare any reservations it has about the treaty (statements made by officials in a country to clarify certain points), for nations to withdraw their reservations at a later time, or denounce the treaty at any time. Finally, amendments to the treaty may be proposed by any nation.

Issues and Concerns with the CoE Treaty

The CoE Cybercrime Treaty is clearly a serious attempt to attack the problem of cybercrime on an international level. However, the treaty was criticized as having significant issues, making some wonder if it could be effective at reducing cybercrime. Some have argued that the treaty will have a limited effect, if any, in halting future cybercrimes.

First, the treaty requires participating nations to provide their police and investigators with more powers of surveillance and interception when investigating cybercrimes. Participating nations are also asked to require Internet service providers to give assistance to investigators who are investigating cybercrimes. Some critics argue that these rules are a way to increase the investigatory powers of the police and therefore increase the government's ability to control the content of the Internet. Critics also argue that these provisions would give government the authority to conduct surveillance on the citizens of another country—even if the citizen is alleged to have broken no laws in his or her home country. Some organizations in the United States point out that the treaty is worded such that

Box 10.2   Outline of the Council of Europe Convention on Cybercrime

Chapter 1: Use of Terms
Chapter 2: Measures to Be Taken at the National Level

Section 1: Substantive Criminal Law
    Title 1: Offenses Against the Confidentiality, Integrity and Availability of Computer Data and Systems
Article 1: Offenses Against the Confidentiality, Integrity and Availability of Computer Data and Systems
Article 2: Illegal Access
Article 3: Illegal Interception
Article 4: Data Interference
Article 5: System Interference
Article 6: Misuse of Devices
    Title 2: Computer-related Offenses
Article 7: Computer-related Forgery
Article 8: Computer-related Fraud
    Title 3: Content-related Offenses
Article 9: Offenses Related to Child Pornography
    Title 4: Offenses Related to Infringements of Copyright and Related Rights
Article 10: Offenses Related to Infringements of Copyright and Related Rights
    Title 5: Ancillary Liability and Sanctions
Article 11: Attempt and Aiding or Abetting
Article 12: Corporate Liability
Article 13: Sanctions and Measures

Section 2: Procedural Law
    Title 1: Common Provisions
Article 14: Scope of Procedural Provisions
Article 15: Conditions and Safeguards
    Title 2: Expedited Preservation of Stored Computer Data
Article 16: Expedited Preservation of Stored Computer Data
Article 17: Expedited Preservation and Partial Disclosure of Traffic Data
    Title 3: Production Order

international law enforcement could carry out surveillance that would not be permitted by U.S. law.

Moreover, some members of civil rights organizations expressed concerns that the increased surveillance powers given to law enforcement agencies in the treaty could undermine the privacy rights of citizens. They point out that under the treaty, Internet service providers could be required to provide customer records to investigators. This could pose a risk to the privacy of those who use the Internet. Additionally, an Internet service provider could be held criminally liable if it fails to monitor customer or user content, or for the criminal actions of their employees. European critics of the treaty are concerned about the possible transfer of their citizens' personal data to agencies outside of Europe.

Another problem with the CoE Cybercrime Treaty is based on differences that may exist between countries when it comes to investigating cyber offenses. Some countries lack adequate resources or trained personnel to investigate cybercrimes. Thus, they may be unwilling to fully implement the requirements pertaining to increased law enforcement. Although some countries have established specific agencies that are responsible for investigating cybercrimes, others have not. For example, the European

Union created a high-tech organization, the European Network and Information Security Agency, which is responsible for coordinating cybercrime investigations within member countries. But many countries do not have such an organization and have no plans to create one. The extent of the investigations done by these different countries may vary widely.

Countries also vary concerning their legal systems. Some countries in Europe have a common-law system (the United Kingdom and Ireland), but others have a civil-law system (most continental countries).[14] This may affect the investigation of crimes and how offenders are treated once arrested.

Differences may also exist between countries regarding the collection, preservation, and analysis of evidence. Countries have established different standards for searches and seizures of criminal evidence. In the United States, for example, the legal requirements that must be met before a search warrant will be granted are quite stringent. Other nations do not allow law enforcement to carry out online investigations of alleged offenders because it is deemed to be an excessive use of police power. Because of the differences in search-and-seizure policies, provisions of the CoE treaty may not be enforced equally or consistently.

Other critics of the convention have pointed out that the countries that choose to participate are not the countries that are lax when it comes to cybercrime. Some countries are known to provide cybercriminals with a safe haven to conduct their crimes. These countries may be the ones that are choosing not to participate in the treaty.

Additional concerns about the treaty may prohibit it from being fully enforced. First, there is no dual criminality in the treaty. This means that if a person in the United States is accused of committing a crime in a foreign country, the United States must carry out a search and seizure for evidence against that person, even if the activity is legal in the United States. In other words, the act may be legal in the United States, but illegal in another country, so the accused may be investigated by U.S. officials at the request of foreign officials. For example, someone accused of certain types of speech, which may be protected in the United States but illegal in other countries, may be searched.

Critics of the treaty argue that many of the provisions are unclear or provide only vague definitions of some terms. For example, the definition of "illegal devices" in the treaty is unclear and may be used by law enforcement as an excuse for investigating individuals who are engaged in legal activity. As another example, the term "service provider" is defined in the treaty as any public or private entity that provides a service via the computer or any entity that stores data for such an online service. Critics say that under this definition a restaurant delivery service could be considered to be a service provider. Because the terms are defined so generally, the treaty will be difficult to enforce.

Critics also argue that there will still be inconsistencies in the laws of different countries, even though the treaty suggests specific laws that need to be passed in order for a country to be part of the treaty. More than likely, the definitions and interpretations of key terms will vary greatly from nation to nation, and there will be many differences in the legislation that

---

Box 10.3 The Takedown of Darkode

One of the major benefits to the growth of network technology and the Internet is the ability to work across borders seamlessly. This same benefit, however, makes it increasingly complex to pursue cybercriminals. This is because traditional jurisdictional boundaries applied in law enforcement do not apply in cyberspace.

However, just because it is difficult does not mean that enforcement across these boundaries is not being done. Recently, there was a particularly good example of international cooperation that exemplified the cross-jurisdictional cooperation necessary in the modern cybercrime landscape.

Darkode was one of the most widely known forums accessed by cybercriminals to share information on malware, rent botnets, and find partners to operate their operations with. Darkode has been around for at least eight years, and was managed by a succession of several hackers who specialized in different forms of cybercrime.

The takedown of Darkode was accomplished through the cooperation of at least 21 law enforcement agencies from around the world. It was led by the FBI but based in Europol's European Cybercrime Center. The operation, code named "Shrouded Horizon," resulted in the arrest of 28 individuals associated with Darkode, including 12 in the United States.

While the FBI and Europol suggested that the takedown of Darkode was a significant blow to the online underground, it is more likely that the users who were not arrested simply moved to other sites. In a way it is ironic. The same technology that helps law enforcement agencies to coordinate their efforts against cybercriminals allows those cybercriminals to move seamlessly once their operations have been shut down. However, the pace of the takedowns is increasing, as more and more law enforcement embrace the international nature of the policing required to address modern issues of cybercrime.

Source: R. Reeve, "Law Enforcement Clears out Darkode Cyber-criminal Forum," *SC Magazine*, July 20, 2015, http://www.scmagazineuk.com/law-enforcement -clears-out-darkode-cyber-criminal-forum/article/426864/.

results. For example, the concepts of fraud vary greatly from nation to nation, as do definitions of pornography. Some countries are prohibited constitutionally from passing certain laws. For example, the U.S. Congress cannot impose restraints on free speech over the Internet. This inconsistency may lead to difficulties with enforcement.

Another reason for the inconsistencies that may appear is that nations are permitted to opt out of certain provisions of the treaty. They can choose what provisions they will enact while ignoring others. The suggestions for laws that were made in the treaty are just that—suggestions. Further, the patchwork of legislation that may result may make investigations and punishments even more complicated. After a crime occurs and the laws are enforced, the penalties imposed may not be sufficient for the harm caused.

On November 7, 2002, the Council of Ministers within the CoE adopted an additional provision that was separate from the Cybercrime Convention. This provision addressed racist and xenophobic materials posted on the Internet. The United States was not a signatory to this provision.

Conclusion

Ultimately, it is unlikely that there will be uniform, international legislation on cybercrime in the near future. However, most international organizations recognize the need for legislation that permits better law enforcement investigations of cybercrimes and better protection of computer systems. The issue, of course, is that countries differ as to their ability to implement policies passed by others, or their willingness to do so. As cybercriminals continue to increase the number and severity of their attacks, international organizations will have to react quickly or it could mean real damage to computers and infrastructures around the world.

Review Questions

1. Provide some examples of laws passed in other countries to combat cybercrime.
2. What actions have international organizations taken to combat cybercrime?
3. Describe the Council of Europe's Cybercrime Convention.

Key Terms

Computer Incident Response Capability (NATO)
Convention on Cybercrime (Council of Europe)
Data Protection Directive (European Commission)
Rapid Reaction Team (NATO)
Senior Officials Meeting on Transnational Crime (ASEAN)

Notes

1. Bert-Jaap Koops and Tessa Robinson, "Cybercrime Law: A European Perspective" in *Digital Evidence and Computer Crime*, ed. Eoghan Casey, 3rd ed. (Boston: Academic Press, 2011), 123–183.

2. "Leaders Join to Fight against Internet Crime," *Chicago Tribune*, May 15, 2000, http://articles.chicagotribune.com/2000-05-15/news/0005160020_1_love-bug-cybercrime.

3. "EC to Force Firms to Disclose Cyber-attacks," *Computer Fraud and Security*, February 2013, 1, 3.

4. European Commission, "Commission Proposal for a Directive Concerning Measures to Ensure a High Common Level of Network and Information Security across the Union," July 2, 2013, http://ec.europa.eu/digital-agenda/en/news/commission-proposal-directive-concerning-measures-ensure-high-common-level-network-and.

5. "EC to Force Firms to Disclose Cyber-attacks."

6. Grainne Kirwan and Andrew Power, *The Psychology of Cyber Crime: Concepts and Principles* (Hershey, PA: Information Science Reference, 2012).

7. NATO, "NATO Rapid Reaction Team to Fight Cyber Attack," March 13, 2012, http://www.nato.int/cps/en/natohq/news_85161.htm?selectedLocale=en.

8. APEC, "Security and Prosperity Steering Group," http://www.apec.org/Groups/SOM-Steering-Committee-on-Economic-and-Technical-Cooperation/Working-Groups/Telecommunications-and-Information/Security-and-Prosperity-Steering-Group.aspx.

9. Association of Southeast Asia Nations, "ASEAN Steps Up Fight Against Cybercrime and Terrorism," May 30, 2014, http://www.asean.org/news/asean-secretariat-news/item/asean-steps-up-fight-against-cybercrime-and-terrorism.

10. OECD, *Cybersecurity Policy Making at a Turning Point*, 2012, http://www.oecd.org/sti/ieconomy/cybersecurity%20policy%20making.pdf.

11. Oliver Silver, "European Cybercrime Proposal Released," *Computer Fraud and Security*, May 2001, 5.

12. Steve Gold, "G8 Cybercrime Meeting Seeks Global Cooperation," *Newsbytes*, May 15, 2000.

13. Bill Hancock, "US and Europe Cybercrime Agreement Problems," *Computers and Security* 19, no. 4 (2000): 306–307.

14. Koops and Robinson, "Cybercrime Law: A European Perspective."

CHAPTER ELEVEN

Conclusion

Introduction

CYBERCRIME WILL NO DOUBT CONTINUE TO EVOLVE AND expand in the next few years as technology continues to evolve. It is hard to predict what will happen in the upcoming years, as the technology and threats change constantly. The number of attacks on individuals, businesses, and governments will only continue to increase and become more severe. Cybercriminals will become more technologically savvy and will continue to seek to profit from their acts or harm other computer systems. The costs associated with cybercrimes will increase as businesses and organizations face more attacks. Not only that, but losses associated with the theft of intellectual property will also increase as more people around the world connect to the Internet.

A successful attack on cybercrime must incorporate multiple avenues: new legislation, and international cooperation. Individuals and businesses must also take actions to protect themselves from becoming a victim of cybercrime.

New Legislation

Governments will need to continue to pass legislation as new cybercrimes emerge. They must also give police the ability to investigate crimes, which means adequate funding. It also means more training for police who respond to reports of cyberattacks. They need to know how to collect evidence from computers in a way to that will maintain its integrity and allow it to be presented in court. New anti-forensic programs make it more difficult for police to find information on hard drives, and police must learn how to disable these programs and find needed information.

Laws that make data handlers liable for losing data or for cyber events are needed. This means increased fines for data breaches, more regulations, and increased notification requirements to not only report the incident to authorities but also to inform customers that their personal information may have been compromised.[1]

Legislation should also require agencies to monitor cybercrime, gather information, and publish data on cybercrime. Legislation should also provide a safe harbor for businesses to report threats and crimes without fear of criminal and civil liability. This will allow companies and the government to make better choices about the risk of cybercrime and policies.

International Cooperation

There must also be international cooperation, as cybercriminals do not respect traditional boundaries. Law enforcement must be given the ability to work across borders, and agencies must provide assistance to others who are investigating possible illegal acts. At the same time, the rights of individuals cannot be ignored, and cultural differences must be respected. International organizations should continue working to devise international cooperation in solving the problems of cybercrime.

Individual Action

Individuals can take precautions to help ensure that they will not become the victim of a cybercrime. Businesses and individuals are often the weakest link in the security chain. They often fail to install adequate security policies and procedures, leaving their systems vulnerable to an attack. In many organizations, information security is often more relaxed than it should be. Many businesses do not prepare adequately for potential incidents. They fail to anticipate what could happen or fail to take proactive steps to prepare their business for an attack. Agencies and organizations of all kinds can play a role in attacking cybercrime by increasing the security of their computer systems. When organizations increase their awareness of cybercrime and place security tools on their systems, it will contribute to a lower risk of cyberattacks. In today's environment, it is essential for organizations to employ a comprehensive cyber forensic program to protect them from an attack.

Many businesses have started to store data on the cloud network This allows businesses easy access to their data, allows employees to be more productive, and in the long run saves money. But there are questions about the security of the cloud, and many businesses are cautious about using cloud-based services.

It is important that businesses and individuals increase their software programs, such as firewalls, to help prevent access by unauthorized users. Firewalls inspect all pieces of information that enter or leave a computer as a way to help to screen out hackers and vandals from stealing personal information or placing malware on the computer system.

Placing antivirus software on a computer system may help to block malware from being installed, and it also removes any viruses that are able to pass through a firewall.

Businesses and individuals can also place email blocking systems, called spam filters, on their computers. These prevent most unsolicited email messages and junk email from appearing in a user's inbox. That way, emails with malware cannot be opened and cannot unleash viruses onto a computer. But these programs are not perfect, and users must be careful about opening emails from unknown or suspicious sources. Often, emails and websites appear to be legitimate. It is important that users are cautious and are educated about the dangers of unfamiliar websites and messages. It may be as simple as encouraging the use of strong passwords that are more difficult for hackers to crack.

To protect key or sensitive data, encryption methods are available. These protect information by changing it before it is transmitted from one computer to another. Once received, the information can be deciphered only with the code. Personal devices such as laptops, cell phones, and flash drives can be encrypted to protect them if they are lost or stolen.

If an attack does occur, immediate action must be taken to stop additional damage or harm, and to preserve any evidence.

All computer systems should be continuously monitored for suspicious activity. Audits should be performed regularly to detect unusual behavior. Companies and individuals must periodically examine their security. Other precautions might include providing a way for employees to report illicit or suspicious activity, limiting access to sensitive files, and providing proper training for employees.

Businesses must also share information about new cyber threats with other organizations and with law enforcement. This can prevent attacks from happening or detect them quickly before harm is caused.

Users should also be careful when using the Internet. While the Internet can be very helpful, it can also pose great danger, and users need to be aware of that. They need be cautious when posting personal information on a social media outlet and need to be cautious about purchasing items online from unknown websites or using public Wi-Fi sources. If a person becomes the victim of a cybercrime, it needs to be reported to law enforcement immediately. Additional tips are listed in Box 11.1.

Box 11.1   Tips to Avoid Becoming a Victim

Identity Theft
- Ensure that websites are secure before submitting a credit card number.
- Never throw away credit card or bank statements in a usable form. Shred them to protect your identity.
- Be aware of missed bills, which could indicate that an account has been taken over.
- Be cautious of scams requiring personal information.
- Never give a credit card number over the phone unless you initiate the call.
- Monitor credit statements monthly for any fraudulent activity. Review a copy of your credit report at least once a year.
- Report unauthorized transactions to bank or credit card companies as soon as possible.

Credit Card Fraud
- If purchasing merchandise, ensure that it is from a reputable source. Do research to ensure the legitimacy of the individual or company.
- Beware of providing credit card information through unsolicited emails.
- Promptly reconcile credit card statements to avoid unauthorized charges.

Phishing/Spoofing
- Avoid filling out forms in email messages that ask for personal information.
- Always compare the link in the email to the link to which you are actually directed.
- Research a company's official website instead of clicking a link from an unsolicited email.
- Contact the actual business that supposedly sent the email to verify if the email is genuine. Do so via your own research or by using the phone number on the back of the card if the message purports to be from a bank or credit card provider or about the statements you receive.

Spam
- Do not open spam. Delete it unread.
- Never respond to spam as this will confirm to the sender that it is a live email address.
- Have a primary and secondary email address: one for people you know and one for all other purposes.
- Avoid giving out your email address unless you know how it will be used.
- Never purchase anything advertised through unsolicited email.

Nigerian Letter or "419" Fraud

- Be skeptical of individuals representing themselves as Nigerian or foreign government officials asking for your help in placing large sums of money in overseas bank accounts.
- Do not believe the promise of large sums of money for your cooperation.
- Guard your account information carefully.

Sources: IC3, *2013 Annual Report*, www.ic3.gov/preventiontips.aspx; FBI, "Internet Fraud," http://www.fbi.gov/scams-safety/fraud/internet_fraud.

Insurance

An emerging type of insurance is cyber risk insurance, though these policies are still rare within the insurance industry. They first appeared in the late 1990s, but as cybercrime grows and threatens businesses with greater financial consequences and long interruptions, more insurance firms have recognized the need for the product. The companies most interested in the insurance are those companies most prone to attacks, such as financial institutions.[2]

Cyber insurance would help a company or organization deal with losses after an interruption in business that may occur after a cyberattack. There may also be damage to digital assets, as with some kinds of cyber extortion. Insurance may provide an emergency response team to help a company handle the immediate aftereffects of a breach. A cyber insurance policy may help with a forensic investigation or with the public relations that are needed after an event. There may also be litigation, depending upon the harm done. The insurance may also help to protect the reputation of a brand if it is under attack. However, the insurance industry has been cautious in providing such products, as there is a wide range of new, complex, and often unknown issues surrounding these crimes.[3]

Conclusion

No individual or organization is able to absolutely prevent a cyberattack or data breach, but some steps can be taken to reduce the risk. By increasing security, the risk can be mitigated. If an event does occur, that incident can be handled efficiently and effectively to minimize the damage to the organization and the individuals involved.

Protecting a company's data and information is more complex now. Threats to a company's security are becoming more common and more serious. Hackers have many weapons that they can use against a business, and these weapons are constantly changing and evolving. It is difficult for information technology (IT) personnel to know how to prevent malware that does not yet exist, so having a course of action is sometimes difficult.[4] It is not possible to have a completely secure system but traditional defenses are no longer sufficient. IT personnel must make the system as secure as possible and ensure that the appropriate policies and procedures are in place. By putting procedures in place, it is possible to mitigate some of the risks posed by cybercriminals.[5]

Cyberattacks occur in businesses because there are often security weaknesses in their computer systems. Many organizations do not keep their security as current as they should and are therefore not adequately protected from potential cyberattacks. This is especially true of smaller companies that do not have entire departments to handle security threats. As cybercrime evolves, cybercriminals are able to develop new and innovative ways to bypass standard security measures, such as firewalls. Cybercriminals can easily breach most traditional IT security systems. Any malware that uses a code or technique that has not been previously identified as malicious will get past security without a problem. The increased security standards that may be required to keep customer data secure may cost the company more money.[6]

While some elements of cybercrime and cybersecurity can be addressed at the company level, the government will also take additional steps in the coming years to address this growing problem. The Center for Strategic and International Studies has produced a list of guidelines for cybersecurity that include a variety of elements, the most important of which is creating a comprehensive national plan to address cybersecurity issues. A more complete explanation of their recommendations can be found in Box 11.2.

Box 11.2   Excerpt from the Center for Strategic and International Studies Recommendations About Cybersecurity

The report begins with the following recommendations for a national strategy.

Create a Comprehensive National Security Strategy for Cyberspace
1.   The president should state as a fundamental principle that cyberspace is a vital asset for the nation and that the United States will protect it

using all instruments of national power, in order to ensure national security, public safety, economic prosperity, and the delivery of critical services to the American public.

2. The president should direct the National Security Council (NSC), working with a new office in the Executive Office of the President (EOP)—the National Office for Cyberspace—and other relevant agencies to create a comprehensive national security strategy for cyberspace. Comprehensive means using in a coordinated fashion all the tools of U.S. power—international engagement and diplomacy, military planning and doctrine, economic policy tools, and the work for the intelligence and law enforcement communities.

3. The United States should open the discussion of how best to secure cyberspace and present the issues of deterrence and national strategy to the broad national community of experts and stakeholders.

The report also asserts that any strategy dealing with the challenges cyberspace will present in the future must address the following 11 areas to be successful. Without addressing these components, any strategy will be incomplete, and therefore likely to fail.

1. Organize for cybersecurity
2. Partner with the private sector
3. Regulate for cybersecurity
4. Secure industrial control systems and supervisory control and data acquisition
5. Use acquisitions rules to improve security
6. Manage identities
7. Modernize authorities
8. Revise the Federal Information Security Management Act
9. End the division between civilian and national security systems
10. Conduct training for cyber education and workforce development
11. Conduct research and development for cybersecurity

Source: Center for Strategic and International Studies, *Securing Cyberspace for the 44th Presidency: A Report of the CSIS Commission on Securing Cyberspace for the 44th Presidency*, December 2008, http://csis.org/files/media/csis/pubs/081208 _securingcyberspace_44.pdf.

However the nation addresses the issue, it is clear that cybercrime is not going anywhere soon. With new technologies constantly evolving and additional threats becoming apparent every day, cybercrime will likely become an increasingly important challenge for law enforcement, government, and private industry. Moreover, as it becomes simpler for criminals to engage in cybercrime, individuals will continue to have to take additional steps to protect themselves.

Notes

1. Nigel Pearson, "A Larger Problem: Financial and Reputational Risks," *Computer Fraud and Security*, April 2014, 11–13.

2. Danny Bradbury, "Insuring against Data Breaches," *Computer Fraud and Security*, February 2013, 11–15.

3. Daljitt Barn, "Insuring Cyber-assets," *Computer Fraud and Security*, September 2012, 5–8.

4. Maria Eriksen-Jensen, "Holding Back the Tidal Wave of Cybecrime," *Computer Fraud and Security*, March 2013, 10–15.

5. "Security Finally Climbs Up the Corporate Agenda," *Computer Fraud and Security*, October 2014, 3.

6. "Further Fallout from the Target Breach as Banks and Retailers Consider Responses," *Computer Fraud and Security*, April 2014, 1, 3.

Timeline of Significant Events

1960

- Telephone calls are switched by computer for the first time.

1967

- The Advanced Research Projects Agency (ARPA) works with U.S. computer experts to form a network of Interface Message Processors (IMPS). The computers act as gateways to mainframes at a variety of institutions in the United States and provide a major part of what would become the Internet in the years ahead.

1969

- The ARPA creates ARPANET, later to be known as the Internet.
- The first computer hackers emerge at MIT.
- Joe Engressia (aka the Whistler) discovers that if he whistles at a certain pitch into a pay telephone, he is be able to make long-distance calls at no cost. He becomes known as the father of phreaking.

1971

- John Draper (aka Cap'n Crunch) notices that a free toy whistle found inside a box of Cap'n Crunch cereal is the same pitch as the sound used by AT&T's long-distance switching system. He uses this to build a blue box that permits phreakers to make free long-distance telephone calls. Later, *Esquire* magazine publishes an article in which they provide instructions to make a blue box. Steve Jobs and Steve Wozniak, the future founders of Apple Computer, use the information to build their own blue box.
- The first email program is written and used on ARPANET. The @ symbol is used for the first time.

1972

- *May*: John Draper (aka Cap'n Crunch) is arrested for phone phreaking. He is later convicted and sentenced to four months in California's Lompoc prison.

1981

- *February*: Ian Murphy (aka Captain Zap) is the first hacker charged with criminal offenses related to breaking into the computer systems at AT&T and altering the internal clocks so customers were charged incorrectly. He is later tried and convicted as a felon.
- *May*: Seventeen-year-old Kevin Mitnick us arrested for stealing computer manuals from the switching center at Pacific Bell. He is prosecuted as a juvenile offender and sentenced to a one year term of probation.

1982

- *May*: Kevin Mitnick cracks the Pacific Telephone system and TRW and destroys data on their computer systems.
- *June*: Members of the 414 gang are arrested after breaking into computer systems of Memorial Sloan Kettering Cancer Center and Los Alamos military computers.

1983

- *June*: The movie *WarGames* is released. In the film, Matthew Broderick plays a teenager who accidentally starts the countdown to World War III. The film helps to shape the public's perception of hackers and glamorizes hackers.
- A 19-year-old UCLA student uses his personal computer to hack into the Department of Defense's international communications system.

1984

- *Summer*: The hacking group Legion of Doom is formed by Vincent Louis Gelormine (aka Lex Luther). Other members (along with their aliases) include Chris Goggans (Erik Bloodaxe), Mark Abene (Phiber Optik), Adam Grant (the Urvile), Franklin Darden (the Leftist), Robert Riggs (the Prophet), Loyd Blankenship (the Mentor), Todd Lawrence (the Marauder), Scott Chasin (Doc Holiday), Bruce Fancher (Death Lord), Patrick K. Kroupa (Lord Digital), James Salsman (Karl Marx), Steven G. Steinberg (Frank Drake), and Corey A. Lindsly (Mark Tabas) as well as Agrajag the Prolonged, King Blotto, Blue Archer, the Dragyn, Unknown Soldier, Sharp Razor, Doctor Who, Paul Muad'Dib, Phucked Agent 04, X-man, Randy Smith, Steve Dahl, the Warlock, Terminal Man, Silver Spy, the Videosmith, Kerrang Khan, Gary Seven, Billfrom RNOC, Carrier

Culprit, Master of Impact, Phantom Phreaker, Doom Prophet, Thomas Covenant, Phase Jitter, Prime Suspect, Skinny Puppy, and Professor Falken.

1986

- *September*: German hackers in the group the Data Travellers breach the computers at NASA and other top-secret computer installations around the world.
- *October*: Congress passes Computer Fraud and Abuse Act.
- German hackers in the group Chaos Computer Club breach the computers at the German Nuclear Power Program during the Chernobyl nuclear crisis.

1987

- *November*: Chaos Computer Club hacks into NASA's computer network.
- *December*: Kevin Mitnick is convicted and sentenced to probation for breaking into computer systems at Santa Cruz Operation and stealing software. Later, he shows experts at the company how he was able to breach their system.

1988

- *June*: The U.S. Secret Service videotapes the SummerCon hacker convention without the participants' knowledge.
- *November*: Robert T. Morris Jr., the son of a scientist at the National Security Agency and a graduate student at Cornell University, delivers a self-replicating worm on the Internet. The malware spreads to some 6,000 networked computers, overloading government and university systems. Morris is convicted of cybercrimes and sentenced to three years' probation along with a $10,000 fine.
- *December*: Robert Riggs (aka the Prophet) and a member of the Legion of Doom hacking group breaks into the computer network of BellSouth. He downloads a document that outlines how the 911 emergency phone system works. Riggs sends the document to the editor of *Phrack*, a magazine for hackers, Craig Neidorf (aka Knight Lightning). Later, Neidorf and Riggs are arrested by federal agents and indicted for theft of the document, allegedly worth $79,449. The trial is halted when it is discovered that the document could be purchased by the public for less than $20.
- *December*: Kevin Mitnick is charged with stealing $1 million in software from Digital Equipment Corporation and causing that firm $4 million in damages.

1989

- Corey Lindsly (aka Mark Tabas), a hacker and former member of Legions of Doom, appears in court to plead guilty to felony charges after hacking into the computers of US West. He is sentenced to five years of probation.

- *January*: Hacker and Legions of Doom member Loyd Blankenship (the Mentor) is arrested and writes the Hacker's Manifesto.
- *January*: Herbert Zinn (aka Shadowhawk) becomes the first person convicted under the Computer Fraud and Abuse Act. Zinn was 16 years old (a juvenile) when he broke into the computer systems of AT&T and the Department of Defense. He is convicted of destroying files worth millions of dollars and publishing secret passwords. He also published instructions outlining the process for breaking into computer security systems. Zinn is sentenced to spend nine months in prison and fined $10,000.
- *June*: A 16-year-old in Indiana hacks into the computer of McDonald's and gives all the workers raises and then changes the phone switches so that a person who called the probation department in Florida would be sent to a phone-sex line in New York. He is sentenced to 44 months on probation and 400 hours of community service.
- *July*: Three members of the Legion of Doom are charged with breaking the computer systems of Bell South and stealing proprietary information.

1990

- *March*: Steve Jackson Games, Inc. is investigated when federal agents discover that Legion of Doom members Loyd Blankenship (aka the Mentor) and Chris Goggans (aka Erik Bloodaxe) have a rulebook to the game GURPS Cyberpunk. The agents believe the book contains instructions for computer hacking. They also seize other documents and equipment.
- *March*: Richard G. Wittman Jr., a 24-year-old from Denver, Colorado, pleads guilty to a count of altering information (a password) to hack into the computer system at NASA.
- *April*: Computer hackers from the Netherlands breach the computers of 34 sites in the U.S. Department of Defense. This gives them access to unclassified but sensitive information on military personnel, travel information, and logistics.
- *May*: Agents from the U.S. Secret Service and the Arizona Organized Crime and Racketeering Bureau carry out raids of computer hackers in Operation Sundevil. Hackers are arrested in Cincinnati, Detroit, Los Angeles, Miami, Newark, Phoenix, Pittsburgh, Richmond, San Diego, San Francisco, San Jose, and Tuscon,
- *June*: Kevin Poulsen hacks into the computer system of KIIS-FM radio station in Los Angeles in order to win a $50,000 Porsche that was to be awarded to the 102nd caller. Poulsen uses his computer to control all of the telephone lines at the station and block all calls but his.
- *July*: Mitch Kapor and John Perry Barlow establish the Electronic Frontier Foundation as a way to defend the rights of people who are investigated and charged with committing computer hacking offenses.

1991

- *April*: Kevin Poulsen (aka Dark Dante) is arrested after hacking into systems at Pacific Bell.
- *July*: Justin Petersen (aka Agent Steal and Eric Heinz) is arrested after breaking into TRW to steal credit cards.

1992

- *January*: Morty Rosenfeld is convicted after he hacked into TRW to steal credit card information and then selling credit reports.
- *July*: Members of the hacking group Masters of Deception are indicted after an investigation involving wiretaps.
- *November*: Kevin Mitnick hacks into the systems at the California Department of Motor Vehicles.

1993

- *July*: The first Def Con hacking conference takes place in Las Vegas, Nevada. The conference becomes an annual event.

1994

- *January*: Masters of Deception founder and hacker Mark Abene (aka Phiber Optik) is sentenced to one year in prison. Afterward, *New York* magazine calls him one of the city's 100 smartest people.
- *March*: Richard Pryce (aka Datastream Cowboy), a 16-year-old music student, is arrested and charged with breaking the computer system at Griffiss Air Force Base, NASA, and the Korean Atomic Energy Research Institute, among others. Pryce pleads guilty to 12 hacking offenses and is fined $1,800.
- *June*: A 23-year-old Russian, Vladimir Levin, carries out the first publicly revealed international bank robbery via the Internet. He is able to steal about $10 million from Citibank by transferring the money to international bank accounts. Levin is caught, convicted, and sentenced to three years in prison. The bank later claims to have recovered all but $400,000 after working with the FBI and Interpol to track down the criminals.
- *August*: Justin Petersen steals $150,000 from Heller Financial through the Internet.

1995

- *February*: Kevin Mitnick is arrested and charged with unauthorized access to the computers of many computer software manufacturers, cellular telephone manufacturers, Internet service providers, and educational institutions. He is also charged with stealing, copying, and misappropriating proprietary computer software from such companies as Motorola, Fujitsu, Nokia, Sun, Novell, and NEC. At the time he is arrested, Mitnick is in possession of 20,000 credit card numbers.

- *May*: After he pleads guilty and is sentenced for multiple crimes, Chris Lamprecht (aka Minor Threat) is the first person to be banned from using the Internet. Some of his crimes involve the theft and sale of Southwestern Bell circuit boards.
- *September*: Golle Cushing (aka Alpha Bits), a 22-year-old hacker, is arrested for selling credit card and cell phone information.
- *November*: Christopher Pile (aka Black Baron) is the first person jailed for writing and distributing a computer virus. Pile is sentenced to 18 months in jail for his virus.

1996

- *May*: The U.S. General Accounting Office reports that computer hackers attempted to break into the computers at the U.S. Department of Defense around 250,000 times in 1995. They also report about 65 percent of the attempts were successful.
- *April*: Christopher Schanot, a 19-year-old honor student from St. Louis, Missouri, is indicted for successfully hacking into national computer networks, military computers, and the credit reporting service for TRW and Sprint. He is indicted for computer fraud, illegal wiretapping, and unauthorized access to corporate and government computers.
- *April*: Hackers access the phone system of the New York City Police Department and change the message played for callers. The altered message says, "Officers are too busy eating doughnuts and drinking coffee to answer the phones." The altered message also informs callers to dial 119 in an emergency.
- *July*: The first federal computer sabotage case takes place after Tim Lloyd is accused of placing a software time bomb in the computer systems at Omega Engineering in New Jersey. When executed, the malware destroys the company's computer network, denying them the ability to manufacture goods throughout the summer of 1996. In the end, the attack caused the company an estimated $12 million, and 80 employees lost their jobs. Because of his crimes, Lloyd is given a sentence of 41 months in jail and ordered to pay more than $2 million in restitution.
- *August*: Eric Jenott, a paratrooper based in Fort Bragg, North Carolina, is accused of hacking into U.S. Army computers to steal passwords. He later provides those passwords to someone from China. Jennot is cleared of charges of spying but found guilty of damaging government property and computer fraud.
- *September*: Kevin Mitnick is indicted for damaging computers at the University of Southern California and stealing files containing passwords. The charges against him include 14 counts of wire fraud.

1997

- *March*: A computer hacker known as Jester is the first juvenile who has federal charges brought against him for a computer crime. He is sentenced to pay restitution to the telephone company and complete 250 hours of community service.
- *May*: A 36-year-old hacker, Carlos Felipe Salgado Jr. (aka Smak), inserts a malware sniffer program to collect credit card information from a dozen companies that sell products via the Internet. Carlos collects around 100,000 credit card numbers and the information to use them.
- *December*: A 21-year-old hacker from Argentina, Julio Ardita (aka El Griton), is sentenced to three years of probation after he hacks into computer systems of Harvard, NASA, Los Alamos National Laboratory, and the Naval Command Control, and Ocean Surveillance Center.

1998

- *February*: The Stuxnet worm infiltrates Iranian nuclear fuel enrichment facilities.
- *March*: A 19-year-old Israeli teenager, Ehud Tenenbaum (aka the Analyzer), is arrested in Israel for hacking into unclassified Pentagon computers to steal software programs. The deputy defense secretary calls the attack "the most organized and systematic attack" on U.S. military systems. Although Tenenbaum worked with other teenagers, he is identified as the ringleader.
- *April*: Shawn Hillis, a 26-year-old former employee of NASA contractor Lockheed Martin from Orlando, Florida, pleads guilty in a federal district court after being accused of using a NASA workstation to gain unauthorized access to computer networks of several Orlando businesses.
- *April*: A juvenile from Alabama launches an email bomb across a NASA network against another person. The young offender is later ordered to a 12-month term of probation.
- *April*: Members of the Masters of Deception hacking group claim that they broke into the networks of multiple military organizations, including the Defense Information Systems Network and the network's Equipment Manager, which oversees the military's global positioning satellites.
- *May*: The Flame virus attacks computers in the Middle East. Cybercriminals identify a flaw in the Microsoft security system that allows them to create a digital security certificate that appears to be an official Microsoft update. Instead of updating computers, the program installs massive amounts of spyware. This is the largest piece of malware discovered to date and is considered to be a complex and sophisticated cyberespionage tool. The Flame virus is undetected for over two years.
- *May*: Members of L0pht (now @stake), a hacker group from Boston, Massachusetts, testify in front of the U.S. Senate about the vulnerabilities of the Internet.

- *June*: Shakunla Devi Singla, a former employee of the U.S. Coast Guard accesses a personnel database and deletes data that takes 1,800 hours to reconstruct. She is able to do this because she helped design the program.
- *July*: During the DEF CON 6 conference, members of the hacking group Cult of the Dead Cow release Back Orifice malware, which allows users to compromise Windows security.
- *September*: Hackers break into the website of the *New York Times* and rename it HFG (Hacking for Girls). After hacker Kevin Mitnick is arrested, they target the newspaper because a *New York Times* reporter coauthored a controversial book about Mitnick. Later, the hackers admitted that they hacked the newspaper because they were bored.
- *December*: Twin brothers from China, Hao Jinglong and Hao Jingwen, are sentenced to death after breaking into the network of the Industrial and Commercial Bank of China and stealing 720,000 yuan (about $87,000). The brothers attempted to transfer the money into accounts they set up under aliases.
- Flu-Shot-3 was a useful program for detecting viruses. Hackers created Flu-Shot-4, which appeared to be an update to version 3, but was actually malware that destroyed critical areas of hard disks and any floppies.

1999

- *February*: A 15-year-old teenager from Vienna, Austria, hacks into the system of Clemson University.
- *March*: The Melissa worm, written by 29-year-old David Smith, is released. The virus infects a document on a victim's computer, causing that document to be sent to others. The virus (named after a stripper in Florida) spreads through emails. The virus affects about 100,000 users and causes $80 million in damages.
- *March*: Jay Satiro, an 18-year-old high school dropout, is charged with computer tampering after he hacks into the computers of America Online and alters some data. Satiro pleads guilty and is sentenced to serve one year in jail and five years without a home computer.
- *April*: Ikenna Iffih, a 28-year-old resident of Boston, Massachusetts, uses a home computer to gain access to multiple computer systems, including those of NASA and the U.S. Department of Defense. Once illegally in the system, he intercepts user log-in names and passwords and delays communications. He is sentenced to 6 months of home detention, placed on supervised release for 4 years, and ordered to pay $5,000 in fines.
- *May*: The White House website (whitehouse.gov) is defaced by the hacker group Global Hell.
- *July*: Back Orifice 2000 malware is released at the annual DEF CON 7 hacker conference.
- *August*: The website for ABC news is defaced by the hacker group United Loan Gunmen.

- *September*: The website for C-Span is defaced by United Loan Gunmen.
- *September*: The website for the Drudge Report is defaced by United Loan Gunmen.
- *September*: The websites for the NASDAQ and American Stock Exchange are defaced by United Loan Gunmen.
- *November*: One of the founding members of Masters of Reverse Engineering, 15-year-old Norwegian Jon Johansen, is part of a group of programmers who release DeCSS, a program designed to beat the Content Scrambling System (CSS) encryption used to protect movies on DVD.

2000

- *February*: A 16-year-old Canadian hacker known as Mafiaboy is able to launch a distributed denial-of-service attack with tools readily available on the Internet. He launches a remotely coordinated attack of Internet Protocol packet requests from zombie servers that takes Yahoo off-line for over three hours. Mafiaboy pleads guilty to hacking charges and is sentenced to eight months in a youth detention center.
- *May*: Auditors from the General Accounting Office are able to gain access to sensitive personal information from the Department of Defense by using a file publicly available on the Internet. The auditors are able to enter the file without using any user authentication. They gain access to Social Security numbers, addresses, and pay information of employees.
- *May*: The Love Bug virus (aka ILOVEYOU virus) is released by a hacker in the Philippines. Michael Buen and Onel de Guzman are suspected of writing the virus.
- *July*: AOL confirms that personal records for more than 500 screen names of its customers were hacked. The records contain the customer's name, address, and the credit card number used to open the account.
- *July*: A member of the Darkside Hackers group, 25-year-old Andrew Miffleton (aka Daphtpunk) of Texas, is sentenced to 21 months in prison and ordered to pay a $3 million fine. Miffleton used unauthorized access devices to fraudulently obtain cellular telephone service through cloned cellular telephones. He also used stolen calling card numbers to gain free long-distance telephone service.
- *September*: Raymond Torricelli (aka Rolex), a 21-year-old from New Rochelle, New York, breaks into computers at NASA's Jet Propulsion Laboratory. He is a member of the hacking group #conflict, which electronically changes the results of the annual MTV Movie Awards. Agents find more than 76,000 discrete passwords on Torricelli's personal computer. He is sentenced to four months in prison.
- *September*: Patrick W. Gregory (aka MostHateD), a 20-year-old founding member of the hacking group GlobalHell, pleads guilty to conspiracy to commit telecommunications wire fraud and computer hacking and is sentenced to

26 months in prison and three years of supervised release. He is also ordered to pay a fine of $154,529.86 in restitution. His group was allegedly responsible for $1.5 million in damages to different corporations and government agencies, including the White House and the U.S. Army. Gregory also admits to stealing telephone conferencing services from AT&T, MCI, and Latitude Communications so he could hold conference calls with hackers around the country.

- *September*: Jason Diekman (aka Shadow Knight and Dark Lord) is arrested by federal agents after they find evidence on his computer that he stole usernames and passwords from many universities, including Harvard, Stanford, and Cornell. Diekman admits to hacking into "hundreds, maybe thousands" of computers. He is sentenced to 21 months in federal prison and three years of supervised release. He is also asked to pay $87,000 in restitution.

- *October*: The FBI arrests two Russian hackers, Alexei Ivanov, age 20, and Vasily Gorshkov, age 25, for victimizing American businesses for two years. To arrest the pair, the FBI opens a bogus computer security firm and calls Ivanov about being employed as a hacker. The men agree to a meeting and fly to Seattle, Washington, where they are arrested by FBI agents.

- *December*: Hackers steal over 55,000 credit card numbers and information from creditcards.com, which processes credit transactions for online companies. About 25,000 numbers are posted online after the company refuses to make an extortion payment.

- *December*: A contractor for the U.S. government, Exigent International, discovers that hackers broke into a restricted federal computer system to steal the code used to control satellite systems.

2001

- *February*: Hackers breach the computer systems of the World Economic Forum, allowing them access to credit card numbers, personal cell phone numbers, and information on passports and travel arrangements for government and business leaders. Among the victims whose information is stolen are Microsoft chairman Bill Gates, Palestinian Authority chairman Yasser Arafat, UN Secretary-General Kofi Annan, former U.S. secretary of state Madeleine Albright and former Israeli prime minister Shimon Peres.

- *February*: The Anna Kournikova virus is released by Jan de Wit (aka OnThe-Fly), a 20-year-old Dutchman. He is later arrested and sentenced to 150 hours of community service.

- *March*: Nineteen-year-old Raphael Gray, from Wales, hacks into the credit card account of Bill Gates.

- *August*: Riggs Bank, based in Washington, discovers that its database of Visa customers has been stolen by hackers.

- *September*: The Nimda worm (the name is "admin" backwards) begins to spread. This malware infects Microsoft Internet Information Servers, which have known software vulnerabilities.

- *November*: The group Hacking for Satan infects the websites of 25 churches.
- *December*: Federal prosecutors accuse Jerome Heckenkamp, a former employee of the Los Alamos National Laboratory, of breaking into the computer systems when he was a student. He was suspected of carrying out attacks on other companies, including eBay and E*Trade.

2002

- *January*: Alicia Kozakiewicz, a shy, 13-year-old girl from Philadelphia, Pennsylvania, chats online with Scott Tyree, a 38-year-old computer programmer posing as a 14-year-old girl. Tyree arranges to meet Kozakiewicz and then abducts her and drives her to a townhouse in Virginia, where she is tortured and raped. Kozakiewicz is rescued after Tyree sends photos of her to an Internet acquaintance who calls the FBI. Tyree is sentenced to spend 19 years and seven months in prison.
- *May*: Max Butler (aka Max Vision and the Equalizer) is sentenced to 18 months in prison after launching a worm that affects hundreds of military and defense contractor computers. Butler also serves as an FBI informant and gives the agency information on the activities of other hackers. At the time, he was running a security firm in Silicon Valley.
- *July*: The hacking group World of Hell defaces 679 websites in one minute.
- *July*: The Code Red worm is released and affects thousands of computers. The malware exploits vulnerabilities in the Microsoft Internet Information Server.
- *July*: Five Russian and Ukrainian men are arrested by U.S. federal agents for a massive credit card hacking spree. The agents allege that the men compromised the information of over 160 million credit card accounts and caused $300 million in losses to the companies involved. The men are charged with stealing usernames, passwords, and other personally identifiable information from NASDAQ, 7-Eleven, JCP, Dow Jones, Euronet, Heartland, and Global Payment, among others.
- *July*: Hackers break into the website of *USA Today* and replace several legitimate news stories with phony articles. Israeli hackers are suspected to be behind the attack.
- *July*: Admissions officials at Princeton University gain unauthorized access to the Yale University website, which contains the personal information of applicants to the school.
- *August*: Police in Italy arrest 14 hackers believed to be responsible for thousands of computer intrusions, including attacks on the U.S. Army, the U.S. Navy, and NASA. The people arrested are members of the Mentor and Reservoir Dogs hacking groups.
- *August*: The website of the Recording Industry Association of America is defaced.
- *October*: A 27-year-old Russian hacker, Vasily Gorshkov, is sentenced to three years in prison after being convicted of 20 counts of conspiracy, fraud, and

other computer crimes. He is also ordered to pay restitution of almost $700,000 to Speakeasy Network of Seattle and PayPal for losses suffered.

- *October*: Microsoft is hacked.
- *November*: A 36-year-old British systems administrator, Gary McKinnon (aka Solo), is indicted for hacking 92 networks run by NASA, the Pentagon, and other military installations as well as networks of private sector businesses. In total, the attacks cause about $900,000 in damages. Officials claim that McKinnon stole passwords, deleted files, and shut down computer networks on military bases.
- *November*: Lisa Chen, a 52-year-old native of Taiwan, is charged with software piracy and sentenced to nine years in prison. Chen is arrested after local sheriffs seize thousands of copies of pirated software estimated to be worth over $75 million.

2003

- The Titan Rain cyberattack, launched against computers at the Department of Defense, is designed to copy sensitive data files. Specifically, the malware is used to attack the U.S. Defense Information Systems Agency, the U.S. Army's Redstone Arsenal and Strategic Defense Initiative, and other computer systems. The hack goes undetected for many months, allowing the criminals to collect large quantities of information. Many officials suspect that the malware originated in China.

2005

- *May*: Sven Jaschan, a 17-year-old German citizen, creates the Sasser worm, which harms computers around the world. Jaschan is later found guilty of cyber vandalism and received a 21-month suspended sentence.

2006

- *May*: A data analyst at the U.S. Department of Veterans Affairs takes electronic data to his home, something he is not permitted to do. His house is burglarized and the data stolen. The information includes names, Social Security numbers, dates of birth, and disability ratings for about 26.5 million veterans and their spouses as well as personal information for about 645,000 members of the armed forces reserves.
- *May*: The State Department's networks are hacked, and unknown foreign intruders download significant amounts of information.
- *April*: Sven Jaschan, a 17-year-old German citizen, is sentenced to 32 months in prison and three years of supervised release for creating the Sasser worm and conspiracy. The sentence is the result of a plan to defraud CitiBank. Flury had obtained the account numbers of stolen CitiBank debit cards, along with

personal identification numbers (PINs) and other personal identifiable information of the account holders. Flury then encoded the information onto blank automated teller machine (ATM) cards and used the counterfeit cards to obtain cash from ATMs. It is thought that he collected in excess of $384,000. Once he had the cash, he transferred $167,000 to the people in Europe and Asia who had supplied the stolen CitiBank account information.

- *November*: Hackers attempt to penetrate networks of the U.S. Naval War College in Newport, Rhode Island, resulting in a two-week shutdown while infected machines are restored. Officials had to disconnect the entire campus from the Internet.
- *December*: NASA blocks emails with attachments before shuttle launches out of fear they will be hacked. *Business Week* reported that unknown foreign intruders had obtained the plans for the latest U.S. space launch vehicles.

2007

- *April*: The U.S. Department of Commerce has to take the Bureau of Industrial Security's networks off-line for several months after they were hacked by unknown foreign intruders. The bureau reviews confidential information on high tech exports.
- *May*: Estonian government networks are attacked by a denial-of-service attack by unknown foreign agents, though most believe the Russian government is behind the attacks. As a result, some government online services are temporarily disrupted and online banking comes to a halt.
- *May*: The National Defense University has to take its email systems off-line because of hacks by unknown foreign intruders that leave spyware on the system.
- *June*: The unclassified email account of U.S. Secretary of Defense Robert Gates is hacked by unknown foreign intruders.
- *August*: The British Security Service, the French prime minister's Office, and the office of German chancellor Angela Merkel complain to China about intrusions on their government networks. Merkel even raises the matter with China's president.
- *September*: British authorities report that hackers, thought to be from China's People's Liberation Army, have attacked the network of the Foreign Office and other key departments.
- *September*: Contractors employed by the Department of Homeland Security and the Department of Defense have their networks hacked.
- *September*: Francis Delon, France's secretary-general of National Defence, states that groups from China have infiltrated France's information systems.
- *October*: Over a thousand staffers at the Oak Ridge National Laboratory receive an email with an attachment that, when opened, gives outsiders access to the lab's databases.
- *October*: China's Ministry of State Security says foreign hackers from Taiwan and the United States stole information from the Chinese. They claim that

spyware was found in the computers of classified departments of China's Aerospace Science and Industry Corporation.

- *November*: Jonathan Evans, the head of Britain's Security Service (MI5), warns 300 businesses of the increased potential online threat from Russian and Chinese state organizations. He claims that China is devoting considerable time and energy trying to steal sensitive technology and obtain political and economic intelligence.
- *November*: An 18-year-old youth from New Zealand, who goes by the name "AKILL," writes software that allows criminals to access millions of bank accounts, resulting in a theft of $20 million.

2008

- *January*: A CIA official says that the agency knows of four incidents overseas where hackers were able to disrupt, or threaten to disrupt, the power supply for four foreign cities.
- *January*: The computer systems at Marathon Oil, ExxonMobil, and ConocoPhillips are hacked, and each company loses data detailing the quantity, value, and location of oil discoveries around the world. One company puts the losses in the millions.
- *February*: Cybercriminals use stolen debit cards to take cash from ATMs in 280 cities and three continents (including the United States, Canada, Japan, Russia, and Hong Kong) simultaneously. Within a 12-hour span, the offenders steal an estimated $9 million in cash. Officials believe the crime was carried out by the Hacker 3 group from Eastern Europe.
- *March*: U.S. officials report that American, European, and Japanese companies are experiencing significant losses of intellectual property and business information to criminal and industrial espionage in cyberspace.
- *March*: South Korean officials claim that China has attempted to hack into the Korean Embassy and Korea military computer networks.
- *April–October*: A State Department memo made public by WikiLeaks reports that computer hackers successfully stole about "50 megabytes of email messages and attached documents, as well as a complete list of usernames and passwords from an unspecified [U.S. government] agency." At least some of the attacks originated from a Shanghai-based hacker group linked to the People's Liberation Army's Third Department.
- *May*: An Indian official accuses China of hacking into government computers. The official states that the Chinese are attempting to gain access to their computers in order to learn how to disable or disrupt networks during a conflict.
- *June*: The networks of several congressional offices are hacked by unknown foreign intruders.
- *September*: The Yahoo email account of U.S. presidential candidate Sarah Palin is hacked during the campaign by David Kernell, who posts some of Palin's personal photographs and messages as a way to embarrass her and derail her

political campaign. Databases at the Republican and Democratic presidential campaigns are also hacked and downloaded by unknown foreign intruders.

2009

- *March*: Reports indicate that plans for a new presidential helicopter, *Marine Corps 1*, have been found on a file-sharing network in Iran.
- *April*: Chinese hackers reportedly infiltrate South Korea's Finance Ministry and attach a virus to emails that appear to be sent from trusted individuals.
- *April*: Articles in the *Wall Street Journal* show that the U.S. power grid is increasingly vulnerable to cyberattack.
- *May*: The Department of Homeland Security Information Network is hacked by unknown attackers who gain data by hacking into an account of a federal employee or contractor.
- *May*: Merrick Bank, a leading issuer of credit cards, reports that hackers accessed their computer systems and saw information on as many as 40 million credit card accounts. Bank officials report that the bank lost $16 million as a result.
- *June*: The interior minister of Germany, Wolfgang Schaeuble, notes that China and Russia are increasing their espionage efforts and Internet attacks on German companies.
- *June*: Unclassified networks at the Johns Hopkins University's Applied Physics Laboratory, which does classified research for the Department of Defense and NASA, are hacked. As a result, the networks are taken off-line.
- *July*: Cyberattacks are initiated against government and other websites in the United States and South Korea. Officials in South Korea accuse hackers from North Korea of being responsible for the attacks. The attacks do not disrupt services but last for many days and receive a great deal of attention in the press.
- *July*: Yxes (an anagram of "sexy"), malware that affects mobile phones, is discovered. When a phone is infected, it forwards its address book to a central server, which in turn forwards a short message service (SMS) text containing a URL to each contact. When a person clicks on the link, the malware is downloaded and installed on the phone. This process is repeated over and over again. The Yxes virus was largely limited to Asia, where it infected at least 100,000 devices.
- *August*: Albert Gonzalez is indicted on charges that he and other Russian or Ukrainian colleagues stole over 130 million credit and debit cards by hacking into the computer systems of five major companies. This is the largest hacking and identity theft crime in U.S. history.
- *October*: Operation Phish Phry, a two-year FBI investigation becomes one of the largest cyberfraud phishing cases. The target is criminals who use financial information stolen from thousands of account holders at U.S. banks to transfer about $1.5 million into their own bank accounts. As a result of the investigation, FBI agents arrest almost 100 people, some in Egypt, and charge them with computer fraud, money laundering, and other crimes.

2010

- *January*: The national security adviser in India reports that his office and other government departments were attacked by Chinese hackers; however, the prime minister's office denies that their computers were hacked.
- *January*: Financial services firm Morgan Stanley reports that it was a victim of a very sensitive break in to its network, as do officials at Google. Reports indicate that the attack was carried out by hackers based in China.
- *March*: Officials at NATO and in the European Union report that the number of cyberattacks against their networks had increased significantly over the previous 12 months. They indicate that Russia and China are among the most active adversaries.
- *May*: A memo leaked from the Canadian Security and Intelligence Service indicates that attacks on computers owned by the Canadian government, universities, private companies, and individuals have increased substantially.
- *May*: Albert Gonzalez hacks into computers of government officials in India and major U.S. businesses and sells the hacked information with customer account information to other criminals for almost $3 million. Later, Gonzalez is convicted and sentenced to 20 years in prison.
- *October*: Australia's Defence Signals Directorate reports a large increase in the number of cyberattacks on military sites.
- *October*: The *Wall Street Journal* reports that hackers used Zeus malware, which is available on cybercrime black markets for about $1,200, to steal over $12 million from five banks in the United States and United Kingdom.
- *October*: Stuxnet, a form of malware, is discovered in Iran, Indonesia, and elsewhere. Some believe the attack is a government weapon geared to bringing down the Iranian nuclear program.
- *October*: Officials at NASDAQ report that their networks were hacked, and it is unclear how far the hackers penetrated the network and how much data may have been compromised.

2011

- *January*: Canadian government officials report that its agencies were victims of a major cyberattack. As a result of the attack, the Finance Department and Treasury Board, Canada's main economic agencies, were forced to disconnect from the Internet. Many government sources claim the offender was China.
- *April*: The FBI reports 20 incidents between March 2010 and April 2011 in which online banking information of small to medium-sized U.S. businesses were breached. The information was then used to transfer money to Chinese economic and trade companies. According to the FBI, as of April 2011, the total losses from the fraud amounted to approximately $20 million; the actual loss to victims was $11 million.

- *April*: Google reports that a phishing effort based out of China compromised hundreds of Gmail passwords linked to accounts of prominent people, including some senior U.S. officials.
- *April*: FBI agents uncover an international cyberfraud operation that attacked up to 2 million computers using botnet malware with the Coreflood virus. The offenders relied on a keylogging program to steal a victim's personal and financial information.
- *April*: Employees at the Oak Ridge National Laboratory receive fake emails with malware attached. As a result, two computers are infected, allowing offenders to access data.
- *May*: Cybercriminals pretending to be from the hacktivist group Anonymous attack the PlayStation network and Sony Online Entertainment and steal personal information from accounts. Sony estimates that data pertaining to over 80 million users was compromised, including names, birth dates, credit card information, and home addresses. They also report that the cost of the breach was over $170 million.
- *June*: Citibank reports the theft of personal credit card data for around 360,000 customers.
- *June*: Computers at the International Monetary Fund are compromised by a foreign government by the use of malware attached to bogus emails. They report that a large quantity of data, including documents and emails, was stolen.
- *June*: The Nintendo gaming system is attacked by hackers, allowing them access to one of the site's servers. They are able to copy and publish a configuration file.
- *June*: Hackers break into a database of Fidelity National Information Services, a Florida company that issues prepaid debit cards. The cybercriminals change the maximum daily withdrawal limits on 22 debit card accounts and then withdraw money from these accounts multiple times, netting $13 million.
- *June*: The social network LinkedIn is hacked, possibly exposing about 6.5 million passwords. The passwords are then dumped onto InsidePro, a Russian password-cracking forum. Officials later determine that only the passwords were stolen, leaving the email addresses secure.
- *June*: DroidKungFu, one of the most technologically advanced viruses, is used to attack mobile phones. The virus includes a well-known exploit that allows it to become an administrator of the phone. This means the virus controls the phone. The virus evades detection by antivirus software.
- *June*: Plankton emerges and remains one of the most widespread Android malware applications. The virus allows the phone to download unwanted ads, changes the home page of the mobile browser, or adds news shortcuts and bookmarks to the phone.
- *July*: The U.S. deputy secretary of defense mentions in a speech that a defense contractor was hacked and 24,000 files were stolen from the Department of Defense.
- *November*: Chinese hackers interfere with two satellites belonging to NASA and U.S. Geological Survey.

2012

- *January*: Hackers attack the online shoe store Zappos.com, compromising the credit card numbers and other personal information of 24 million customers.
- *February*: The media reports that hackers from China have stolen classified information about the technologies onboard F-35 Joint Strike Fighters.
- *March*: The U.S. Department of Homeland Security issues alerts warning of a possible cyberattack on U.S. gas pipelines. The potential attack is described as a sophisticated spear-phishing campaign that will begin with a single source.
- *June*: LinkedIn and eHarmony are attacked, and 65 million passwords are stolen and posted online.
- *July*: More than 10,000 email addresses of top Indian government officials are hacked, including officials in the prime minister's office; in the defense, external affairs, home, and finance ministries; and in intelligence agencies.
- *August*: A piece of malware nicknamed "Gauss" infects 2,500 systems around the world. The virus appears to be aimed at Lebanese banks.
- *September*: A hacker group from Iran, Izz ad-Din al-Qassam, launches Operation Ababil, which uses denial-of-service attacks to targeted bank websites. Targets of the malware include Bank of America, the New York Stock Exchange, Chase Bank, Capital One, SunTrust, and Regions Bank.
- *December*: Two power plants in the United States are infected through employees' use of unprotected USB drives.
- *December*: The Wells Fargo website is attacked by denial-of-service malware.

2013

- *January*: The *New York Times*, *Wall Street Journal*, *Washington Post*, and *Bloomberg News* are all victims of persistent cyberattacks thought to originate in China.
- *January*: The Japanese Ministry of Foreign Affairs reports that it was hacked and at least 20 documents, including highly classified documents, were stolen.
- *February*: Officials at the U.S. Department of Homeland Security report that between December 2011 and June 2012, cybercriminals attacked 23 gas pipeline companies to access information that could be used for sabotage. Data pointed to China as the culprit.
- *May*: Chinese hackers breach computer systems at the U.S. Department of Labor and at least nine other agencies.
- *June*: Federal prosecutors charge eight people with attempting to steal $15 million from customers in an international cybercrime scheme. The hackers gained unauthorized access to computer networks and then diverted customer funds to bogus bank accounts and prepaid debit cards. Among the companies targeted were Citigroup, eBay, PayPal, JPMorgan Chase & Co, and TD Ameritrade Holding Corporation.

- *September:* The U.S. Navy reports that Iran hacked into unclassified networks.
- *September:* FakeDefender, the first ransomware for Android mobile phones, emerges. The virus locks an infected phone and requires the victim to pay a ransom to retrieve the phone's contents. The phone must be reset to factory settings in order for it to function again.

2014

- *January:* An online breach at the U.S. retail company Target allows offenders to steal the credit card and personal information of over 100 million customers. The breach costs the company $148 million.
- *January:* Neiman Marcus, a major retailer in the United States, is attacked. The credit card information of over 350,000 individuals is stolen, and over 9,000 of the credit cards have been used fraudulently since the attack. The breach went undetected for months, allowing criminals to gather a large amount of data.
- *January:* The computer system at retail store Michaels is hacked. The hacking affects the payment cards of 2.6 million people.
- *January:* Yahoo! mail services for 273 million users are hacked. The company does not release the specific number of accounts affected.
- *April:* For a period of two weeks, an inside hacker has access to AT&T computers and uses the data to gain personal information.
- *May:* A cyberattack on eBay results in the accounts of eBay employees and customers being hacked.
- *May:* Five Chinese hackers are indicted for computer hacking and economic espionage of companies in the United States.
- *June:* P.F. Chang's China Bistro is hacked, and credit and debit card information from 33 of their restaurants is stolen and sold online.
- *June:* A data breach at the Montana Health Department may have affected over 1 million people.
- *June:* Domino's Pizza is hacked by the Re Mundi group, which steals records of over 600,000 Belgian and French customers. In exchange for not publishing the personal data, which includes names, addresses, emails, phone numbers, and favorite pizza toppings, Mundi demands that the company pay $40,000 in cash. They threaten to publish the customer information online if the ransom is not paid. Domino's refuses to comply and reassures customers that financial and banking information was not stolen.
- *August:* Information from over 60 UPS stores is compromised.
- *August:* Reports indicate that several major U.S. banks, including JPMorgan Chase, have been hacked, compromising information for 76 million households and 7 million small businesses.
- *August:* The computers of the contractor responsible for security clearances at the Department of Homeland Security are hacked. Personal information of their employees is compromised.

- *August*: A hacking group known as Lizard Squad claims responsibility for a denial-of-service attack on the PlayStation Network, Sony Online Entertainment, and Blizzard's video game servers.
- *September*: The credit card information of about 56 million customers of Home Depot is breached.
- *September*: Hackers get into Apple iCloud computers and steal passwords used to access online data storage. These events led to the posting of celebrities' private photos.
- *September*: Goodwill Industries International is hacked, and information for about 868,000 customers is stolen.
- *October*: The contact information for 76 million households and 7 million small businesses at JP Morgan Chase is compromised. The hackers may have originated in Russia.
- *October*: Credit and debit card information from 395 Dairy Queen restaurants is stolen.
- *October*: Servers at the U.S. Postal Service are hacked, exposing employees' names, addresses, and Social Security numbers.
- *October*: The computer systems at the National Oceanic and Atmospheric Administration at the U.S. Department of Commerce are hacked, skewing the accuracy of some National Weather Service forecasts.
- *October*: The Department of State reports possible breaches of its unclassified networks. The department is forced to shut down the entire unclassified email system to repair damage. A month later, there is suspicious cyberactivity on a White House computer network. The White House reports that no classified networks were breached.
- *October*: Gameover Zeus, or Zbot, is a Trojan horse malware that infects millions of computers. It is transferred through an email, usually as an apparent invoice. When the bill is opened, the malware is installed on the computer. The malware is used to gain access to a bank account.
- *November*: Sony Pictures Entertainment is hacked. Some data is deleted, and employees' personal information and unreleased films are posted online. An FBI investigation reveals that North Korea is behind the attack.

2015

- *February*: The computer systems of Anthem, a U.S. health insurance company, are hacked. The personal information of 80 million customers is stolen from an unencrypted database.
- *May*: The Internal Revenue Service reports that identity thieves stole personal information from the tax returns of 100,000 taxpayers. They accuse criminal operations from Russia for the attack.

Selected Bibliography

Ablon, Lillian, Martin C. Libicki, and Andrea A. Golay. *Markets for Cybercrime Tools and Stolen Data: Hacker's Bazaar*. RAND Corporation, 2014. http://www.rand.org/content/dam/rand/pubs/research_reports/RR600/RR610/RAND_RR610.pdf.

Altheide, David. *Terrorism and the Politics of Fear*. Oxford: AltaMira, 2006.

Arquilla, John, and David Ronfeldt. "Cyberwar Is Coming!" *Comparative Strategy* 12 (1993): 141–165.

Brenner, Susan. *Cybercrime: Criminal Threats from Cyberspace*. Santa Barbara, CA: Praeger, 2010.

Brenner, Susan. "Organized Cybercrime: How Cyberspace May Affect the Organization of Criminal Relationships." *North Carolina Journal of Law and Technology* 4 (2002): 1–50.

Broadhurst, Roderic, Peter Grabosky, Mamoun Alazab, and Steve Chon. "Organizations and Cybercrime: An Analysis of the Nature of Groups Engaged in Cybercrime." *International Journal of Cybercriminology* 8 (2014): 10–20.

Caldwell, Tracey. "Spear-phishing: How to Spot and Mitigate the Menace." *Computer Fraud and Security* (January 2013): 11–16.

Carter, David L., and Andra J. Katz. *Computer Crime: An Emerging Challenge for Law Enforcement*. East Lansing: Michigan State University, 1997.

Casey, Eoghan. *Digital Evidence and Computer Crime*. London: Academic Press, 2000.

Cavelty, Myriam Dunn. *Cyber-Security and Threat Politics: US Efforts to Secure the Information Age*. New York: Routledge, 2007.

Center for Missing and Exploited Children. Key Facts. 2015. http://www.missingkids.com/KeyFacts.

Chen, Thomas M. *Cyberterrorism after Stuxnet*. Carlisle Barracks, PA: Strategic Studies Institute and U.S. Army War College Press, 2014.

Citron, Danielle Keats. *Hate Crimes in Cyberspace*. Cambridge, MA: Harvard University Press, 2014.

Clarke, Richard A., and Robert K. Knake. *Cyber War: The Next Threat to National Security and What to Do about It*. New York: HarperCollins, 2010.

Clemmitt, Marcia. "Computer Hacking: Can 'Good' Hackers Help Fight Cybercrime?" *CQ Researcher* 21 (2011): 757–780.

Clemmitt, Marcia. "Internet Regulation: Are Stiffer Rules Needed to Protect Web Content?" *CQ Researcher* 22 (April 13, 2012): 325–348.

Computer Security Institute. "2010/2011 Computer Crime and Security Survey." http://gatton.uky.edu/FACULTY/PAYNE/ACC324/CSISurvey2010.pdf.

Cruz-Cunha, Maria Manuela, and Irene Maria Portela. *Handbook of Research on Digital Crime, Cybersecurity, and Information Assurance.* Hershey, PA: Information Science Reference, 2015.

"Cybersecurity Policy Making at a Turning Point." Organisation for Economic Co-operation and Development. 2012. http://www.oecd.org/sti/ieconomy/cyber security%20policy%20making.pdf.

Dalziel, Max. *How to Defeat Advanced Malware: New Tools for Protection and Forensics.* Waltham, MA: Syngress, 2015.

Dunham, Ken. *Android Malware and Analysis.* Boca Raton, FL: CRC Press, 2014.

Elisan, Christopher C. *Malware, Rootkits & Botnets: A Beginner's Guide.* New York: McGraw-Hill, 2013.

Eriksen-Jensen, Maria. "Holding Back the Tidal Wave of Cybercrime." *Computer Fraud and Security* (March 2013): 10–15.

Etzioni, Amitai. *Privacy in a Cyber Age: Policy and Practice.* New York: Palgrave MacMillan, 2015.

Federal Bureau of Investigation, Internet Crime Complaint Center. 2014 Internet Crime Report. https://www.fbi.gov/news/news_blog/2014-ic3-annual-report.

Flamini, Rolando. "Improving Cybersecurity: Is the United States Safe from Internet Criminals?" *CQ Researcher* 23 (2013): 157–180.

Furnell, Steven. *Cyber Crime: Vandalizing the Information Society.* London: Addison Wesley, 2002.

Gartzke, Erik. "The Myth of Cyberwar: Bringing War in Cyberspace Back Down to Earth." *International Security* 38 (2013): 41–73.

Gitlin, Marty, and Margaret J. Goldstein. *Cyber Attack.* Minneapolis, MN: Twenty-First Century Books, 2015.

Gragido, Will, Daniel Molina, John Pirc, and Nick Selby. *Blackhatonomics.* New York: Syngress, 2012.

Gray, Collin S. *Making Strategic Sense of Cyber Power: Why the Sky Is Not Falling.* Carlisle, PA: Strategic Studies Institute and U.S. Army War College Press, 2013.

Group-IB. "Threat Intelligence Report" 2013. http://report2013.group-ib.com.

Hansen, Brian. "Cyber-crime: Should Penalties Be Tougher?" *CQ Researcher* 12 (2002): 305–328.

Hathaway, Melissa E. *Best Practices in Computer Network Defense: Incident Detection and Response.* Washington, DC: IOS Press, 2014.

Hollis, D. "Cyberwar Case Study: Georgia 2008." *Small Wars Journal,* 2011. http://smallwarsjournal.com/blog/journal/docs-temp/639-hollis.pdf.

Holt, Thomas J. *Becoming a Computer Hacker: Examining the Enculturation and Development of Computer Deviants.* New York: Oxford University Press, 2010.

Holt, Thomas J., ed. *Crime On-line: Correlates, Causes and Context.* Durham, NC: Carolina Academic Press, 2010.

Holt, Thomas J., and Bernadette H. Schell, eds. *Corporate Hacking and Technology-driven Crime: Social Dynamics and Implications.* Hershey, PA: IGI Global, 2010, 190–213.

Jackson, Gary M. *Predicting Malicious Behavior: Tools and Techniques for Ensuring Global Security.* Indianapolis, IN: John Wiley, 2012.

Jacobson, George V., ed. *Cybersecurity, Botnets and Cyberterrorism.* New York: Nova Science Publishers, 2008, 1–35.

Jaishankar, K., ed. *Cyber Criminology: Exploring Internet Crimes and Criminal Behavior.* Boca Raton, FL: CRC Press, 2011, 65–77.

Jewkes, Yvonne, and Majid Yar, eds. *Handbook of Internet Crime.* Cullompton, UK: Willan, 2010.

Johnson, David R., and David Post. "Law and Borders: The Rise of Law in Cyberspace." *Stanford Law Review* 48, no. 5 (1996): 1367–1402.

Kagel, Laura Tate. *Cybersecurity and National Defense: Building a Public-Private Partnership.* Athens, GA: Dean Rusk Center, 2015.

Katz, Rita. *Terrorist Hunter: The Extraordinary Story of a Woman Who Went Undercover to Infiltrate the Radical Islamic Groups Operating in America.* New York: Ecco, 2013.

Levy, Stephen. *Hackers: Heroes of the Computer Revolution.* New York: Penguin Group, 1984.

Libicki, Martin. *Cyberdefense and Cyberwar.* Santa Monica, CA: Rand, 2009.

Libicki, Martin, David Senty, and Julia Pollak. *Hackers Wanted: An Examination of the Cybersecurity Labor Market.* Santa Monica, CA: Rand, 2014.

"Malware Report: The Economic Impact of Viruses, Spyware, Adware, Botnets and Other Malicious Code." *Computer Economics,* 2007. http://www.computer economics.com/page.cfm?name=Malware%20Report..

Marshall, Patrick. "Cybersecurity: Are U.S. Military and Civilian Computer Systems Safe?" *CQ Researcher* 20 (2010): 169–192.

Martinez-Prather, Kathy, and Donna M. Vandiver. "Sexting Among Teenagers in the US: A Retrospective Analysis of Identifying Motivating Factors, Potential Targets, and the Role of a Capable Guardian." *International Journal of Cyber Criminology* 8, no. 1 (2014): 21–35.

McAfee. "McAfee Virtual Criminology Report: Organized Crime and the Internet." 2006. http://i.i.cbsi.com/cnwk.1d/html/itp/mcafee_ww_virtual_criminology _FINAL.pdf.

McAfee. "Net Losses: Estimating the Global Cost of Cybercrime." June 2014. http://www.mcafee.com/us/resources/reports/rp-economic-impact-cybercrime2 .pdf.

McCarthy, N. K. *The Computer Incident Response Planning Handbook: Executable Plans for Protecting Information at Risk.* New York: McGraw-Hill, 2012.

Mehra, Salil K. "Law and Cybercrime in the United States Today." *The American Journal of Comparative Law* 58 (2010): 659–685.

Mulvenon, James C., and Gregory Rattray. *Addressing Cyber Instablility.* Vienna, VA: Cyber Conflict Studies Association, 2012.

"Networks and Netwars: The Future of Terror, Crime, and Militancy." *Cost of Cyber Crime Study* (2013): 239, 288. http://media.scmagazine.com/documents/54/2013_us_ccc_report_final_6-1_13455.pdf

Norton. "Norton Cybercrime Report." 2012. http://now-static.norton.com/now/en/pu/images/Promotions/2012/cybercrimeReport/2012_Norton_Cybercrime_Report_Master_FINAL_050912.pdf.

Ponemon Institute. *Cost of Cyber Crime Study: United States.* October 2013. http://media.scmagazine.com/documents/54/2013_us_ccc_report_final_6-1_13455.pdf.

Powers, Shawn M. *The Real Cyber War: The Political Economy of Internet Freedom.* Urbana: University of Illinois Press, 2015.

Richards, Jason. "Denial-of-Service: The Estonian Cyberwar and Its Implications for US National Security." *International Affairs Review* 18 (2009). http://www.iar-gwu.org/node/65.

Rid, Thomas. *The Cyber War Will Not Take Place.* Oxford: Oxford University Press, 2013.

Schell, Bernadette H., John L. Dodge, and Steve S. Moutsatsos. *The Hacking of America: Who's Doing It, Why and How.* Westport, CT: Quorum, 2002.

Schmallenger, Frank, and Michael Pittaro, eds. *Crimes of the Internet.* Upper Saddle River, NJ: Pearson, 2009, 336–355.

Shimeall, Timothy, Phil Williams, and Casey Dunlevy. "Countering Cyber War." *NATO Review* 49 (2001): 16–18.

Silver, Oliver. "European Cybercrime Proposal Released." *Computer Fraud and Security* (May 2001): 5.

Skibell, Reid. "Cybercrimes and Misdemeanors: A Reevaluation of the Computer Fraud and Abuse Act." *Berkeley Technology Law Journal* 18 (2003): 909–944.

Slatalla, Michael, and Joshua Quittner. *Masters of Deception: The Gang That Ruled Cyberspace.* New York: HarperCollins, 1995.

Springer, Paul J. *Cyber Warfare: A Reference Handbook.* Santa Barbara, CA: ABC-CLIO, 2015.

Steinmetz, Kevin F. "Becoming a Hacker: Demographic Characteristics and Developmental Factors." *Journal of Qualitative Criminal Justice and Criminology* 3, no. 1 (2015): 31–60.

Steinmetz, Kevin F., and Jurg Gerber. "The Greatest Crime Syndicate since the Gambinos: A Hacker Critique of Government, Law, and Law Enforcement." *Deviant Behavior* 35 (2014): 243–261.

Sterling, Bruce. *The Hacker Crackdown: Law and Disorder on the Electronic Frontier.* New York: Bantam, 1992.

Symantec. "Internet Security Threat Report." 2014.

Thomas, Douglas, and Brian Loader, eds. *Cybercrime: Law Enforcement, Security and Surveillance in the Information Age.* London: Routledge, 2000.

Timm, Carl, and Richard Perez. *Seven Deadliest Social Network Attacks.* Burlington, MA: Syngress/Elsevier, 2010.

United Nations, Office on Drugs and Crime. *Comprehensive Study on Cybercrime.* 2013. https://www.unodc.org/documents/organized-crime/cybercrime/CYBER CRIME_STUDY_210213.pdf.

United Nations, Office on Drugs and Crime. *The Use of the Internet for Terrorist Purposes.* New York: United Nations, 2013.

United States Department of Defense. "The DoD Cyber Strategy." 2015. http://www.defense.gov/home/features/2015/0415_cyber-strategy/Final_2015 _DoD_CYBER_STRATEGY_for_web.pdf.

United States Department of Homeland Security. "Strategic National Risk Assessment in Support of PPD 8: A Comprehensive Risk-Based Approach toward a secure and Resilient Nation." December 2011. http://www.dhs.gov/xlibrary /assets/rma-strategic-national-risk-assessment-ppd8.pdf.

United States Department of Justice. "Computer Crime and Intellectual Property Section." http://www.justice.gov/criminal/cybercrime/.

United States Government Accountability Office. *Communications Networks: Outcome-Based Measures Would Assist DHS in Assessing Effectiveness of Cybersecurity Efforts: Report to Congressional Requesters.* Washington, DC: U.S. Government Printing Office, 2013.

United States House of Representatives, Committee on Homeland Security, Subcommittee on Cybersecurity, Infrastructure Protection and Security Technologies. *Cyber Threats from China, Russia, and Iran: Protecting American Critical Infrastructure: Hearing before the Subcommittee on Cybersecurity, Infrastructure Protection and Security Technologies.* Washington, DC: US Government Publishing Office, 2014.

United States House of Representatives, Committee on Homeland Security, Subcommittee on Cybersecurity, Infrastructure Protection and Security Technologies. *Examining the Cyber Threat to Critical Infrastructure and the American Economy Hearing before the Subcommittee on Cybersecurity, Infrastructure Protection, and Security Technologies of the Committee on Homeland Security.* Washington, DC: Government Printing Office, 2012.

United States House of Representatives, Committee on Homeland Security. *Examining the President's Cybersecurity Information-Sharing Proposal Hearing before the Committee on Homeland Security, House of Representatives, One Hundred Fourteenth Congress.* Washington, DC: U.S. Government Publishing Office, 2015.

United States House of Representatives, Committee on Homeland Security, Subcommittee on Oversight, Investigations, and Management. *America Is under Cyber Attack: Why Urgent Action Is Needed: Hearing before the Subcommittee on Oversight, Investigations, and Management.* Washington, DC: U.S. Government Printing Office, 2013.

United States House of Representatives, Committee on Small Business. *Small Business, Big Threat: Protecting Small Businesses from Cyber Attacks: Hearing before the Committee on Small Business.* Washington, DC: U.S. Government Publishing Office, 2015.

United States Working Group on Unlawful Conduct on the Internet. "The Electronic Frontier: The Challenge of Unlawful Conduct Involving the Use of the

Internet: A Report of the President's Working Group on Unlawful Conduct on the Internet." 2000. http://purl.access.gpo.gov/GPO/LPS5093.

Valeriano, Brandon, and Ryan C. Maness. *Cyber War Versus Cyber Realities: Cyber Conflict in the International System.* Oxford: Oxford University Press, 2015.

Wall, David S. "Cybercrime and the Culture of Fear: Social Science Fiction(s) and the Production of Knowledge about Cybercrime." *Information, Communication & Society* 11 (2011): 861–884.

Wall, David S. "Cybercrime, Media, and Insecurity: The Shaping of Public Perceptions of Cybercrime." *International Review of Law Computers and Technology* 22 (2008): 45–63.

Wall, David S. "Cybercrimes: New Wine, No Bottles?" In *Invisible Crimes: Their Victims and Their Regulation*, edited by P. Davies, P. Francis, and V. Jupp. London: Macmillan, 1999, 105–139.

Weimann, Gabriel. "Cyberterrorism: The Sum of All Fears?" *Studies in Conflict and Terrorism* 28 (2005): 129–149.

White House. "The Comprehensive National Cybersecurity Initiative." https://www.whitehouse.gov/issues/foreign-policy/cybersecurity/national-initiative.

Williams, Matthew. *Virtually Criminal.* New York: Routledge, 2006.

Xuxian, Jiang. *Android Malware.* New York: Springer, 2013.

Yar, Majid. "Computer Hacking: Just Another Case of Juvenile Delinquency?" *The Howard Journal of Criminal Justice* 44, no. 4 (2005): 387–399.

Zhengchuan Xu, Qing Hu, and Chenghong Zhang. "Why Computer Talents Become Computer Hackers." *Communications of the ACM* 56, no. 4 (2013): 64–74.

Index

About the Authors

Joshua B. Hill is an Assistant Professor of Criminal Justice at The University of Southern Mississippi and a Fellow at the Office of Global Perspectives and Metropolitan Center at the University of Central Florida. He teaches courses in terrorism, homeland security, and criminal justice, particularly focusing on politics and theory within each of these areas. His research interests range widely, from criminal justice to cybercrime, with a particular emphasis on the social and political implications of crime and criminal justice. Dr. Hill previously worked for the Institute for the Study of Violent Groups as a lead analyst. In addition to his current faculty role at the University of Southern Mississippi, Dr. Hill serves as the Co-Director of the Center for Justice and Security. He holds a bachelor of arts in international relations as well as a master of arts and a PhD in criminal justice from Sam Houston State University. He is the coauthor of *Homeland Security in America* with Nancy Marion and *Ohio's Criminal Justice System*, with Nancy Marion, R. James Orr, III, Kendra Kec, and Kevin Cashen, as well as numerous journal articles and book chapters.

Nancy E. Marion is a Professor of Political Science at the University of Akron and a Fellow with the Bliss Institute of Applied Politics. Dr. Marion instructs classes on public policy, policy analysis, criminal justice, and organized crime. Her research interests include the intersection of crime and politics, including the politics of homeland security, terrorism, and cybercrime. She holds a master of science degree in criminal justice from the American University as well as a master of arts and a PhD in political science from the State University of New York at Binghamton. Dr. Marion is the author of *Making Environmental Law: The Politics of Protecting the Earth* (Praeger, 2011) and coeditor of *Drugs in American Society*.